MW01253015

NOTHING TO FIX

SEXUALITIES

General Editor: Gautam Bhan

Other Books in the Series:

NOTHING TO FIX
Medicalisation of Sexual
Orientation and Gender Identity

Edited by
Arvind Narrain and Vinay Chandran

 www.sagepublications.com
Los Angeles • London • New Delhi • Singapore • Washington DC

First published in 2016 by

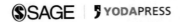

SAGE Publications India Pvt Ltd
B1/I-1 Mohan Cooperative Industrial Area
Mathura Road, New Delhi 110 044, India
www.sagepub.in

YODA Press
268 AC Vasant Kunj
New Delhi 110070
www.yodapress.co.in

SAGE Publications Inc
2455 Teller Road
Thousand Oaks, California 91320, USA

SAGE Publications Ltd
1 Oliver's Yard, 55 City Road
London EC1Y 1SP, United Kingdom

SAGE Publications Asia-Pacific Pte Ltd
3 Church Street
#10-04 Samsung Hub
Singapore 049483

Published by Vivek Mehra for SAGE Publications India Pvt Ltd and printed at Chaman Enterprises, New Delhi.

Library of Congress Cataloging-in-Publication Data Available

ISBN: 978-93-515-0890-8 (HB)

Contents

III. HUMAN RIGHTS

Foreword

DR. SHEKHAR SESHADRI

In India, disciplinary boundaries have been generally difficult to bridge. Be it law or medicine, professionals in each field tend to work within their sector without necessarily collaborating across sectors. An example of inter-sectoral collaboration emerged particularly in the context of the impetus to decriminalise homo-sexuality. The criminalisation of homosexuality had become a tool of harassment and violence against the LGBT community, hampering public discussions on homosexuality and contributing to discriminatory attitudes towards LGBT persons in society.

The genesis of the inter-sectoral collaboration in this context can be traced to a seminar organised in the National Law School of India University (NLSIU), Bangalore, in September 1997. While exemplary activist work has been done in other parts of India, this was the first collaboration between lawyers, activists, mental health professionals as well as artists to begin work towards removing the law. This proved a significant starting point for continued conversations across disciplines with a view to improving the status of LGBT persons in Indian society.

Thereafter, there has been significant progress although only in specialised sectors like NGOs, informal support spaces, legal initiatives and individuals who were helped by individual doctors or endocrinologists. However, as the movement progressed, though the sparks were many, the interventions were still fragmented and unsynchronised. There was an absence of protocol-driven initiatives, institutionalised responses, or established inter-sectoral collaborations that worked synergistically to provide the most effective form of intervention to people in need.

As the momentum gathered, inter-sectoral collaborations improved. The movement against Section 377 of the Indian Penal Code achieved a degree of success with the decision of the Delhi High Court which effectively decriminalised consenting homosexual relationships between adults. Following this, 15 Hindu, Muslim and Christian religious groups filed petitions appealing the High Court judgement. It was at this moment that lawyers and the medical fraternity (mental health professionals) collaborated to draft a persuasive scientific affidavit which would place proven medical facts before the Court.

Simultaneously, individuals in the health sector who were thus far working on the basis of personal conviction began to do more training programmes for colleagues and students as a result of which health-driven protocols have become more and more institutionalised. The hope is that irrespective of where a person goes, for instance, for certification of sex reassignment procedures, international standards and protocols of assessment would be followed and legally accepted documentation can be provided. The capacity to provide this will reside in the institution and not necessarily in any one individual. Increasingly, the same processes are being applied to other health and medical interventions such as counselling.

In the context of sex reassignment surgery it is also important that various health-professionals involved—psychiatrists, endocrinologists, surgeons, gynaecologists, and others—need to be networked in a manner that the benefit to the individual, seeking help, is not fragmented. In the past, an individual has often had to run around to seek out these services on his or her own. The emerging need now is to consolidate all these services within the same institution, either a general hospital or through a nodal person to coordinate between different players. Some states in India are already providing subsidies for many of these medical processes and procedures.

However, it is important for all the players involved in such inter-sectoral collaborations to understand the triangulation between medical systems/processes/responses; pathologising/de-pathologising of sexual orientation and gender identity; and law/procedural/human rights for central, coherent and synergistic interventions.

This book is a true example of the start of the discourse on this central point.

Acknowledgements

The editors are grateful for the Sarai/CSDS Fellowship, New Delhi, without which this book could not have been put together. Many friends and colleagues have supported us along the way and we thank everyone for their insights and comments on this book as it was taking shape. Chiefly, all our friends at Alternative Law Forum (Lawrence Liang, Clifton d'Rosario, Maitreyi Krishnan, Aarti Mundkur, Namita Malhotra, Siddharth Narrain, Danish Sheikh and Raghupathy) and the Swabhava Trust (Patrick Wilson, Suresh Jayaram, Owais Khan and Kevin Joseph) were invaluable and deserve our gratitude. Dr. Shekhar Seshadri, apart from writing the foreword, was also a guide and support throughout the framing of this book. Thanks also to Arpita Das and Gautam Bhan for sharing our belief that this book would help with the debates on sexual orientation and gender identity.

Introduction

The emergence of queer struggles that insistently question the normative understanding of gender and sexuality have broadened our understanding of what we mean by the 'political'. If previously it was taken for granted that those born as women dress as 'women' and fall in love with and marry 'men,' today this norm is being questioned. There are women and men who choose to fall in love with others of the same gender; there are women and men who choose to transition from their assigned gender at birth to the other gender; and there are those that reject the binaries of two genders altogether. Equally there are questions being raised about whether intersex children should be made to conform to a gender through surgical intervention. This questioning of some of the fundamental norms of society emerges from the perspective of the queer movement that seeks to bring about an understanding of the numerous *loci* through which the heteronormative social order is being produced.

The queer movement encompasses

> a multiplicity of desires and identities, each and all of which question the naturalness, the rightness and the inevitability of heterosexuality... By proudly calling themselves queer, homosexual people are not only re-appropriating a word historically used as part of a language of oppression, they also reject the power of the oppressor to judge them in the first place. The term 'queer' is, in some ways, both a deeply personal identity and a defiant political perspective.[1]

The term 'heteronormative' refers to the dominant social norms that regulate identities, sexualities and relationships. Heteronormativity assumes that a 'family' unit comprises a man, woman, and their children. It is also taken as given that they are each heterosexually identified. Hence, 'appropriate' gender and sexual roles are not only expected but also imposed on them. Within the queer movement, these assumptions are challenged and diverse ways of establishing social and intimate relationships as well as sexual or gender identities are welcomed. The queer perspective, in effect, empathises with the experiences of those who are pushed to the margins of a heteronormative society and seeks to foreground the narratives of all those who feel left out.

A queer perspective with its focus on the zone of private and intimate relationships adds another dimension to the concerns of social movements. Social movements, as traditionally conceptualised, occupy a public space and struggle for justice of marginalised groups against oppression by the state. The first to broaden this notion of a movement was the feminist movement which insistently raised the question of the personal as political. The feminist movement put institutions such as family, marriage and relationships between the sexes under the scanner and sought to expose the relationships of power, which underpin seemingly 'natural' institutions such as the family. The notion of the political itself was broadened by feminist thought and practice as they moved beyond just looking at incidents of violence against women to raising questions about the structural roots of such violence in social institutions such as the family and marriage.

This spirit of intensive questioning was taken to even include seemingly apolitical institutions such as the medical establishment and its practices. Applied particularly to the field of mental health, the concern was whether what the medical establishment viewed as 'pathological' had embedded within it patriarchal biases and whether one could propose alternative feminist therapies. Within the Indian context, the work of Bhargavi Davar has been of germinal importance as, for the first time, the field of mental health became the subject of serious academic work from a perspective which emerges from outside the mental health field. Davar's contribution has been to move the debate beyond the polemical position of diagnosing all madness as a form of protest against the social order to actually facilitate a dialogue between professionals (psychiatrists/ psychotherapists) and feminists.[2]

If one compares the queer movement with the feminist movement, it is clear that the queer movement too is deeply concerned with the norms which govern the zones of intimacy within which we all function. Questions about the 'appropriate' gender roles imposed on the respective sexes and the expectations of heterosexual marriage resulting in procreation on each individual are illustrative of the queer movement's challenge of the normative understanding of gender and sexuality.

The most visible site of the queer movement's struggle has been Section 377 of the Indian Penal Code (IPC) that criminalises consensual sex between people of the same sex.[3] However, while the law might be a more visible symbol of queer oppression, it is by no means the only site through which social pressure to conform both in terms of sexual orientation and gender identity is generated. The other key and just as powerful sites through which the ideal (heterosexual) man/woman is produced includes the media and the medical establishment.

If the heteronormative social order is produced through numerous social sites then it is clear that we need to begin understanding how this process of constructing ideals of both masculinity/femininity as well as normative heterosexuality works. An exclusive focus on legal change will mean that other equally important sites of oppression are ignored. This realisation underlies the diversity of spaces, frames and practices within the queer movement. This book is part of such efforts and it focuses on one key site on which we aim to shed more light: the medical establishment.

Both the theory and practice of medicine remains central to concerns of persons identified as lesbian, gay, bisexual, transgender, intersex or others (LGBT). Individuals who have homosexual desires or feel transgender or are born intersex are taken often against their will to the medical professional. Often this is due to the pressure of their parents or due to feelings of self-guilt or their own desire to change. But once within the medical system, instead of receiving affirmative support, distressing experiences of violence and violations occur. The narratives of such violence and violation include treatments offered for converting homosexuals to heterosexuals, humiliation of transgender people within the institution and emergency surgeries of intersex infants who, due to the collusion between surgeons and parents, face the scalpel to convert them into an 'acceptable' gender. Everyday struggles of LGBT persons like suicidality and depression are dealt with less sensitively owing to the pathologisation of their identities.

The centrality of the medical discourse to the concerns of the LGBT community are undeniable yet there has been little systematic work to understand the impact of such 'medicalisation'.

Since the Humjinsi *Resource Book on Lesbian, Bisexual, Gay Rights* published in 2002,[4] there have been scattered efforts at making sense of how the medical establishment deals with questions of sexual orientation and gender identity. The question of what is popularly called 'shock therapy' (which is referred to by the medical establishment as 'aversion' or 'conversion' therapy) dominated the initial discussions around the role played by medicine in 'converting' or 'curing' the homosexual. Yet there is a broader diversity of issues that fall within the ambit of understanding interactions between queer communities and the medical establishment. These include issues pertaining to the medical category of 'ego-dystonic homosexuality', the treatment of transsexuals and of people born as intersex, and the social role played by scientific discourses in shaping the legitimacy of normative behaviour. There is also the question of the medical curriculum and how it remains influenced by both the legal framework as well as by outdated medical concepts.

In fact there is a lot to be done in terms of activism within the medical profession so that attitudes to homosexuality, gender identity, transsexuals and intersex people change, and the terms within which treatment is proffered is radically revised. In fact, a change in classification systems within medicine is only one step in trying to change a medical 'culture' that functions largely within the frame of heteronormativity. The larger challenge will be to change mindsets of doctors who are still insistently focused on changing their patients' sexual orientation or still exhibit prejudice when it comes to dealing with their transgender patients.

Perhaps a starting point for change is the writing, both within the medical profession as well as from emerging queer activism, which is beginning to question heteronormativity within the field of medicine. This book attempts to put together some of the initial writings in one place as a resource for activists, doctors and medical professionals. There is still a long way to go as seen by the fact that neither the association for Indian Psychiatrists nor Indian Psychologists or even the Indian Council of Medical Research (ICMR) has come out with any guidelines or treatment protocols for working with sexual orientation and gender identity.[5]

The questions which a queer engagement with the mental health establishment must inevitably raise include: how is the mental health establishment complicit in producing gender as binary and sexual orientation as always directed towards the 'opposite' sex? What are the other ways in which the mental health profession (re)produces the norms of gender and sexuality? How do these practices of the mental health profession impact the question of human rights? What can be done by mental health professionals to de-pathologise sexual orientation? These are some of the questions this volume seeks to engage with.

The starting point of our engagement was when we, as members of Bangalore's queer community, started hearing stories of aversion therapy being given to gay men to 'convert' them to heterosexuality. We realised the importance of documenting these stories and trying to push for progressive change within the medical establishment. The more stories we heard of how doctors were treating homosexuals, the more questions arose. The way this book has been structured indicates the kinds of questions which we had to grapple with as well as some tentative answers to how we can respond to the medicalisation of sexual orientation and gender identity.

The book is divided into three sections. The first section, Medicalisation, outlines the frameworks on which the mental health and other medical sectors have posited homosexual desire and transgender or intersex identities. The second section, De-pathologisation, argues that sexual orientation and gender identity are not to be seen as pathologies and suggests forms of engagement that are more affirmative of LGBT identities. The third section, Human Rights looks at the interface between law, medicine and human rights as perhaps the beginning of a change in the perception of LGBT persons.

Medicalisation

Narrain and Chandran in the first essay approach the question of the treatment of sexual orientation through looking at the history of medical efforts to treat homosexuality as well as through documenting the contemporary practice of mental health professionals in Bangalore. The implicit question being the way treatment can violate the rights of the queer community and the imperative to move away from 'treating' homosexuality to de-pathologising homosexuality.

The second essay in this section by Reddy attempts to explore the attitudes of medical students towards the question of sexual orientation. In Reddy's understanding, an outdated medical curriculum which pathologises homosexuality (as one prescribed medical textbook notes, 'Lesbians who are morbidly jealous of one another when rejected may commit homicide, suicide or both') plays a strong role in moulding a homophobic student body.

Ranade in her essay also documents the fact that though homosexuality may not be considered an illness per se, conversion therapy is still used by doctors in Pune and Mumbai to treat homosexuality. The interviews with the doctors, which Ranade documents, show that there is still a long way to go in terms of de-pathologising homosexuality. Both Ranade's study and the Narrain and Chandran essay give us an insight into how homosexuality is still viewed by counsellors and psychiatrists across three cities. The regressive nature of the medical practice reflects poorly on the knowledge of mental health professionals.

The essay by Fernandez focuses on the concerns of lesbians

within the mental health profession, addressing the paucity of material on lesbians and bisexual women. Fernandez essays a gender-specific understanding of how the issues faced by women in dealing with the mental health field are different from the issues men face. As she notes, 'in marked contrast to the gay male clients who approach (mental health professionals) specifically to "become heterosexual" ... none of the women had come to the mental health professionals requesting to "become heterosexual."' The interviewees 'reported distress, grief, anxiety and or depression about a range of other issues such as break-up of relationships, pressure to marry, bad marriages, etc.'.

A completely different lens is cast on the role of the medical establishment, when it comes to the treatment of transsexualism. Here it's not possible to merely assert as gay rights activists have asserted in the case of homosexuality that 'if it ain't broke, don't fix it'. Many in the transgender community while being averse to considering gender identity disorder as a psychiatric disorder would definitely want it to be treated as a non-psychiatric medical condition warranting medical intervention to bring their body in alignment with their deeply felt sex. Chakrapani's essay documents the trials and tribulations of the Aravani community with the allopathic medical establishment, quacks, self-emasculation and emasculation by the elders in the hijra community. Chakrapani essays an understanding of what is lacking in Indian medical practice and what could be done to ensure that Aravanis/hijras are treated with dignity and full humanity by both wider society and the medical establishment.

The final essay by Suresh raises concerns (for the first time in the Indian context) about the treatment of intersex children by the medical profession. The essay notes the serious potential for the violation of basic rights of the child if surgery is performed without consent and the necessity for evolving treatment protocols. Suresh also raises the important question as to whether the category of intersex entails a medical emergency or a 'socio-cultural emergency where the body of the intersex infant must be made to conform to culturally defined notions of a male and female body'.

De-Pathologisation

While there is the human rights approach to the question of treating homosexuals, it is also important to note the efforts within the mental health field to bring about changes in the perception of homosexuality as pathology. Empirical explorations within the field of mental health research played a pivotal role in de-pathologising sexual orientation.

Reddy's empirically based study is of pioneering significance because it adapts the classic study by Evelyn Hooker to the Indian context by comparing 30 homosexuals and 30 heterosexuals of similar socio-economic backgrounds to assess if there is any significant difference between the two groups with respect to psychological health, social relationships and relationship to the environment. Reddy's conclusion (like Hooker's) that there is no statistically significant difference between the two groups is an important starting point in the efforts to de-pathologise homosexuality.

Sebastian in her study takes on the question of whether ego-dystonic homosexuality is a phenomenon associated with intra-psychic factors or with external social factors. Sebastian concludes that ego-dystonic homosexuality is positively correlated with external factors such as lack of family acceptance, religious intolerance, lack of support structures, etc., and therefore there would have to be a radical rethinking of the way homosexuality is dealt with in the medical establishment. One of the important points made by Sebastian in her essay, in seeming contradiction to Reddy, is the higher incidence of suicidality, depression and other mental health problems in homosexual populations. But an understanding of 'minority stress' (stress experienced by individuals owing to their social, often minority, status) and social stress theory (conditions in the environment as sources of stress) can explain this contradiction. Reddy's essay, like Hooker's, reflects on the misconception that homosexuality is inherently pathological. Sebastian's essay considers the effects of stigma and internalised homophobia on homosexuals wanting to 'change' their orientation. Both provide the same conclusion that health professionals should stop pathologising homosexuality, and need to develop skills that can actually be helpful to those homosexuals who experience severe mental health crises.

The essays by Chandiramani and Hemchand are personal reflections. Chandiramani reminds therapists that, 'the way sexuality issues are looked at by most people does influence, to some extent, the way therapists view and respond to these issues.' She urges therapists to be aware that the language they could use may reflect heterosexist biases and how use of sensitive language can itself communicate that the therapist is not judgemental about homosexual orientation and gender non-conformity. Hemchand documents her personal journey as a psychologist who because of her association with the LGBT community realised the grave injustice to LGBT people if she continued to use the ICD-10 classification and give them treatment to change their identity.

Sathyanarayanan and Bhola's essay is an understanding of what would be required of practitioners if they viewed transgenders outside the framework of pathology. By drawing on their clinical experience, the authors address the different issues transgender persons face and the kinds of medical attention that could be offered.

The question which often arises when it comes to medical practice is how one deals with often complex concerns around sexual orientation and gender identity in a concrete counselling scenario? What do doctors or counsellors actually do when patients come to them with concerns around sexual orientation and gender identity? The documented experiences in India in the last decade or so and the experiences globally in working with queer people provide some preliminary answers to this very important question.

The counsellor's guide by Chandran, which is based upon counselling experiences with LBGT persons, attempts to lay out some of the issues that counsellors face and also indicates ways in which these issues can be tackled. Even the listing of the range of issues which counsellors might face from LGBT clients such as conflicts around identity, pressure to get married, coming out, safer sex, loneliness, negative reactions to being gay and relationship problems communicates concretely the LGBT counselling contexts.

Two significant issues which counsellors might have to face with respect to the queer context are the question of coming out to family and the conflict of religious beliefs with one's sexual orientation. With respect to coming out to family, Chandran's essay narrates the documented experiences of coming out in India and the learning from that experience of how coming out can be negotiated. The other piece by Chandran and Narrain deals with the question of conflict of religious faith with sexual orientation and how counsellors can help individuals to reconcile two seemingly irreconcilable positions.

Human rights

The discourse of human rights and the discourse of medicine have often functioned on parallel tracks. What this section seeks to document is the interface of law and medicine and its role in protecting the rights of LGBT persons.

Narrain documents the impact of the medical discourse in decriminalising homosexuality and goes on to argue that the law in turn might have set a new benchmark with respect to how one views homosexuality. The Naz judgement views the sexual act as being linked to the realm of feelings, emotions and the profound human need for establishing attachments and relationships and this might have implications not just for the medical field but a wider social field.

The extract from the PUCL-K Report on Human Rights violations against the transgender community, specifically addresses rights violations by the medical establishment of the hijra and kothi communities. The recommendations include both specific ones for change within the medical practice as well as those meant for society and state.

The final piece addresses transgender and intersex persons' rights by including relevant parts of the Yogyakarta Principles on Sexual Orientation and Gender Identity as well as the International Bill on Gender Rights. The idea here is that these progressive laws could provide a normative framework within which one can think of the relationship between transgender and intersex identities and rights.

Taking things forward

When we started working on the issue of the medical treatment of sexual orientation way back in 1999, ours was a lonely voice. However today the sheer diversity of essays in this volume, which we have been successful in collating, points to the increasing attention being paid to the medicalisation of sexual orientation and gender identity from both within the medical profession and from the queer movement. This book, therefore, represents the coming together of perspectives which are solidly grounded within the professional context as well as perspectives which emerge from a queer context. As such there would be questions about methodological rigour from the point of view of scientists and equally questions about the ideological framework from those who come from a queer perspective. One hopes that the questions aid a more productive engagement with another worldview, instead of becoming a point of closure.

The gaps in an anthology such as this are enormous and one only hopes that it will be seen as an initial effort which will stimulate fresh enthusiasm and interest in the way gender identity and sexual orientation are being treated by the medical profession. One of the clear limitations of this anthology is that while there are a few pieces which do reference systems of treatment other than allopathy, we have not systematically focused upon the impact of homeopathy, ayurveda and the vast informal system of faith healers and others who undoubtedly service the needs of a large majority of the Indian population. One hopes that these missing perspectives are addressed by emerging Indian scholarship in the near future.

Caveats aside, this anthology aims to incubate serious and sustained work on the centrality of the medical establishment to queer lives. One needs to broad base the concerns of the queer community beyond the debates on Section 377 and this anthology is be a step in that direction. We need sustained attention to be given to the other sites which reinforce the second class citizenship of queer persons and this anthology attempts that as well. In particular, building on the insights of the feminist movement, this anthology seeks to understand and document the heteronormative frame within which much of the medical establishment functions. It seeks to highlight issues such as the criticality of the medical establishment to queer lives, identities and the queer movement for a wider public. We hope that the range of insights and critiques in this anthology will make the medical establishment more responsive to the concerns of those who because of their sexual orientation or gender identity have been subjected to inhumane and degrading 'treatments'.

Notes

[1] A. Narrain and G. Bhan (eds), *Because I Have a Voice* (New Delhi: Yoda Press, 2005), p. 3.

[2] See B. Davar (ed.), *Mental Health from A Gender Perspective* (New Delhi: Sage Publications, 2001). In this volume, Davar brings together papers by practising psychiatrists and psychologists as well as feminists who participated in a conference on Indian women and their mental health in 1996.

[3] The provision was challenged before the Delhi High Court where it was read down and on appeal the Supreme Court reinstated the provision.

[4] B. Fernandez (ed.), *Humjinsi: A Resource Book on Lesbian, Gay, and Bisexual Rights in India* (Mumbai: Combat Law Publications, 2002).

[5] This is in stark contrast to progress in the medical field globally. ICD-10 which is the classification system authored by the WHO as well as DSM-IV have both de-pathologised homosexuality.

I. Medicalisation

'It's not my job to tell you it's okay to be gay...' Medicalisation of Homosexuality

A Queer Critique[1]

ARVIND NARRAIN and VINAY CHANDRAN

... Homosexuality has a biological basis and if we find this basis, we can treat homosexuality. I think they will definitely find a treatment. For example in some mental illnesses, especially depression, if we treat the T2 receptors using drugs, the patient feels better. Similarly, if you compare normal heterosexuals and homosexuals and do a neuro-imaging and see the difference in biological parameters then one can pinpoint possibly two or three factors and try and change them.

—PE, Psychiatrist

However in today's world, young people have to fight both against peer pressure and the media, both of which are very strong. I believe that people should be free, but not free to commit suicide or to commit homosexuality. When we talk about freedom, we should ask the question, if God would want you to do that particular act.
    —LCA, Lay Counsellor, affiliated to a religious centre
    Sodomy is illegal in India.

—CPC, Clinical Psychologist

I. Introduction

Historically, medical discourse always pathologised most non-procreative, non-marital sexual desire. Alongside religion and law, medicine sought to control what it perceived as 'deviant' sexual behaviours. Medical classifications were created to control such deviance and while applying to a large majority of sexual behaviour they affected homosexuals the most. This was because classifying homosexuality as inherently pathological, medicine sought to control the very expression of homosexual desire. It wasn't until the second half of the twentieth century, with the rise of the queer rights movement, that pathologisation of homosexuality was challenged. These challenges were aided by several path-breaking studies demonstrating homosexuality as a natural variant of human sexuality.

While there has been a lot of documentation in the west of the struggles against pathologisation, there is a paucity of material even on the way medical professionals 'treat' homosexuality in India. This essay charts the rise of the medical discourse on homosexuality, and we show how medical professionals in India deal with homosexuality in everyday practice. The field evidence suggests that even as medical discourse in the west moved beyond pathologising homosexuality towards affirming the rights of persons with different sexual orientations, mental health professionals in India by and large continue to still treat homosexuality as pathology.

The essay documents contemporary treatment of homosexuality in India. We learn that 'treatments' are themselves nothing more than expressions of deep-rooted prejudice (that are also influenced by law and religion) against homosexuals. We listened to the voices of both mental health professionals and the homosexual clients they have 'treated' and conclude two things: first, medical professionals need to stop viewing homosexuality as pathological and second, that alternatives to treatments and pathologisation lie in building affirmative support group structures that enable homosexuals to become comfortable with themselves.

Methodology

Conceptually, this essay adopts a historical approach to understand the way mental health professionals have dealt with homosexuality. The research for this essay was conducted in several stages. First, the effort was to use literature reviews to trace the origins of the categories into which homosexuality was classified in medical discourse. Second, to understand how these categories have been deployed in Indian settings, we surveyed editions of the *Indian*

Journal of Clinical Psychology up to 2001 and of the *Indian Journal of Psychiatry* between 1982 and 1995. Third, to understand day-to-day practice in India, with respect to the treatment of homosexuality, we interviewed 14 mental health practitioners including clinical psychologists, psychiatrists, sexologists, and lay counsellors. The interviews were conducted through snowball sampling. Finally, we interviewed a few individuals who had been subjected to medical treatment for their homosexual desires. In fact, the impetus for studying the way the mental health system treats homosexuals emerged from our experiences as part of Bangalore's queer community where we met a number of homosexuals who have been through 'treatment' (for their homosexual desires) administered by mental health professionals across India. Invariably, the 'treatment' has had a negative impact on the persons' sense of self, something that has been documented in various research studies.[2] We were interested in mapping out the history of a health discourse that inflicts different forms of violence on the homosexual client. The original study was conducted in 2003, under the SARAI/CSDS Short Term Independent Fellowships. In the study, we held a series of interviews with practitioners from different mental health fields. The interviews used open-ended questions related to the general practice that respondents had, types of illnesses treated, types of sex-related complaints among patients, eliciting of sex/sexuality history, kind of complaints related to homosexual desires, practitioner responses to homosexual patients, and practitioner responses to families of homosexual patients. The study set out to understand how contemporary mental health professionals understand and work with homosexuality in their practice.

II. History of western approaches to mental health and homosexuality

The status of homosexuality is a political question, representing a historically rooted, socially determined choice regarding the ends of human sexuality. It requires a political analysis.[3]

Within the field of allopathic medicine there are many ways

of thinking about sexuality. Disciplines as diverse as sexology, psychology and psychiatry have produced vast bodies of literature that have documented and analysed deviations from the sexual norm (i.e., the heterosexual marital relationship) in terms like sexual perversion, pathology, and abnormality, which stigmatises difference as deviance. This classificatory enthusiasm is not completely innocent of the grids of knowledge and power as Foucault is apt to remind us.[4] The social function served by this detailing out and classification of deviations from the norm is actually to stabilise the norm. As Weeks (1981) notes:

> ... the negative side of this classificatory enthusiasm was a sharp reinforcement of the normal ... the debates over the causes of the perversions and the eager descriptions of even the most outrageous examples inevitably worked to emphasize their pathology, their relationship to degeneracy, madness and sickness, and helped to reinforce the normality of heterosexual relationships.[5]

This essay will trace the trends in allopathic traditions in thinking about abnormal sexuality and the shifts that have happened in the way the abnormal is conceptualised. The reason why the history of these traditions is important is that these discourses about the abnormal have become implicated in the workings of contemporary medical practice in India. This essay will also look at the role that psychology and psychiatry played in constructing the notion of the homosexual as abnormal as well as the various ways in which this notion of abnormality began to be questioned.

Homosexuality as a part of Psychopathia Sexualis

Diversity in sexual behaviour can be categorised in multiple ways. One way is to classify sexual behaviour into what is the norm and what is a deviation from the norm. Another is to view sexual diversity in the same way one views diversity with respect to the colour of hair or colour of eyes, i.e., without moral judgement.

If the discourse on sexuality has been marked by the tradition of viewing the spectrum of sexuality through the normal/abnormal framework, it is thanks to the Viennese psychiatrist, Richard Krafft-Ebbing. In his work *Psychopathia Sexualis* (1894), he classified all forms

of sexual behaviour that did not result in procreation as examples of 'psychopathia sexualis' (i.e., psychopathic sexual desire). This classification of sexual desire as normal and abnormal influenced the prevailing discourse of the time and Krafft-Ebbing's book was hugely popular. 'Deviations from this "normal" (i.e. procreative) pattern Krafft-Ebbing viewed as perversions, diseases to which he and others applied such names as sadism, masochism, necrophilia, urolagnia, fetishism, nymphomania, satyriasis, homosexuality, voyeurism and exhibitionism.'[6]
Bristow (1997) notes that:

> Given the overwhelming quantities of evidence that Krafft-Ebbing subsequently produces on the topic of sexual perversion, *Psychopathia Sexualis* makes the distinct impression that the highest form of heterosexual love is menaced on all sides by an epidemic of perverse sexual behaviours. The numerous case histories included in his chapters on sadism, masochism, fetishism and homosexuality attest to what he considers are widespread sexual disorders among men.[7]

Although Kraft-Ebbing wrote his work towards the end of the nineteenth century, the conceptual framework of classifying non-procreative sexuality as pathology remained remarkably resilient. To illustrate this point, one needs to only look at a textbook on abnormal psychology that was used extensively in Bangalore until recently. In it, the author notes in a manner reminiscent of Kraft Ebbing:

> ... it is a wrong notion with some persons that homosexuality is characteristic of only children and adolescents. In fact, this perversion may be found in any person at any age and in both the sexes. Innocent children and adolescents pick up this habit through association with perverted persons. Homosexuality in women may be found in those who are either unmarried, widows or deserted by or separated from their husbands on certain grounds. Such women seek partnerships with other such women who also desire their sexual gratification through the same process....[8]

While the contribution of Krafft-Ebbing can be evaluated in quite a straightforward manner, the legacy of one of the most influential thinkers of the twentieth century, Sigmund Freud, is a bit more complex. Freud propounded a theory where he suggested that all people were born bisexual and that sexual development resulted in a proper sexual object choice. As he framed it, '...one of the tasks implicit in the object choice is that it should find its way to the opposite sex'. This development of a heterosexual orientation according to Freud went hand in hand with:

> ... the social instincts such as friendship, camaraderie, and the 'general love of mankind' all [of which] derived their strength, their erotic component from the unconscious homosexual impulses of those who had achieved the capacity for heterosexual relationship.[9]

In his famous 'Letter to an American mother', Freud noted that:

> ... homosexuality is assuredly no advantage, but it is nothing to be ashamed of, no vice, no degradation, it cannot be classified as an illness; we consider it to be a variation of the sexual function produced by a certain arrest of the sexual development.[10]

What is apparent in Freud's analysis is a tension between the acknowledgement that homosexuality is not an illness and the idea that it still remains an 'arrest of the sexual development' and not a proper 'sexual object choice'. This ambivalence on the part of Freud towards the very perception of homosexuality resulted in a pessimistic attitude towards treating homosexuality. As Freud notes:

> By asking me if I can help, you mean I suppose, if I can abolish homosexuality and make normal heterosexuality take its place. The answer is in a general way, we cannot promise to achieve it.... What analysis can do for your son runs in a different line. If he is unhappy, neurotic, torn by conflicts inhibited in his social life, analysis may bring him harmony, peace of mind, full efficiency whether he remains a homosexual or gets changed....[11]

However, this Freudian ambivalence towards homosexuality was completely rejected by his followers in what was to become the hegemonic way of conceptualising and treating homosexuality. Sandor Rado rejected Freud's theory of a constitutional bisexuality and instead asserted that everyone has the heterosexual drive and that the turn to homosexuality is not an instinctual response but rather a phobic response to heterosexuality. Rado's position was continually elaborated by other psychoanalysts who sought to demonstrate the pathological condition of homosexuality, thereby completely overturning the last remnants of Freud's ambivalence and returning to the conclusions that Krafft-Ebbing reached, but now using the discourse of psychoanalysis.

Foremost among these psychoanalysts was Irving Beiber who, in a study of 100 homosexuals and 100 heterosexuals, concluded that homosexual orientation was a result of a pathogenic family with a domineering mother and a detached or absent father. Beiber in his study went on to pathologise various aspects of homosexual existence. He noted that, '... because of its pathological status, the possibility of establishing a stable and intimate homosexual relationship is precluded ... hence there is ceaseless, compulsive, anonymous cruising ...'.[12]

This conclusion by psychoanalysts reinforced efforts to treat what was considered a 'pathological' condition. Even prior to the influence of psychoanalysis there were efforts to treat homosexuality through the use of surgical techniques. For example, Dr. Stienach in 1917 was the first to use a surgical technique to attempt to cure homosexuality. He performed a unilateral castration on a homosexual man, and then transplanted testicular tissue from a heterosexual man into the castrated patient, in the hope that a cure would be achieved. Silverstein (1991) notes dryly, 'At least 11 men were operated on from 1916 to 1921. The experiments were not successful.'[13]

In 1962, Roeder introduced a new surgical technique involving the hypothalamus region of the brain. Since then 75 men considered sexually abnormal were subjected to hypothalamotomies. Most of these men had either been imprisoned or involuntarily committed to medical institutions for committing sexual offences.[14] These experiments do not seem to have been particularly successful either. Apart from these surgical experiments there were also attempts to treat homosexuality by using hormones—based on the assumption that the presence of homosexual desire in men indicated that they were inadequately masculine and the same in women indicated that they were overly masculine.

Behaviour therapy

The therapeutic method that achieved a culturally hegemonic status in the western world was behavioural therapy. Behavioural therapy was based on the work of physiologist Ivan Pavlov who showed that a previously neutral environmental stimulus (for instance, a bell) when temporarily preceding a naturally occurring automatic response (for instance, salivation in the presence of food) could acquire the power to elicit the automatic reaction after many such pairings. This phenomenon was later described as 'classical conditioning' and a number of the current treatment strategies used by behaviour modifiers are derived from these basic principles of classical conditioning.

Following from the work of Pavlov, B.F. Skinner formulated the empirical law of effect. Hersen et al. (1975) write that according to Skinner:

> ... the rate of a particular response could be controlled by its relation to environmental events (i.e. its consequences). He specifically described the process of positive reinforcement wherein a particular response followed by a contingent (reinforcing) environmental event resulted in a high probability of that response being emitted in the future. By contrast, in the case of punishment, if the same response was followed by a contingent (reinforcing) environmental event, the probability of the behaviour being emitted was decreased in the future. These two relationships constituted the empirical law of effect.[15]

When behavioural therapy was applied to the treatment of homosexuality, it took the form of exposing the patient to nude or sexual images of persons of the same sex and subjecting the patient to a mild electric shock so that the patient could link the imagery to feelings of pain. This was followed by techniques wherein the patient was encouraged to experience increased pleasure in heterosexual desire. One of these techniques was 'orgasmic reconditioning' which is described below:

... involves masturbation to 'deviant' imagery, with a heterosexual image substituted just before ejaculation. The appropriate image is then gradually substituted at an earlier stage of the masturbatory sequence until it becomes its sole content. Case studies have demonstrated the usefulness of this technique for increasing heterosexual arousal in subjects seeking treatment for homosexuality.[16]

The curious thing about behavioural therapy is the complete lack of clarity on what exactly it is meant to cure. Is behavioural therapy only changing the existing sexual behaviour or does it actually alter existing erotic fantasy structure in its entirety? Is the achievement of abstinence from same-sex sexual behaviour or the ability to 'perform' heterosexually, a measure of the 'cure'? At any rate, the gap between the diagnosis and the proposed treatment is also quite inexplicable. If studies in the aetiology of homosexuality insist on pointing to a pathogenic family as the cause, and if homosexual orientation is a product of a deep psychic process, as many psychoanalysts claim, then behavioural therapy does not address the aetiology question and instead equates a change in 'behaviour' to a change in 'orientation'.

Questioning homosexuality as Psychopathia Sexualis

What accounted for the dominance of the paradigm established by *Psychopathia Sexualis*? Why did this form of knowledge and this particular therapeutic practice gain cultural hegemony? Was it because there were no interventions in the field of knowledge positing an alternative viewpoint? Or was it that alternative viewpoints were rendered marginal in a socio-political climate that was hostile to any deviation from the norm? And conversely, what accounted for the changes in the perception of homosexuality as being a form of pathology?

Bayer (1981) in his study notes that the pathologisation of homosexuality has always been questioned. Apart from the ambivalence of Freud, there were extensive studies by Havelock Ellis, Magnus Hirschfield and Karl Ulrichs in the field of sexology, which saw homosexuality as a natural variant of sexual behaviour. For example, Breecher (1976) believes that Havelock Ellis anticipated the later studies of Alfred Kinsey by suggesting that '...homosexuality and heterosexuality are not opposites, like up and down; they are present or absent in varying degrees.'[17]

In the United States, Ford and Beach conducted a study of 76 societies. In this study they showed that in 64 per cent of them, homosexual activities were considered normal and socially acceptable at least for certain members of the community.[18] Evelyn Hooker in her study of 30 homosexual and heterosexual men found that there was no difference in psychological indicators of mental health of both groups.[19] Hooker, in fact, questioned the basis of viewing homosexuality as a pathology attributing the supposed pathological behaviour of homosexuals to social causes. She noted:

> ... with fear of public exposure and humiliation dominating the homosexual's life, it was extraordinarily difficult for relationships to last. What was a source of security for the heterosexual was a source of risk for the homosexual. Thus, it was the social reaction to homosexuality that generated the fear of intimacy cited by clinicians as evidence of homosexual pathology.[20]

However, it was not till the emergence of the gay and lesbian movement that the hegemonic status of the pathology paradigm was seriously ruptured. It was the beginning of gay rights militancy after the Stonewall Riots,[21] which resulted in a dramatic transformation of the existing social milieu and attitudes to homosexuality. While previously organisations working for homosexuals requested inclusion and stressed a gradualist approach, the actions following the Stonewall riots changed the nature of gay activism. As one of the activists noted, 'We consider the Stonewall riots to mark the birth of the gay liberation movement, as that was the first time that homosexuals stood up and fought back.'[22] This new culture of militancy found it unacceptable that homosexuals were classified as mentally ill and treated for *being* homosexuals. Gay activists used various strategies to question the framework of pathology.

First, the authority of psychiatry to speak on behalf of a silent population was questioned. Gay activists such as Frank Kameny questioned the right of psychiatrists to speak on their behalf. Kameny quite simply asserted that:

... I for one am not prepared to play a passive role in controversies over psychopathology letting others dispose of me as they see fit. I intend to play an active role in the determination of my fate.... *We are the true authorities on homosexuality whether we are accepted as such or not.*[23] (*emphasis ours*)

This viewpoint was taken forward by repeatedly asserting the right to speak in forums of psychiatrists where homosexuality was the subject of discussion. This was an important strategy since homosexuals who were until then defined only as an object of study began to assert their subject-hood.

Second, many activists and authors feel that the critique was successful because the strategy built upon the new culture of fighting back as opposed to reasoned speech. Activists disrupted the functioning of psychiatric conferences through sit-ins and what were called 'zaps'. Conferences were disrupted with gay activists taking the microphone and denouncing psychiatry as the enemy incarnate. Bayer concludes:

To those who had so boldly challenged the professional authority of psychiatry it was clear that only the threat of disorder or even of violence had been able to create the conditions out of which such a dialogue could occur. That lesson would not be forgotten.[24]

Third, the critique of pathologisation tapped into a cultural current, which de-linked sex from pleasure. The hegemonic status of the ideology of sex as being equivalent to procreation was questioned by the rise of the feminist movement as well as the emergence of the student revolution of the late 1960s. What was central to the challenge posed by both movements was the relentless critique of mainstream institutions such as marriage and family. Again, as Bayer puts it:

That ethos [linking sex with procreation and not pleasure] has all but crumbled in the West, subverted by profound social changes, battered by movements no longer bound to its influence, and increasingly deserted by the population over which its strictures held sway. Not only have procreation and pleasure been divorced, but also the priority of the former has been displaced by that of the latter. It is in this context that the struggle on the part of homosexuals for the social legitimisation of their sexual orientation ... must be understood.[25]

Finally, activists arrived at a more political understanding of the cultural power of psychiatry. Psychiatry was no more seen as a science but rather an elaborate body of knowledge, which had replaced religion as the arbiter of social values. The critique of psychiatry's inclusion of homosexuality in fact drew upon a wider critique of the very process of the medicalisation of social life. It drew upon the work of anti-psychiatrists such as Thomas Szasz who in their work went on to:

> ... expose the ways in which psychiatry, masquerading as a medical discipline, had assumed the social function previously performed by religious institutions. As a guarantor of the prevailing social ethos, he argued, it sought to redefine deviations from ethical, political and legal norms by first the invention and then the expansion of the concept of mental illness. Since psychiatry placed itself in the tradition of scientific medicine, this defence of values took the form of a value neutral defence of health.... At the same time, Szasz argued, psychiatry camouflaged its own quest for power as a benevolent extension of medical authority.[26]

Shifts in diagnostic categories

> Categories are the outcomes of historical development, cultural influence and political negotiation. Psychiatric categories, though mental illness will not allow us to make of it whatever we like, are no exception.[27]

Owing to the criticism by the LGBT movement, the classification of homosexuality as a mental illness under the Diagnostic and Statistical Manual (DSM II) came under increasing pressure. Ultimately, in 1973, after years of bitter dispute, the Board of Trustees of the American Psychiatric Association (APA) approved the deletion of homosexuality as a mental disorder. The rationale for deletion, as formulated by Robert Spitzer, was that:

> For a mental or psychiatric condition to be considered a psychiatric

disorder, it must either regularly cause subjective distress, or regularly be associated with some generalized impairment in social effectiveness or functioning.... Clearly homosexuality, *per se*, does not meet the requirements for a psychiatric disorder.... Many homosexuals are quite satisfied with their sexual orientation and demonstrate no generalized impairment in social effectiveness or functioning.[28]

This recognition that homosexuality is not a psychiatric disorder went hand in hand with the approval of a far reaching civil liberties resolution, which clearly opposed discrimination against homosexuals and called for a repeal of anti-sodomy laws. In support, the APA noted,

... Whereas homosexuality in and of itself implies no impairment in judgement, stability, reliability, or vocational capabilities, therefore, be it resolved, that the American Psychiatric Association deplores all public and private discrimination against homosexuals in such areas as employment, housing, public accommodation....[29]

However, despite this removal, the APA felt that the category of those homosexuals who are troubled or distressed by their homosexual feelings should be able to access psychiatric help. For this purpose another classification, the 'sexual orientation disturbance', was created. The APA noted that:

This category is for individuals whose sexual interests are directed primarily towards people of the same sex, and who are disturbed by, in conflict with, or wish to change their sexual orientation. This diagnostic category is distinguished from homosexuality which by itself does not constitute a psychiatric disorder.[30]

Following this historic development, the opponents of the decision asked for a referendum on the decision by the entire membership of APA. Through a democratic process, the APA, by a majority vote of 58 per cent who supported the decision versus 37 per cent who opposed it, decided that homosexuality was not a mental disorder.[31] This vote by the entire membership of the APA, rather than showing them in a good light, in effect made a mockery of the scientific process of expert review. What it showed was that *the question of the inclusion or deletion of homosexuality was a deeply political question* thereby throwing into question the nature of the 'science' underlying both its inclusion and its deletion.

Thomas Szasz was critical of the celebration that followed the APA's decision. He believed that what had remained unchallenged was the power of psychiatry to classify illnesses and thereby define aspects of existence using the label of pathology. As he put it:

> Celebrating the APA's abolition of homosexuality as a psychiatric diagnosis tacitly acknowledges that they have the knowledge and the right to decide what is and what is not a mental illness. I think the homosexual community is making a big mistake by hailing the APA's new stand as a real forward step in civil liberties. It's nothing of the sort. It's just another case of cooptation.[32]

The relevance of Szasz's critique strongly emerged in the successive debates that took place around the writing of the Diagnostic and Statistics Manual III (DSM III). There were proposals to include the new term, *dyshomophila*, which later changed to 'homosexual conflict disorder' and finally settled on 'ego-dystonic homosexuality'. Ego-dystonic homosexuality was defined as: '… a desire to acquire or increase heterosexual arousal so that heterosexual relations can be initiated or maintained and a sustained pattern of overt homosexual arousal that the individual explicitly complains of is unwanted as a source of distress.'[33]

This classification of ego-dystonic homosexuality was subject to critique on the grounds that it reinforced the pathological nature of homosexuality, particularly because there was no such equivalent concept of ego-dystonic heterosexuality. Following this critique, DSM III R dropped even this residual category. When the DSM III was revised in 1987, 'ego-dystonic homosexuality' was deleted as a separate diagnostic entity because '… in the United States, almost all people who are homosexual first go through a phase in which their homosexuality is ego-dystonic.'[34]

However, even this deletion was accompanied by adding a category that is non-specific with respect to gender of the person one is sexually attracted to, i.e., 'sexual disorder not otherwise specified', defined by the presence of '… persistent and marked distress about one's sexual orientation'.[35] DSM IV follows DSM III R in dropping ego-dystonic homosexuality but includes the category of 'sexual disorder not otherwise specified'.

The position adopted by DSM IV should be understood in the context of the various APA statements made since 1973, which have been supportive of gay and lesbian civil rights. Among the most recent is a 1998 statement regarding 'reparative' or 'conversion' therapies. It states that:

> ... the American Psychiatric Association opposes any psychiatric treatment, such as 'reparative' or 'conversion' therapy which is based upon the assumption that homosexuality *per se* is a mental disorder or based upon the *a priori* assumption that the patient should change his/her sexual orientation.

In specific regard to the issue of civil unions, in 2000, the APA's Board of Trustees voted to affirm that, 'The American Psychiatric Association supports the legal recognition of same-sex unions and their associated legal rights, benefits, and responsibilities.'[36]

In the contemporary American context a lot of the concerns around homosexuality are being played out over the question of behavioural therapy. While the battle regarding diagnostic categories has settled with DSM-IV removing any reference to homosexuality, the residual category of 'sexual disorder not otherwise specified' still allows for psychiatrists to provide treatment for those who were distressed by their orientation.

Questioning the logic, rationale and effectiveness of conversion therapy

Conversion therapy also known as reparative therapy, as noted earlier, aims at converting homosexual and bisexual orientation to a heterosexual orientation. It is based on the assumptions of the behaviouralist school that homosexuality is a behaviour which can be modified through treatment. However, the scientific objectivity and neutrality of the behavioural therapist and indeed the very methodology of behavioural therapy have come under increasing scrutiny and criticism, particularly in a social context in which the queer voice is being increasingly heard. The scrutiny to which this form of therapy was subjected took the following forms.

First, there was the emergence of literature that pointed out the inefficacy of the supposed 'cure' which behavioural therapy was supposed to bring about. Haldeman notes that:

> Even the most enthusiastic of conversion therapists claim roughly a 30% 'success' rate. This low frequency is typically explained by the fact that sexual orientation is very difficult to change. Where others might consider a 30% success rate as less than optimal, in the domain of conversion therapy it is the accepted standard. The apparent lack of concern on the part of conversion therapists regarding their treatment 'failures' is significant. Only recently, for example, has the obvious question been raised—what about the other 70%?[37]

Second, there were serious questions about what exactly was being converted. The key problem that has been pointed out to in the literature on conversion therapy is that the 'expansion of the sexual repertoire towards heterosexual behaviour is viewed as equivalent to a shift of sexual orientation.[38] As Haldeman goes on to note:

> Eager to equate heterosexual competence with orientation change, these researchers have ignored the complex questions associated with the assessment of sexual orientation, which includes biological, gender-based, social, and affectional variables. No researchers who conducted conversion studies have displayed any such thoughtfulness in their assessment or categorization of subjects.[39]

What conversion therapists in effect do, can be more appropriately described in the words of Shildo and Shroeder as 'homosexual behaviour management'. This term is used to: 'Identify the range of cognitive and behavioural tools taught in conversion therapy to diminish and cope with same-sex desire and behavior and to increase heterosexual desire and behavior.'[40]

Third, there was a shift from merely raising the question as to the success of aversion therapy to raising questions as to whether aversion therapy itself had any harmful consequences for the patient concerned. Again, Haldeman in his study has documented various consequences of conversion therapy from depression, inability to conduct a relationship (intimacy avoidance), sexual dysfunction, de-masculinisation, to exacerbating conflicts with spirituality.[41] The issue of negative consequences of conversion therapy is a largely unexplored area in literature that tends to focus almost single-mindedly on the question of success of the procedure in getting the patient to exhibit heterosexual behaviour.

Additionally, Haldeman's empirical study illustrates that in a culture where homosexuality is stigmatised, behavioural therapy only exacerbates the sense of shame at feeling same-sex desire. This heightened sense of shame has implications for the clients' abilities to accept themselves, which in turn affect their ability to conduct relationships and perform sexually. The 'success' of conversion therapy is a false notion based as it is on the sole parameter of ability to exhibit heterosexual behaviour. To take one of the many case studies that Haldeman cites:

> This treatment was not successful in changing Jim's sexual orientation. It did however, leave him extremely confused and conflicted about his natural homoerotic feelings.... Additionally he had deeply rooted shame related to his sexual response partly as a result of his culture, and partly having been reinforced by his conversion therapy....[42]

Fourth, there was the emergence of a social critique of conversion therapy. These critics sought to shift attention from the individual patient to the wider societal implications of conversion therapy. As Bagelman notes:

> [The efforts of behavioural therapists to reorient homosexuals to heterosexuality] *by their very existence constitute a significant causal element in reinforcing the social doctrine that homosexuality is bad.* Indeed, the point of the activist protests is that behaviour therapists contribute significantly to preventing the exercise of any real option in decision making about sexual identity, by further strengthening the prejudices that homosexuality is a 'problem behaviour,' since treatment may be offered for it. As a consequence of this therapeutic stance, as well as a wider system of social and attitudinal pressures, homosexuals tend to seek treatment for being homosexuals. Heterosexuals on the other hand, can scarcely be expected to seek voluntary treatment for being

heterosexual especially since all the social forces arrayed—including the non-availability of behaviour therapy for heterosexuality—attest to the acknowledgement of the idea that whatever 'problems' heterosexuals have it is not due to their sexual orientation. The upshot of this is that contrary to the disclaimer that behavioural therapy is 'not a system of ethics', the very act of providing therapeutic services for homosexual problems indicates otherwise[43] (*emphasis ours*).

While there were these four important positions of critique of behavioural therapy, conversion therapy was not without defence. While some proponents of conversion therapy conceded that the days of treating homosexuality as a mental illness per se were over, there was still the need for treating those who came to the therapist seeking treatment. For example, Mark Yarhouse makes three arguments in favour of treating persons who are distressed by their sexual orientation. First, he defends conversion therapy on the grounds that clients are autonomous and should have the right to choose treatment. Second,he argues that conversion therapy is successful for *some persons*. Finally, he suggests that it would be wrong for the doctor to deny treatment to a client who would like to 'cure' his or her homosexuality as the patient could feel that his religious beliefs (which stigmatise homosexuality) are more important than his or her sexual identity.

> For some it is easier, and less emotionally disruptive to contemplate changing sexual orientation than to disengage from a religious way of life that is seen as completely central to an individual's sense of self and purpose. However we may view this choice, or the psychological underpinnings thereof, do we have the right to deny such an individual treatment that may help him to adapt in the way that he has decided that is right for him? I would say that we do not. That is why the mental health organisations have adopted advisory policies that do not ban the practice of conversion therapy outright....[44]

Yarhouse's arguments are answered comprehensively by the APA Task Force study of sexual orientation change efforts (2009). To the first argument of client autonomy the APA's stance is that:

> Self-determination cannot be considered without an understanding

of the individual, community and social contexts that shape the lives of sexual minorities. By understanding self-determination as context-specific and by working to increase clients' awareness of the influences of context on their decision making the mental health professionals can increase client self-determination and thereby increase their ability to make informed life choices (APA 2009).

The second argument that conversion therapies can succeed is not borne out by the weight of empirical evidence.In fact in the APA's assessment that 'enduring change to an individual's sexual orientation is uncommon. The participants ... continue to experience same-sex attractions following sexual orientation change effort and did not report significant change to other-sex attractions that could be empirically validated.' Further, there was also some evidence to indicate that individuals experienced harm from this effort to change. 'The negative side effects included loss of sexual feeling, depression, suicidality and anxiety.' The APA Task Force believes firmly that mental health professionals who offer such therapies '... abdicate the responsibility ... to provide competent assessment and interventions that have the potential for benefit with a limited risk of harm'(APA 2009).

The third argument for conversion therapy is that some LGBT people choose to go in for therapy because of their desire to live a life in congruence with the teachings of their religion. The APA's response to this is to note that while it is true that 'many religious individuals desired to live their lives in a manner consistent with their values (telic congruence), however, telic congruence based on stigma and shame is unlikely to result in psychological well-being' (APA 2009). Mental health professionals could also refer to both groups and individuals who have resolved this conflict through personal effort and retain their sexual identity while continuing to practise their faith.

III. Mental health and homosexuality in the Indian context

Homosexuality in India was never a subject of furious debates as a medical category as it was in the West. Within India, medical categories were themselves complex, encompassing traditional systems of medicine such as *ayurveda, unani* and included homeopathy, which were positioned in opposition to the allopathic system. Outside the framework of these systems of medicine there still exist various faith healers, god-men and other peddlers of miracle cures for a whole series of ailments. Particularly in the area of sexuality, the informal system of medicine undoubtedly serves a significant part of the Indian population. The 'treatment' of homosexuality is located within this complex field of competing systems of medicine. However, this chapter focuses on the effects of the only system of medicine to be backed systematically by colonial power—allopathy.

Most discussions around the introduction of western medicine into India have focussed on the interrelationship between diseases such as plague and the role that western medicine played as one of the technologies of colonial power.[45] Comparatively, there has been little discussion on the history of the mental health field in India. The few accounts we have are descriptive in nature and link the birth of psychiatry to the establishment of asylums in the Indian context. As Venkoba Rao notes: 'The history of psychiatry in this country is the history of establishment of mental hospitals and then increasing their accommodation from time to time as the exigencies of time demanded.'[46]

The earliest asylum was established around 1787 in Calcutta. However it took over another hundred years for the first psychiatry department in a general hospital to be established in 1938 in Bombay. Post independence, psychiatry became established as a field of practice both in hospitals and private clinics.

Apart from looking at the history of institutions as a part of the history of psychiatry, it is equally important to understand the basis on which psychiatry makes its interventions. Treatment is dependent on the classification of diseases and disorders that allows for diagnosis of conditions of ill health. This classification is based on both the DSM and ICD diagnostic manuals. The DSM manual, as mentioned earlier, is adopted by the APA in the US and the International Classification of Diseases (ICD) manual is adopted by the WHO.

Diagnostic manuals such as the ICD and DSM are heuristic tools or standardised measures for estimating distress in clinical settings. The diagnostic manuals themselves are produced after much debate within the scientific community and are the 'officialese' spoken by practising clinicians of diverse ideologies and clinical practices and is constantly under vigilance.[47]

A critique of classification of diseases

The classification of diseases has been subject to two serious critiques.

The first critique that has been put forward of the classification of diseases is its insensitivity to diverse cultural contexts. This critique brought to the fore that psychiatry was primarily a western discipline that was mostly insensitive to other cultural contexts, such as in India. For example, in the scheme of the ICD, that most Indian medical professionals use, bulimia is defined as a disorder. The critique suggests that while bulimia may be a predominant concern in western societies, it was definitely not a huge concern in India. This critique of cultural insensitivity prompted the acceptance of specifically South Asian disorders in the ICD-10.[48] One such entry, the *Dhat* syndrome (also referred to as semen-loss anxiety), was listed as a neurotic disorder in the manual. *Dhat* syndrome, the contribution of Prof. Wig, is defined thus:

> As early as 1960, he described cases of young adult males complaining of involuntary passage of white discharge per urethra during micturation or defecation leading to multiple somatic symptoms along with anxiety and depression features. Many subsequent workers have confirmed this phenomenon, which is perhaps unique to the culture of South Asia.[49]

This critique of the classification adopted by the mental health field on the grounds of culture did not disturb the foundations of the ICD system. Instead, this resulted in the inclusion of what was perceived as culture-specific disorders within the system. However, no debate arose around the social implication of bringing semen-loss anxiety (something that actually reinforces patriarchal notions of masculinity) within the field of neurotic disorders.

A more wide-ranging critique emerged from outside the mental health field, through the sustained interrogation of mental health practice. This critique takes up the issue of how some human contexts of distress get seen as illnesses and serious enough to merit medical attention while others do not. The critique brings to light the nature of value frameworks and political contexts that result in this process of classification. A brief look at the history of classification can help us understand what accounts for these choices.

Very clearly, since the history of psychiatry is interwoven within the history of colonialism, there were perceptions of the colonised and the oppressed that became a part of the history of medical categories. As Davar notes:

> Dr. Cartwright proposed the term 'drapetomania' which was a disease of the slaves, characterised by an 'irrestrainable propensity on the part of slaves to run away to escape from slavery'. Similarly, 'in the Indian context, the colonisers characterised movements of protest in Eastern India as the work of *pagols*.[50]

It is this political basis of classification that Davar sees as particularly problematic from a feminist lens. The persistent assumptions and prejudice about certain behaviours and the nature of a mental health discourse that takes classification and treatment for granted, has been interrogated from a perspective that does not see the *normative* as being necessarily *just*. In Davar's viewpoint what gets classified as disease is also an ideological preference for conformity or adjustment to what is often simply a patriarchal status quo. This particularly impacts women who might not be ill but merely deeply uncomfortable with the range of mainstream choices available to them. In such contexts, mental health professionals, instead of validating women's choices, might be imposing the unjust requirement of conformity on women.

The value of this critique emerged quite strongly in the context of our interviews with mental health professionals. The condition of *vaginismus*, for instance, is understood as '... where there is a spasm of the outer one third of the vagina during an attempt or in anticipation of an attempt at sexual intercourse thereby making penetration impossible.[51] In one of the interviews we conducted the doctor told us that *vaginismus* is a condition that makes it impossible for the penis to penetrate the vagina. However, a speculum used by a doctor penetrates the vagina easily. The doctor stated that a woman was treated for *vaginismus* using behaviour therapy. There was neither debate nor attention paid to the reasons due to which a woman might find a penis unwelcome.

Critique of ego-dystonic homosexuality

In spite of the fact that there has been some amount of work on the critique of classification of diseases, there has been no discussion on the classification of ego-dystonic sexual orientation as a disorder in the Indian context.The Indian medical establishment—i.e., the Medical Council of India, the Indian Medical Association and the Indian Psychiatric Association—has adopted the WHO system of classification of mental and behavioural disorders known as ICD-10 (1992). This system specifically mentions ego-dystonic sexual orientation associated with heterosexuality, homosexuality and bisexuality as psychiatric disorders (see Code F. 66.1, ICD). In its previous edition, ICD-9, homosexuality was listed under 'Sexual Deviations and Disorders' with the following statement: 'Exclusive or predominant sexual attraction for persons of the same sex with or without physical relationship. Code homosexuality here whether or not it is considered a mental disorder.'[52]

ICD-10 did away with homosexuality per se as a disorder and introduced the category of ego-dystonic sexual orientation. ICD-10 defines ego-dystonic sexual orientation as: 'The gender identity or sexual preference (heterosexual, homosexual, bisexual or pre-pubertal) is not in doubt, but the individual wishes it were different because of associated psychological and behavioural disorders, and may seek treatment in order to change it.'

ICD-10 also has two other problematic diagnoses:

Sexual Maturation Disorder (Code F 66.0): The patient suffers from uncertainty about his or her gender identity or sexual orientation, which causes anxiety or depression. Most commonly this occurs in adolescents who are not certain whether they are homosexual, heterosexual or bisexual in orientation, or in individuals who, after a period of apparently stable sexual orientation (often within a longstanding relationship) find that their sexual orientation is changing.

Sexual Relationship Disorder (Code F66.2): The gender identity or sexual orientation (heterosexual, homosexual, or bisexual) is responsible for difficulties in forming or maintaining a relationship with a sexual partner.

The important shift from ICD-9 to ICD-10 is that homosexuality per seis not a sexual perversion. But the other shift that the classification makes is to not specifically mention homosexuality but rather subsume it under the broader rubric of supposedly neutral categories like ego-dystonic sexual orientation. Obviously, despite its avowedly neutral classification, those who get treated are invariably homosexual or bisexual. In effect the category of ego-dystonic sexual orientation is meant to allow for 'converting' homosexuals and bisexuals into heterosexuals. What the inclusion of the three categories noted above—ego-dsytonic sexual orientation, sexual relationship disorder and sexual maturation disorder—actually do is legitimise the idea that if people are distressed by homosexuality or bisexuality, that distress can be treated by 'changing' sexual orientation. The very existence of the category in effect justifies the practice of conversion therapy as homosexual orientation gets subtly coded as a disorder in need of 'conversion'. And again, the origin of the distress remains unquestioned and unchallenged.

Indian literature on ego-dystonic homosexuality and treatment
A survey of the professional literature indicates that some of the causes attributed for homosexuality include birth order (either the youngest child or the oldest child), paternal loss and detached fathers, close binding seductive mother and early homosexual seduction.[53] All the studies that we found in the review focussed on male homosexuals. There was no data on women.

In another study, 'A Case Study of Unusual Sexual Perversion', the author finds a psychodynamic explanation for homosexuality. He notes:

There is evidence of castration anxiety, guilt which manifests in form of searching for partner of same sex. The patient feels seduced by his mother and feels threatened after the arrival of his younger sister, which has resulted in hatred for young females. The other possible reason for his homosexuality could be his unconscious desire to prove himself more powerful and masculine than other males.[54]

The literature documents use of aversion therapy equipment along with positive and negative reinforcement.[55] Positive reinforcement in the documented literature has taken the form of pictures of women with erotic content along with the use of soft music and perfumes that the patient found desirable. The literature has also documented positive reinforcement in the form of 'acquisition' of social skills (for instance, assertive training for submissive behaviour and feminine ways of dressing is of great potential in assisting the transition from homosexual to heterosexual social adaptation).[56] The negative reinforcement has consisted of shocks administered by the doctor on viewing same-sex pictures of probable erotic content that the patient considered attractive.

The disturbing part of the surveyed literature was the indication of 'success' rates in conversion therapy. The 'success' rates were measured in terms such as the clients getting 'successfully married' or having sexual intercourse with a woman. The professional literature does not seem to enter into the debate on whether sexual orientation is limited to sexual behaviour and the decision to get married. By focussing only on the ability to function heterosexually, the literature refuses to take seriously the complexity of sexual orientation and ends up with a definition of 'success' that is based on a limited understanding of sexual orientation. In effect, what the literature actually ends up positing is that the only problem with the male homosexual individual is the inability to have sex with women. And if this can be achieved, the therapy is considered successful. Considering sexual orientation to include components such as erotic fantasy structure, arousal cue response, self-labelling and affectional patterns don't seem to have entered this discourse at all.

As the APA notes,

Sexual orientation refers to an individual's patterns of sexual, romantic and affectional arousal and desire for other persons based on those persons' gender and sex characteristics.... Tied to physiological drives and biological systems that are beyond conscious choice and involve profound emotional feelings such as 'falling in love'(APA 2009).

In addition, the literature that concludes that 'marriage' is a successful conclusion of therapy does not address the ethical problem of what such a marriage would mean for the wife who enters into such a marriage.

The further question as to what are the 'costs' to patients of the 'success' is entirely ignored by the Indian literature. The evidence as to the implications of conversion therapy for the patients is present within the study but ignored by their focus. As one study noted, 'Out of the 13 patients, six of them began to suffer from depression', a factor that is mentioned without any need for explanation. According to the authors, 'In five of our patients the depression was accompanied by an anxiety that they may lose their sexual drive totally and be neither homosexual nor heterosexual.' Instead of addressing the fact that conversion therapy might itself cause depression, it is sought to be explained away as 'an accompaniment of the change to heterosexuality'.[57] The work of Haldeman and the comprehensive survey by the APA (2009) has shown several health-based consequences of behaviour therapy that professional literature has ignored for too long. The question of intimacy avoidance and depression are documented consequences of conversion therapy. But the academic literature has not engaged with this issue in the Indian context.

IV. Ego-dystonic homosexuality: What do doctors mean?

In this section, we examine how the mental health professionals we interviewed have understood and interpreted 'ego-dystonic' homosexuality. In response to our questions, four kinds of opinions were expressed.

The *first* opinion was from those counsellors who believed that ego-dystonicity was a relevant categorisation and had to be treated.

Ego-dystonicity is a Freudian term and is to do with the lack of coherence of the self. The *dystonic* patient is often deeply distressed over his/ her condition. As a psychiatrist, I cannot ignore the patient's distress. It is not my job to tell him that it is okay to be gay, but rather my duty to deal with the patient's distress by treating him. I have to help the individual.

PB, Psychiatrist

When people come with homosexuality as a problem, I need to refer to the debate on homosexuality—with one extreme saying it is normal, and the other saying it is a psychological problem. Today there is a consensus in psychological classification that homosexuality becomes a psychological problem only when the person who is homosexual is unhappy with his or her own sexual orientation, i.e., he is distressed by his condition. If the person is perfectly happy such a person is not labelled anything. The WHO classification system is neutral towards homosexuality as it classifies ego-dystonic sexuality as a disorder regardless of sexual orientation. I believe if a patient is in distress because of his sexuality, I cannot say be adjusted, it's okay.

PE, Psychiatrist

If a person comes to us and says that he wants to change, the reason being very genuine distress with himself, then we try and help him out. If someone does not want to change we let him be. Sometimes due to pressure from parents to get married the boy gets married and finds that he cannot consummate the marriage. Thus if someone is trying to change because of social reasons but does not have a deep-rooted desire for change, we find that it is difficult to change that person. One cannot in such cases develop an aversion to heterosexuality through any therapy, as the pleasure which one gets through sex is unique.

CPC, Clinical Psychologist

What emerges through these narratives is how the category of ego-dystonic homosexuality is closely connected with the subjective feeling of distress. The clear implication is that ego-dystonic homosexuality is about being distressed about one's sexuality and therefore the role of the doctor is to alleviate that distress. Within this framework, as has been argued earlier, there are no questions about why people are distressed about their homosexuality, but instead a rather strong focus on treating the distress associated with homosexuality. As PB(Psychiatrist) succinctly summarises, '*It is not my job to tell him that it is okay to be gay* but rather my duty to deal with the patient's distress by treating him.' However, what appears to complicate the picture is the origin of the distress. In CPC'sunderstanding distress itself can be either a deep 'genuine' distress or a distress that is solely related to social pressure. In this case, the first situation warrants treatment and the second does not. Thus, even within the category of those who utilise the framework of ego-dystonic homosexuality there are those who completely ignore the question of the origins of distress and those who are troubled by what they consider as not 'genuine' distress that does not warrant treatment. The strong impulse towards treatment is itself driven by the pressure exerted either by the clients themselves or the family of the client, all of whom desperately seek a more 'normal' life.

The *second* opinion on ego-dystonicity is expressed by those who feel that the category is not entirely useful. These practitioners base this opinion upon clinical practice and the inability to achieve any cure through treating ego-dystonic homosexuality.

> Through my clinical practice, I have arrived at the conclusion that ego-dystonic homosexuality, in most cases, does not exist. There might be a few cases in which there is no space for heterosexual experience even through fantasies might exist, however, the majority are cases where patients have homosexual fantasies and in such cases change is not possible. If patients come to me asking that their orientation be changed, I used to tell them that it is not possible to change their orientation and refer them to other doctors.
>
> PA, Psychiatrist

> I am not comfortable with technical terms like ego-dystonic homosexuality, because I feel it often allows the doctors not to think. It becomes easy for us to deal with homosexuals once you categorise them.
>
> PD, Psychiatrist

> The problem is much more when the person is not distressed about homosexuality but about its consequences. Since you cannot separate

the individual from the society, the attraction leads to a problem.

CPC, Clinical Psychologist

Within these narratives it appears that clinical practice helps frame the challenge to medical categorisation. Clinical categories can also aid in embedding a certain heterosexist bias in the practitioner that often remains unacknowledged. The uncritical use of the category of ego-dystonic homosexuality can itself become a means for mental health professionals to disguise their discomfort and loathing at the very thought of homosexuality.

The *third* opinion is expressed largely by those from a sexological tradition preferring to use the Kinsey scale, which sees homosexuality as a natural variant of sexuality.

> Homosexuality is just a sexual preference and if a person is comfortable being homosexual there is no need for treatment. If a person is not comfortable with his sexuality, then we make him comfortable with it.
>
> SB, Sexologist

This viewpoint traces its origins to the discipline of sexology. Sexology has its roots in the thinking of people like Havelock Ellis who consciously eschewed the viewpoint of homosexuality as pathology and instead chose to focus on homosexuality as a natural variant of human sexuality. However, this was not a uniform viewpoint among the sexologists we interviewed and there were others who believed in converting homosexuals to heterosexuality, as indicated in later narratives.

The *fourth* kind of opinion on ego-dystonicity is presented by those who see dystonicity as an illegitimate colonial imposition upon a traditional ethos, which is more accepting of sexual difference.

> ... feel that psychiatry intersects with their lives primarily because their condition is constructed as medical pathology. This is a major factor in handling issues such as transsexualism and homosexuality as what has happened is 'deviations' of sexual expressions come within the framework of medicine and pathologisation. There is a colonial legacy in the role that biomedicine plays in constructing sexual difference as pathology. In rural India, sexual variations are not pathologised, it is only in the urban context that sexual difference is medicalised and this

impacts the life worlds of people, however this is not studied very seriously in the Indian context.

PC, Psychiatrist

Homosexuality is still seen as a subject of therapy by medical experts. Psychiatrists generally tend to treat problems faced by their patients in clinical diagnostic terms. The psychiatrists are hugely influenced by the medical system and hence deal with all forms of 'deviant' sexuality as a diagnostic problem.

CPA, Clinical Psychologist

The above two narratives illustrate the role of the discipline of medicine in constructing notions of normality and abnormality. Both the doctors are aware that there is a relationship between the discourse of medicine and the wider social world and how sometimes medical ways of looking at the world might not do justice to their clients. Within this framework, there is nothing inherently pathological about homosexuality; however, the very use of the medical framework places what might be accepted and tolerated in society within the realm of abnormality.

Thus, if one were to summarise the medical opinion on ego-dystonic homosexuality, there appears to be a balance between those who feel that treatment for ego-dystonicity is necessary as dystonicity causes distress to the patient, and those who for various reasons refuse to accept the category of dystonicity and refuse to treat it. The basis of a critique of the category of ego-dystonic homosexuality can be clinical experience itself, or it can come from within the framework of sexology, or it can be from looking at psychiatry as a colonial category which is insensitive to the way sexuality is framed and understood in India.

V. The ceaseless aetiological preoccupation: How did it happen?

What flows from the classification of homosexuality as a disease is the obsessive focus on finding out the 'cause' for it. Every practitioner had an opinion on the question.

I feel that young people are being trapped in Bangalore, on the roads, in pubs, they are enticed by offer of food and drinks and once they get addicted then they feel there is no way out...In a meeting with gay activists, I told them that you are trapping people into homosexuality; they kept quiet because they knew it was the truth.

LCA, Lay Counsellor, affiliated to religious organisation

I believe that sexual orientation is determined by early childhood experience, in most cases, homosexual orientation goes hand-in-hand with a female *habitus* and hence is biologically determined. When patients have a repertoire of behaviour that is feminine, then it gets imprinted as desirable and such patients turn out homosexual. So sexual orientation is really determined with the degree of pleasantness associated with early childhood experiences.

PA, Psychiatrist

At a particular age the person of the opposite sex appears very mysterious and there is no outlet in our society, so what people do is that to release sexual tension they adopt whatever is available and get fixated on it. People do have friends of the same sex and they can care a lot about each other.... What is the aetiology? When did this orientation become a fixation?

CPC, Clinical Psychologist

Homosexuality doesn't do any good ... the homosexual himself was not the problem but his condition was due to poor parenting. People who feel they are homosexuals and want to change should come in early to cure the problem ... if a homosexual is happy then there's no problem, but if they aren't then I will help them.

LCB, General Physician, Lay Counsellor,
affiliated to religious organisation

The answers themselves illustrate the way the issue of aetiology has been elaborated by existing discourse. Among the most powerful influences has been the discourse of psychiatry with the theories of homosexuality resulting from a pathogenic family. Thus the 'homosexual fixation' is explained by the lack of normality in the family environment, which could include the 'victim' suffering from child sexual abuse. A further theorisation contends that the fixation, which interferes with the normal route of sexual development, might be the result of a particularly Indian context, where the two sexes are rigorously separated. There is also the link between early childhood experience and pleasure, which could lead to a homosexual orientation being formed. Finally, homosexual orientation is also linked to the trapping of young boys, by people who are already homosexual, a viewpoint which asserts that homosexuals 'recruit' new members for their community. Within this discourse there is a vigorous resistance to the idea that homosexuality could be a natural variant of human sexuality and an insistence that one needs to understand the 'reasons' for why some people are homosexual.

What this quest, to find the 'truth' behind homosexuality, does is to leave heterosexuality as the unquestioned norm. Heterosexuality becomes the unexamined normative position from which one tries to understand homosexuality. The entire focus of medical science in trying to understand homosexuality produces an intricate web of knowledge about the homosexual, which simply reinforces the idea that heterosexuality is the norm. As David Halperin notes,

> ... By constituting homosexuality as an object of knowledge, heterosexuality also constitutes itself as privileged stance of subjectivity—as the very condition of knowing—and thereby avoids becoming an object of knowledge itself, the target of possible critique.[58]

If we take seriously the Foucauldian dictum about the relationship between knowledge and power, then we need to understand how knowledge forms constitute the homosexual within relationships of power. In medical science, one gets to 'know' the homosexual within a series of classifications.

> If biology is playing a role in determining homosexuality then it is not distressing as it is inbuilt or true homosexuality. Acquired homosexuality on the other hand is not biological. The approach to treatment would be different for both. However, there are other cases in which, for example, the boy has a sexual outlet through his homosexual experience, that is, he sleeps next to his brother, lives

in his hostel, sleeps with other boys. This is what I call inevitable homosexuality. Most of these, which is 8 to 10 cases a year, want to marry, want to enjoy with women, etc., therefore in such cases, therapy works.

CPC, Clinical Psychologist

There are two classifications of homosexuality: primary and secondary. Primary homosexuality is when a person right from adolescence has always had homosexual fantasies, has never masturbated to female images and has no heterosexual orientation whatsoever. There is a biological basis to primary homosexuality. With respect to secondary homosexuality, it refers to a person who has heterosexual fantasies, but *suddenly* has preference for sex with males. Normally, it is related to circumstances such as a person being in an all-male prison, in which case homosexual activity steps up. When the person is released such homosexual activity normally stops in secondary homosexuality. Secondary homosexuality is easier to treat.

PE, Psychiatrist

The need to classify also seems to be endless. Right from primary and secondary to inbuilt and inevitable there is a constant need to define homosexuality within a grid of problematic classifications. This classificatory grid is not innocent of power and the work of Michel Foucault has shown how these forms of knowledge are linked to power. As Foucault noted,

> ... the implantation of perversions is an instrument-effect. It is through the isolation, intensification and consolidation of peripheral sexualities that the relations of power to sex and pleasure branched out and multiplied, measured the body, and penetrated modes of conduct. And accompanying this encroachment of powers, scattered sexualities rigidified, became stuck to an age, a place, a type of practice....[59]

There are thus serious concerns around how classification of homosexuality and theorising on its origins becomes a node of power. This intricate web of knowledge about the homosexual subsumes the sexually diverse universe within a medical framework and hence produces the homosexual as a more 'knowable' subject who is then subject to a whole series of controls within medical practice.

VI. The received meaning about homosexuality— The physician's discourse

> The power which thus took charge of sexuality set about contacting bodies, caressing them with its eyes, intensifying areas, electrifying surfaces, dramatizing troubled moments. It wrapped the sexual body in its embrace.[60]

What is the basis for exercising power over the homosexual body? What are the ideas which form part of the way the physician thinks? Where do these ideas come from? This section argues that the physician's discourse is a product of both what the medical field has to say as well as the ideas prevalent in the wider society emanating from the two other discourses that we mentioned at the beginning of this essay—law and religion.

The relationship between the doctor and the client becomes of crucial importance when a heterosexual doctor is counselling a homosexual client. Very often, there is a wide gap between what the heterosexual person sees as 'right behaviour' and what the homosexual person's behaviour is. These gaps emerge dramatically through the attitudes of the counsellor on issues such as cruising, gay marriage, notions of effeminacy and masculinity, multiple-partner relationships, casual and anonymous sex, etc. The interviews with the mental health professionals in this study provided a glimpse into their deep-rooted beliefs about homosexuals and homosexuality.

> For example, homosexual people, because of the societal pressure, do not have relationships which last long. They change their partners frequently. They have issues of how to deal with the pain of break-ups etc...there are those who go to seek sexual satisfaction by paying others for sex. Some of my patients have gone to a park with the objective of getting sex for payment and have met up with unhealthy people who have tried to blackmail them. One of them was in fact beaten up by one of those who had sexual relationships with him.
>
> PD, Psychiatrist

The entire issue of multiple partners can create depression, feelings of rejection, jealousy when break-ups happen, as there is no support within the group for partners who experience this form of rejection....

PC, Psychiatrist

I feel that gays also have other problems such as depression, personality disorders, etc. Some of these are due to a lifestyle with multiple sexual partners....

CPB, Clinical Psychologist

In the narratives above, the beliefs about unstable and distressing homosexual relationships first constructed by Bieber, Rado, and Socarides in the early twentieth century find voice through the experiences of mental health practitioners in Bangalore. Experiences that these counsellors had with a few homosexual clients get extrapolated as 'truths' about the entire homosexual community. Multiple-partners, cruising for sexual contact, lack of long-term relationships, rejection and depression, are all mentioned as problems that homosexual people have to face without exception. 'Instability' in homosexual relationships is alluded to without any acknowledgement of the hostile social environment within which such relationships are formed.

Development of interest in the opposite sex is natural. However, if they get fixated (on same-sex), then they continue with their homosexual behaviour...the question I want to ask is, is acquired homosexuality a result of abuse? This question has to be researched.

CPC, Clinical Psychologist

There was one young man who was pulled into homosexuality by his seniors and started enjoying it. However when he got to a marriageable age, because of societal pressure, he started thinking of marriage, having a family and bearing children. I asked him if he would like to get out of it and encouraged him to be near women for some time. Since he was comfortable being near women, I then referred him to a psychiatrist who helped with behavioural therapy.

LCC, Lay Counsellor

Clearly, conservative notions of relationships as being monogamous, single-partner, marital and procreative only, permeate these narratives. The assumptions that several mental health professionals have about the origins of homosexuality operate as a pervasive background ideology, which determines the way they treat homosexuals. The assumption by all the counsellors is that heterosexuality is the natural end of sexual development and that people are homosexual because of unhealthy fixations on same-sex experimentation, sexual abuse and peer pressure.

The assumption of inevitable heterosexuality echoes the Freudian assumptions of homosexuality as arrested development. Additionally, several practitioners in this study pose heterosexual desire as being 'superior' to homosexual desire. The following example speaks about how the counsellor, a sexologist, views these differences between homosexuality and heterosexuality using a rather unfortunate analogy about scooters and cycles.

> In another case, a patient told me that he was standing in a bus and another man with his erect penis poked him. I told him that he should not feel guilty that he had enjoyed. I instead told him that he was going to have better and better enjoyment once he got more and more involved with girls. If you are riding a cycle you are happy just riding it. But once you know that a scooter is better than a cycle you would prefer to ride the scooter....
>
> SA, Sexologist

When counselling practices are based on an explicitly religious framework, it is only male-female sexual relationships within the framework of marriage that are seen as legitimate and any sex falling outside this framework is seen as a sin. But, in our study, we found that counsellors affiliated to a religious organisation often freely used 'scientific' language about poor parenting and other pathogenic causes for homosexuality. They also made explicit links between HIV, STDs and homosexual sex.

> I consider homosexuality akin to an addiction like alcoholism and drug abuse and many boys and young men who, because of homosexual sex, have sexual diseases like AIDS, and some boys wore colostomy bags because of anal tears...homosexuals who came to change obviously

felt there was a deficit in their lives compared to heterosexuals....

LCA, Lay Counsellor, affiliated to religious organisation

A few practitioners believed that homosexuals who articulate their identities are 'flaunting' it or 'wearing it on their sleeve'.

> The problem we have had in our hospital is that it being a teaching institute we have presentations on homosexuality. I have always felt we should look at it objectively and not get too carried away by activism. Even in this hospital we have some people who wear their sexuality on their sleeve. This, I feel, is unnecessary as heterosexuals do not assert their sexuality all the time.

CPB, Clinical Psychologist

In a socio-political context where heterosexuality gets constantly constructed in public through every sector in society (advertising, film, education, etc.) as being normal and natural, individuals begin to see heterosexuality as the unfailing norm. All areas of social life right from the family to the workplace and media representations presume the heterosexual couple as the social ideal. In this context, if even one homosexual speaks about his or her identity, it is considered 'flaunting'. Such a viewpoint is only indicative of how any questioning of the 'norm' of heterosexuality provokes a vigorous defence of the norm.

The narratives above examine these various beliefs that counsellors hold on homosexuality. Starting with classifying homosexuality itself as a mental illness to looking at it as a habit or addiction, many counsellors pathologise homosexuality. They talk of multiple-partner relationships, which lead to instability in the relationship, jealousy, rejection and depression, these being seen as usual outcomes of homosexuality. They understand the distress faced by homosexuals as a condition intrinsically linked to the condition of being homosexual rather than seeing it as a wider phenomenon arising from an experience of social bigotry and lack of acceptance. The physician's lack of experience or knowledge about the LGBT community results in an inability to deal empathetically with the problems faced by homosexual patients.

VII. Subject position of counsellor/ doctor— The possibility of neutrality

Can a health practitioner or counsellor be outside contemporary social mores that shape and influence opinions about homosexuality? The objectivity of a counsellor is considered a central aspect of all counsellor-client relationships, according to most doctors. The question that emerges sharply is whether such a position of empathetic neutrality is at all possible. If one considers that counsellors and doctors too are a part of a society, which believes that heterosexuality is the norm, it's likely that they too will share in some of the prejudices of the wider society. Some counsellors located themselves as coming from homophobic surroundings and it is necessary to note these narratives because they influence the counsellor's perspective while they deal with homosexuals as patients.

> I have never had problems with homosexuality though I come from a background where others in my family were homophobic. I've never had a problem with treating homosexuals as anything other than normal…. My personal stance is that we are all basically bisexual and in most instances, this bisexuality solidifies into homosexuality based on early childhood experiences. This is a Kinseyan kind of a view. I believe there's nothing wrong with being gay. The way I deal with people who are gay is by counselling them to expand their comfort zone. Of course it's easier said than done, because the problem is that in most cases they have to go back to their peer group who is not accepting of their sexuality.
>
> PA, Psychiatrist

Other counsellors put forward a cultural argument against homosexuality invoking the idea of Eastern cultural values versus Western decadence. But the irony of invoking the cultural argument to support a clearly western category of ego-dystonic homosexuality and a western mode of treatment, behavioural therapy, was lost on the interviewee.

> … the rest of the world may be liberal minded but India has a more conservative tradition. There is no systemic preoccupation with

sexuality in India. We cannot blindly ape what goes on in the west....

PB, Psychiatrist

The associations, which even sensitive counsellors make when talking about homosexual clients, sharply reinforce the idea of homosexuality as a form of pathology. If one, even unconsciously, associates homosexuality with murderers, thieves and other similar categories of social outcasts rather than with desire, family, affection or other such concepts it merely reflects the latently phobic perception of homosexuality.

> Our main issue is to deal with the feelings of the person and ensure that the person is at peace with himself regardless of whether he is a murderer, homosexual, etc. All are just labels to me. My role as a counsellor is to be neutral and leave my prejudices behind when I am talking to a client.
>
> LCC, Lay Counsellor

Sometimes the associations are unspoken and indirect. Moral values imbibed from religious traditions often complicate notions of objectivity and make it impossible for a client to get any perspective other than that of homosexuality as a sin. There is no scope for objectivity within a religious framework where it is believed that God has already ordained the nature of the male-female relationship as a part of the natural order.

For example, LCB (lay counsellor and medical doctor affiliated to religious organisation offering counselling services) said that she felt gays and lesbians were very aggressive, as she had seen them in TV shows abroad. She also said that she had read in a forensic medicine paper when she was a post-graduate student that more homosexuals than heterosexuals commit murders out of jealousy. She justified her opposition of homosexuality on the basis that homosexual sex spreads diseases and that homosexuals are violent criminals as well as victims of psychological maladjustments.

In a context where the client has to enter a counsellor's office, which is deeply rooted in a religious tradition based on negative associations towards homosexuals, there is no space for an objective provision of services to the homosexual client. Additionally, when practitioners invoke cultural differences between the West and India, their value framework for dealing with homosexuals cannot be considered empathetic. Even when doctors claim objectivity, the associations they make with murder, violence, diseases, etc., show how the very claim of objectivity is based on a pre-existing value framework.

Lastly, what the mental health professional thinks when he or she encounters a homosexual patient is often not known. Does the mental health professional share an anxiety about even being in the presence of a homosexual person? In one rare self-reflective interview, the counsellor said,

> Many heterosexual doctors are often very uncomfortable with the issue of homosexuality and when they deal with homosexual people, there is distaste and an anger, which gets expressed. The expression hides under the labels of ego-dystonicity. Many doctors often mock homosexuals, they feel they are threatened by homosexuals because the sexual difference has some affinity with themselves—for example, in Jungian terms, the anima (female side) is something which doctors are personally uncomfortable with. One should learn to accept one's own feminine side before one is able to deal with homosexuals with a degree of comfort. It is distasteful to deal with homosexuals even speaking personally and it takes some preparation before one is even willing to be compassionate.
>
> PD, Psychiatrist

VIII. The contemporary 'treatment' of homosexuality

In a recent testimony, a young gay man spoke of being taken to a psychiatrist by his parents to cure him of his 'affliction'. According to him, the psychiatrist observed that: 'There are three ways in which we can approach this condition. One, homosexuality might be caused by hormonal imbalances. Two, it could be a result of some tumour in the brain. And third, it could be caused by some other mental disorder.'[61]

Some mental health professionals in India continueto assert such opinions and prescribe several kinds of treatment for homosexuality. There are three predominant avenues of treatment still being prescribed.

First, there is the mode of prescribing behavioural therapy including aversion therapy.

> How aversive technique works is by giving the person a mild aversive stimulus when the person is watching something with homosexual content. The aversive stimulus is removed the moment the picture changes to a heterosexual image.... The idea is to decrease interest in homosexuality and increase interest in heterosexuality. That apart, we use treatments like orgasmic reconditioning—which is basically a treatment to redirect a person's stimulus for pleasure. For example, if a person can be made to think of a woman instead of a man at the moment of orgasm, then we succeed in reconditioning their pleasure in the female direction. Treatment is intensive; we have a six to eight week period of treatment with 30 to 45 sessions. We make the person get an erection with physical stimulus; the person is then made to imagine a person of the opposite sex and made to masturbate. We start by showing pictures of the same sex but move towards replacing it with pictures of the opposite sex. As an adjunct to orgasmic reconditioning we also use aversive therapy (10 to 20 sessions). We may follow up with booster sessions, which may be for four to five days consecutively.
>
> CPC, Clinical Psychologist

> I believe in behaviour modification, the positive way. What I do... is to show a series of pictures of heterosexual activity. Combined with this I teach him how to enhance pleasure by the use of lubricant. I try and introduce him to the idea that a woman feels nice and the pleasures of living together and how sex is the root cause of that. I give him an idea of what is the vagina and how one can masturbate with lubricant so that the organ slides into the vagina. I create a sense of anticipation about the vagina so that when he finally encounters a vagina he feels pleasure. My objective is to replace the feeling of

pleasure in homosexuality by pleasure in heterosexuality. This is what I call replacement therapy. I have an 80–90% success rate in all my cases.

SA, Sexologist

As one homosexual client who was subject to aversion therapy said:

She (the counsellor) first explained to me about three kinds of sex—'straight, homo and bisex'. She said that she could change me to bisexual and not 100% straight. For the first 2 days, she counselled me for around 45 minutes each. On the third day, she started treatment. She asked me to get photographs or magazines of men and women I thought sexy. So I went and bought some magazines. Then she brought a machine that looked like a small tape recorder. It didn't look like it had been used for a long time. She said that they weren't using the machine and that this was a rare case. She connected some wire to my left hand and tried the machine, but it didn't work for some time. She repaired it and then asked me to look at man's photo. I saw the photo for some time and she gave me a shock. Then she asked me to change and look at a woman's photo. Like this she kept asking me to change and giving me shock when looking at the man's photo. The shock was very painful. I couldn't continue after two or three and told her I wanted to stop. So she discontinued the treatment.

Mr. V

There seems to a widespread understanding that homosexuality is simply a sexual behaviour and one can get patients to stop expressing that form of behaviour through therapy, positive reconditioning, orgasmic therapy and other ways. The violence of the process of behavioural therapy has its roots in its very beginnings. A comprehensive textbook of psychiatry notes that, in the experiment conducted in Pavlov's laboratory it was discovered that:

As usual, the unconditioned stimulus was food powder and the unconditioned response was salivation. In this case the conditioned stimulus was a mild electric shock on the dog's skin, which might be expected to elicit defensive reactions competing with salivation.... Still, the conditioning was going well up until the point when the shock was administered to one new location after another on the animal's skin. When this was done, conditioning broke down, and the animal developed a lasting disturbance of its overall behaviour.[62]

The 'violence' of the process lies not only in the physical pain of a mild aversive shock which increases in intensity going up to 10 amps, but in the exposure of one's deepest fantasies to a clinical gaze of judgement. The fantasy is the subject of the doctor's gaze as pleasure is monitored, calibrated and judged. There are 'right' forms of pleasure and 'wrong' forms of pleasure. The patient gets the approval of the doctor when he is 'successfully' able to exhibit the 'right' kind of pleasure. When we speak of the clinician's gaze, the gaze not only functions to capture the homosexual body in an embrace of power but also aims to change the direction of desire under its relentless judgmentality.

The violence thus lies most painfully in the process of this judgement. When the client is told repeatedly that his/her pleasure is illicit and needs to move towards becoming a form of pleasure which society can approve of, the client's sense of self and internal coherence instead of being validated is being questioned. As one doctor noted, behavioural therapy provides and accentuates a sense of low self-esteem in the client as she is told through verbal and physical means that what she feels is wrong and needs to change.

Second, drug therapy as a mode of treatment, remains popular.

I personally do not use drug therapy with respect to homosexuality but recently had this case of a young man who was given male hormones by his family physician who wanted to cure him of homosexuality.

PA, Psychiatrist

He indulged in high-risk behaviour and violence. The man's homosexuality was only one component of his pathological behaviour. It is difficult to differentiate this from other behaviour. When the parents came to me for treatment asking that he be treated, they wanted the entire gamut of high-risk behaviour to be treated including his homosexuality.

PB, Psychiatrist

However, in cases of homosexuality where there is a major psychological disorder like schizophrenia, then one would need to treat with drugs as well. To take an example, I had a patient who thought he was female and that he should have sex with males. He was confused about his gender identity and felt the need to have sex with men. This was part of his schizophrenic illness due to some neuro-chemical imbalance; once I treated the schizophrenia with drugs he became normal with even the male-female angle disappearing.

PA, Psychiatrist

In the above cases of prescription of drugs, there are two strands, which are visible. First, there is the equating of homosexuality with an excess or deficit of the required hormones. Therefore the homosexual man is really insufficiently male and hence needs to be masculinised. This of course has its roots in medical history with the sexological assumption itself being that 'inverts' were those who were basically men trapped in women's bodies and vice-versa and providing the right hormones would help them become appropriately masculine or feminine. Second, there is the belief that homosexuality happens to be a part of a complex of illness and if other mental health conditions needed drug therapy, the homosexual desire was equally susceptible to treatment. There seems to be an easy collapsing of homosexuality into illness and reading it as part of a continuum of illness including high-risk behaviour, violence and schizophrenia. It's vital that treatment protocols deal with the complexities associated with sexual orientation and schizophrenia as two separate components so that the client can be helped to disentangle the two different aspects of identity and be helped to work through the complexities associated with the different characteristics of selfhood.[63]

Third, religion-based therapy, as a form of 'treatment' is also being offered to homosexuals. This therapy provides homosexuals, through prayer and belief, the opportunity to become heterosexuals. International organisations like Exodus International (which have travelled to India to offer their expertise on 'treating' homosexuality) pride themselves on having members who have 'successfully' converted from homosexuality to assert heterosexual identities using these 'treatments'. Their practices are also endorsed internationally by another organisation called National Association for Research and Treatment of Homosexuality (NARTH), an association that believes that homosexuality can be cured and offers aversion therapy. The confusion and anxiety that arises from this faith-based counselling service damages sense of self and lowers self-esteem. Global developments show that even founders of Exodus International now state that their programmes were 'ineffective … not one person was healed'. They stated that the programme often exacerbated already prominent feelings of guilt and personal failure among the counselees; many were driven to suicidal thoughts as a result of the failed 'reparative therapy'.[64]

Apart from all these forms of treatment that many practitioners offer, there are a few counsellors who reject all forms of treatment.

I don't believe the classifications of ego-syntonic and dystonic homosexuality is useful. This is because the stress related to sexual identity has a long background. Very often, the stress is related to social pressures, which the patient is subject to. Therefore, treating a person for ego-dystonic homosexuality does not make sense. We refer patients to support groups so that they can be comfortable with themselves.

PC, Psychiatrist

I stopped administering aversion therapy after meeting gay people, which opened a new world to me. I had already read about aversion therapy not being useful and then meeting regular gay identified people only increased the knowledge about the impracticality of aversion therapy.

CPA, Clinical Psychologist

When I met the son he told me that he couldn't have sex with women and that he was comfortable with being homosexual. I then spoke to the parents and counselled them to accept their son as he was as there was nothing wrong with him. The parents blamed me saying that though they had paid around Rs. 500 I still was not able to change their son. In fact they told me that they would speak to me only if I was ready to convert their son.

SB, Sexologist

I do not try to treat my patients out of their homosexual identity. I try to deal with the pain that they have. Many patients ask me the question of why they are like that. My own feeling is that sexual identity is not a genetic but a social problem. Sexuality starts as an amorphous entity and attachment to either sex depends on the social situation such as the family, etc. Easy acceptance of sexual identity is still very hard for the patients themselves. When families say that they want their children to change, I tell them that we'll take them to therapy and see if they are genuinely like this. If we find that they do have a homosexual identity after a couple of sessions then we cannot undo it. Even if patients come to me, and say that they want to change their identity, after a couple of sessions of discussion, they normally change their mind.

PD, Psychiatrist

When one tries to isolate the reasons for this position, how does this category of admittedly small number of doctors exist in spite of the powerful discourses outlined above? Is it the nature of a singular pro-active empathy for patients or does the articulation point to the beginnings of another discourse?

Would we be right in following Foucault to note the formation of a counter-discourse? As Foucault said:

There is no question that the appearance in 19th-century psychiatry, jurisprudence and literature of a whole series of discourses on the species and sub-species of homosexuality, inversion, pederasty, and psychic hermaphroditism made possible a strong advance of social controls into this area of 'perversity'; but it also made possible the formation of a reverse discourse: homosexuality began to speak on its own behalf, to demand that its legitimacy or 'naturality'be acknowledged, often in the same vocabulary, using the same categories by which it was medically disqualified. There is not, on one side, a discourse of power, and opposite it, another discourse that runs counter to it.[65]

There is a hint that it is really the emergence of a gay and lesbian voice that has resulted in the abandonment of 'treatment' of homosexuality. There is also the understanding that the availability of new research in contemporary psychiatry has thrown into question the disease model of homosexuality. The question of clinical practice, which shows that treatment does not work, is also hinted at. Thus, one can note that there is the incipient formation of a counter discourse that questions the heterosexist assumptions around the treatment of homosexuality.

IX. Science, religion and law—a common approach?

The science of mental health is based upon the adjustment theory whereby the effort is to make the non-normative conform to the norm. Medicine constructs homosexuality as a sickness. Based on this construction of illness, the discipline of psychiatry proceeds to treat it, so that individuals begin to exhibit normative behaviour. There is a striking parallel to the role of religious discourse in similarly constructing the non-normative as sinful and hence needing conversion. A similar parallel can be drawn from the law, which in Section 377 of the Indian Penal Code (IPC) continues to treat the homosexual act as a crime and hence justifying punishment. Medicine thus functions not in conflict with law and religion but rather in an easy co-existence with both in order to control what they consider a 'deviance'.

One of the research pathways science has taken is to find the biological basis of homosexuality.[66] The interest in this question is not limited to scientists who contemplate a cure for homosexuality.[67] There are thousands of homosexual men and women to whom the search for the 'gay gene' is a search for affirmation that being homosexual is not a choice but a biological disposition that nobody has a choice over. But, in the hands of 'objective' scientists, this research on homosexuality takes on rather disturbing colours. This is demonstrated in what this psychiatrist had to say, 'There is research that shows that there are transmitters in the brain that can be switched on and off to induce hetero/homo behaviour.' When asked if this were not a dangerous trend, PB (Psychiatrist)said, 'Progress of science is not subject to social control.'

> Homosexuality has a biological basis and if we find this and if we find this basis we will be able to treat homosexuality. I think they will definitely find a treatment. For example in some mental illnesses especially depression, if we treat the T2 receptors using drugs, the patient feels better. Similarly if you compare normal heterosexuals and homosexuals and do a neuro-imaging and see the difference in biological parameters then one can pinpoint possibly two or three factors and try and change them.
>
> PE, Psychiatrist

What was deeply troubling about these narratives was the sub-stratum of the reasoning, i.e., that homosexuals could yet be converted to heterosexuals. Since the scientific method of conversion therapy could not be considered a definitive success, maybe the answer lay in more advanced forms of treatment which could deal with homosexuality at its biological root. These new possibilities which scientific research could throw up still lay very much within the framework of adjustment theory.

This current bent of scientific thinking is also functioning in easy collusion with attitudes, which emerge out of the framework of religion and which use the language of love. They are best described as a form of what has been called compassionate moralism. Compassion is very clearly a part of their ideology but it is linked to a moral framework. For example as one faith-based counsellor noted,

> However in today's world, young people have to fight both against peer pressure and the media, both of which are very strong. I believe that people should be free, but not free to commit suicide or to commit homosexuality. When we talk about freedom, we should ask the question, if God would want you to do that particular act.
>
> LCA, Lay Counsellor, affiliated to religious organisation

Till recently, the discourse of law, very much like the discourse of religion and medicine was disposed towards a regime that defines heterosexuality as the norm. The law did this by defining and punishing the homosexual act and by simultaneously investing heterosexual sex with the legitimacy of marriage. The fact that homosexual sex used to come within the framework of illegality and was punishable with imprisonment, which could go up to life, had been internalised by the mental health profession.[68]

> Sodomy is illegal in India.
>
> CPC, Clinical Psychologist

However the decriminalisation of homosexuality by the Delhi High Court in 2009 opened a window of opportunity for changing the terms of discourse. The fact that the Delhi High Court relied upon scientific and medical evidence as well as evidence of human rights abuses to decriminalise homosexuality meant that the legal norm could be a signpost for bringing about significant change in wider social attitudes as well as medical practice.

X. Formation of a counter discourse— Queer resistance to medicalisation

While the existence of Section 377 was an issue around which the queer community had mobilised, it is by no means the sole locus of oppression. As the People's Union of Civil Liberties–Karnataka (PUCL-K) has noted in a study, human rights violations against sexual minorities is not just a matter of law but something in which media, family and the medical establishment are equally complicit. As the PUCL-K put it:

> The ideology of heterosexism pervades all dominant societal institutions such as the family, the medical establishment, popular culture, public spaces, workspaces and household spaces. We will examine each of these sites through which sexuality minorities are silenced and oppressed individually. [69]

One of the sites of queer oppression with which there has been some amount of activist engagement is the medical establishment. One of the key moments of this engagement was when the petition was filed before the National Human Rights Commission (NHRC) challenging the medical treatment of homosexuality on human rights grounds.

Apart from the public debate around Section 377, the medical profession too has come in for some amount of public scrutiny for the way it deals with homosexuality. The NHRC has been conceptualised as being in the vanguard of human rights struggles in India. If the NHRC fulfils its mandate, it must not only inquire into complaints but also link up with understandings of human rights globally and locally. It must promote human rights cultures by effectively linking up global developments in human rights with local initiatives.

It is in this context that we must understand the petition filed in the case of a patient at the All India Institute for Medical Sciences (AIIMS), who had been undergoing treatment by a doctor in the psychiatry department for four years to cure him of his homosexuality. The patient went to Naz Foundation India (an organisation working with men having sex with men [MSM] issues), and the coordinator of the MSM project, Shaleen Rakesh, filed a complaint with the NHRC alleging psychiatric abuse. The client noted that:

> [M]en who are confused about their sexuality need to be given the opportunity to go back to heterosexuality. I have never been confused but was nevertheless told that I had to be 'cured' of my homosexuality. The doctor put me on drugs, which I have been taking for four years.[70]

The treatment reportedly involved two components: counselling therapy and drugs. During counselling therapy sessions, the doctor explicitly told the patient that he needed to curb his homosexual fantasies, as well as start making women rather than men the objects of his desire. The doctor also administered drugs intended to change the sexual orientation of the patient, providing loose drugs from his stock rather than disclosing the identity of the drugs through formal prescription. The patient reported experiencing serious emotional and psychological trauma and damage, as well as a feeling of personal violation.[71]

The moment the petition was filed, there was a wide

mobilisation of the queer community and a number of letters were written to the NHRC urging it to protect the rights of the affected individual. The NHRC, after admitting the complaint (#3920), finally chose to reject it. Informal conversations with the Chairman of the NHRC revealed that the Chairman believed that until Section 377 was repealed nothing could be done and in any case most of the organisations were foreign-funded, without any real grassroots support. According to another NHRC source, 'homosexuality is an offence under IPC, isn't it? So, do you want us to take cognisance of something that is an offence?'[72]

Regardless of the negative outcome of the complaint in the NHRC, what is significant is the framing of a medical issue within human rights terms. As a letter of protest written by students, researchers and faculty of the National Law School of India University notes,

> This complaint 3920 illustrates the necessity for formal standards to prevent discrimination and abuse on the basis of sexual orientation in medical and psychiatric care. There is no doubt that in the absence of these standards, physicians cannot be held accountable for such human rights violations against lesbian, gay, bisexual and transgender individuals occurring in psychiatric and medical contexts throughout India.[73]

The complaint marked a moment of LGBT assertion, which was dismissed on the specious ground that Section 377 made homosexuality an offence. However now that Section 377 has been provisionally declared unconstitutional, the NHRC cannot refuse to look into a complaint made against the treatment of homosexuality by the mental health profession. The connections between human rights violations and the mental health profession are poised to enter the public arena in a much bigger way in a post-Section 377 climate.

XI. Conclusions—Challenging medicalisation and offering alternate structures

While the challenge to viewing homosexuality within the framework of a medical pathology has to some extent come from human rights discourse, the human rights language remains unable to mount an epistemological challenge to the very categories within which homosexuality is discussed. Queer discourse apart from being an activist intervention can also be seen as an epistemological intervention, which challenges the very foundations within which homosexuals have been defined and treated. The key analytical category through which this challenge has been mounted is the understanding of how heterosexism and homophobia pervade the discourse of medicine. The queer perspective, apart from challenging the very concept of medicalisation, also proposes an alternative.

Challenging heterosexism and homophobia

When it comes to violence against homosexuals, the first conceptualisation was the notion of 'homophobia'. George Weinberg introduced the word homophobia into literature in 1972 in a publication titled *Society and the Healthy Homosexual*. He defined homophobia as, 'the dread of being in close quarters with homosexuals which is consistent with the formal criteria for a phobia in psychological literature'.

However, Plummer (1999) notes that:

> There are five key differences that distinguish homophobia from a true phobia. First, the emotion classically associated with a phobia is fear, whereas homophobia is often characterised by hatred or anger. Second, a phobia generally involves recognition that the fear is excessive or unreasonable, but homophobic responses are often considered understandable, justified, and acceptable. Third, a phobia typically triggers avoidance, whereas homophobia often manifests itself as hostility and aggression. Fourth, a phobia does not usually relate to a political agenda, while homophobia has political dimensions including prejudice and discrimination. Finally, unlike homophobia, people suffering from a phobia often recognise that it is disabling and are motivated to change.

It is also interesting to note that unlike other phobias where the client suffering from the phobia is provided treatment, in homophobia, treatment is being provided to homosexuals, not to the individuals who are homophobic. Apart from these reasons as to why homophobia might be a mischaracterisation of the violence faced by homosexuals, much can be learnt from feminist efforts to grapple with the reasons for the violence faced by women. Bhargavi Davar argues for a feminist understanding of domestic violence:

> ... the relations society deems appropriate—that is, white heterosexual male dominance and the concomitant subordination of women, people of colour, homosexuals, and the poor—can only be maintained by constant assertion and enforcement of that regime. This is the true perspective from which we must look at the otherwise incredible information that one-fourth to two thirds of men in relationships have used violence toward 'their wives'. When behaviour is that widespread you can't very well call it pathology unless you want to say that the whole perpetrator class is sick.[74]

What we learn from Davar's critique is that violence, which is a socio-political phenomenon,cannot be reduced to pathology. Doing so results in an absurd situation where all the men who beat their wives are seen as sick. Similarly the use of the term homophobia implies that those who perpetrate homophobic violence suffer from a form of sickness. And this clearly fails to take into account the fact that the discrimination which homosexuals face is a socio-political phenomenon much like racism and sexism.

To take this analysis further, instead of viewing hatred of homosexuals as a phobia alone, we must look at how various social institutions are ideologically predisposed to presume heterosexuality. This is referred to as heterosexism. Heterosexism becomes the basis of intolerance for any deviance from the norm. As the PUCL-K Report notes,

> This report makes the argument that the extent and nature of violence can only be explained by paying close heed to its roots in social institutions such as the family, the law, the media and the medical establishment which constantly reinforce the idea that the norm is for the biological male to behave in a gender appropriate manner.[75]

If one were to identify a heterosexist framework within the mental health field one can note that the object of study is ego-dystonic homosexuality, not heterosexuality. Behavioural therapy is prescribed for homosexuality and not heterosexuality. It is constantly assumed that heterosexuality is the natural outcome of sexual development, not homosexuality. Thus medical discourse as a system of knowledge rigidly constructs homosexuality as the problem, leaving heterosexuality as the unquestioned norm.

De-medicalising sexual orientation: Support groups as an alternative

What queer discourse has done is to show that both the classification of homosexuality as an illness and the concept of ego-dystonic homosexuality are products of heterosexism. If such is indeed the understanding of why homosexuality has been produced as a medical condition, then what are the alternatives? What forms of support and social structures can homosexual communities create to provide a non-judgemental, affirmative environment for personal development?

To answer this question we looked at the role that support groups for homosexual communities play in dealing with the anxieties of being homosexual in a largely heterosexist world. We conducted a focus group discussion with the Bangalore-based support group Good As You (GAY) in order to make this possible. GAY was formed in February 1994 and was envisaged as a space 'which was a little more private than a pub and a little more constructive than a good bitching session!'[76] The group meets every Thursday and has provided a safe space for those who are not identified as 'exclusively heterosexual'. The group has a floating membership with over a thousand people attending its meetings since its inception. The group's agenda is to provide a place for queer people to talk about issues that mattered to them in a safe space.

In the focus group, open-ended questions were posed to members who attended the session that day. Members were asked why they initially came to the group meeting and how they had learned about it. They were asked about their perceptions about the group both before they joined it and their current perceptions. They were also asked why they continued attending the group meetings. Some of the responses are reproduced below:

I got to know about the group from my friend. I was confused about my identity, and how to take my life forward. I was discussing this with him in detail. He asked me to come for the meeting and see how it is. He said that even if I did not want to introduce myself, or discuss or answer questions it was fine. The first month was not very comfortable, but down the line I got comfortable. There was a confidence to talk about problems.

A, 29 years

When I shifted from Delhi, I had no friends in Bangalore. I wanted to meet a group of people.... K, who I met, said that Good As You was the right place for me. So I came here. It took me a week to get comfortable.

B, 28 years

I heard that people gather here to bitch, and that there was a place on Double Road where a lot of gay guys meet. My initial impression was that it was just about cruising. Finally, after hearing a lot of things I found out that this was a space where people are comfortable. The first time I was not very comfortable as I was not sure if I have to give my name. I was apprehensive about it being a public forum.

C, 24 years

What the responses indicated was that even for the most comfortable GAY members, the initial step to contact GAY was taken with a great deal of trepidation. There was a sense of isolation combined with a discomfort with oneself and one's sexuality. This sense of isolation really emerges from the fact that other spaces of socialisation including family, workspace, etc., do not provide space to express homosexual desire or romantic or sexual feelings and emotions.

After a year I wanted to talk about things. I was tired of hanging out with my office crowd. I forced myself and came back to the group. It helped me sort out many issues in my mind and learn about different views.

D, 34 years

When participants came to GAY for the first time, they were

not 'comfortable' with their sexuality. They often felt 'isolated', 'confused' and lonely. However, over a period of time, which varied from a week to a year, there was a change in the way the members felt.

> 'I thought I was bisexual and wanted to marry. Now I'm very comfortable being gay. There's nothing wrong with me. I have seen myself go from zero to completely positive about homosexuality.'
>
> E, 28 years

> Earlier, I was pretty uncomfortable with my sexuality. But coming to the group was like coming to a school. I learnt many things about people around me and myself. Soon I came out to my parents. After learning all these years, I feel I like can teach now!
>
> F, 29 years

> It helped me sort out many issues in my mind and learn about different views. We even discussed religion, spirituality. It was fantastic to discuss these issues with others who are going through the same thing. It was wonderful. It is comfortable to meet people with the same experiences.
>
> G, 34 years

> I came to Good As You in two phases. This is my 60th time. The first time I came I was in a relationship. I had had friends, etc. After a few years, this deteriorated and I did not have anyone to fall back on.
>
> H, 35 years

The question, which needs to be answered, is what accounts for this shift from 'lonely', 'isolated' and 'confused' to 'very comfortable', 'completely positive', and a 'perspective that gay guys can also do something'?

One part of the answer is that Good As You was a community space that allowed for the expression of a part of the self, which was silenced in the wider world. The creation of a safe space where one could freely express one's feelings is an important step in the construction of selfhood. This self-expression was also in a social context in which there were others who felt similarly. As such it allowed for a collective exploration and articulation of an aspect of human experience, which was not possible in a wider social setting. The increasing comfort with oneself was a process of collective learning with members learning from each other's experiences and getting more comfortable as they observed other group members. Members got a sense of individuality and self-esteem through contact with others who have gone through similar experiences. It was also a space where the dominant understanding of homosexuality was challenged.

Some of the key shifts were from understanding homosexuality from a purely sexual context to seeing other queer people as a supportive network of friends. As one respondent noted,

> Initially I thought gay guys were only for sex. When I came here I got the perspective that gay guys can also do something. The more your social circle widens, the more acceptance comes in.
>
> I, 24 years

> I told my boyfriend that I love you but I need my set of friends as a support system. I need to look at life beyond my boyfriend.
>
> H, 35 years

The importance of this shift in perspective is to move from seeing homosexuality from a relational context to seeing it from an affiliative perspective. That is, one does not see other gay people as only sexual contacts or as relationship material but rather as people who fulfil the roles of friends, brothers, sisters and even parents. This widens the social network and provides a social space for the articulation and management of stress relating to sexual identity. As some studies have noted:

> The presence of social support has been identified as a key variable in moderating the effects of threatening life events, which push the individual towards mental distress. The range of social relations available to an individual provides a mechanism whereby the burden of individual stress can be relieved and the objective sources of stress managed in a collective manner.[77]

Of course it cannot be argued that a queer support group succeeds at all times in alleviating distress relating to sexual orientation. As one respondent noted:

> A few people who have come here have not yet been able to take anything back. With old age, insecure feelings have come, and people have not taken the decisions they should have. Things (in Good As You) that have given us the strength have not given them the same strength.
>
> J, 36 years

However, the point, which needs to be made, is that there is a rough congruence between the feelings of distress with which clients approach practitioners for treatment and the feeling of confusion and isolation with which individuals enter a group like GAY. Of course, the clients who go to the practitioner might be more disposed to getting 'converted' while individuals who come to GAY are more disposed to becoming 'comfortable'. But in several instances in the group, counsellors or practitioners who knew about the group have referred members to it. In these instances, even while the clients came in originally with distress about their sexuality, meeting others like themselves and listening to experiences of other individuals enabled them to become comfortable with their identities.

Hence, it is vital that even before embarking on therapy, practitioners need to make the effort to make clients understand that they are not alone in their desires and that they can be 'comfortable' with themselves. Practitioners might help the client further by sharing more information about groups like Good As You and encourage clients to meet such groups. Since there is the possibility that clients might get more comfortable with their sexual orientation, if practitioners send out such messages, a support group might play a vital role in aiding patients to arrive at this sense of comfort.

As one respondent put it:

> I was out as a gay man before coming here. Even as an out gay man I have self doubts. A place like this reinforces my identity.
>
> K, 25 years

However this is a difficult journey and one cannot presume success even after becoming a part of the group. Support groups are not a magical solution to the problems that emerge from a wider heterosexist frame. However, the emergence of this space does allow for some people to benefit from a 'range of social relations', which provides a mechanism whereby 'the burden of emotional stress can be relieved and the objective sources of stress can be managed in a collective manner'. This pull of social relations has been referred to as the fund of sociality which is composed of intimacy, the network of common concerns, the ability to develop supportive social relations, the confirmation of one's prestige and the feeling of alliance with others who provide a supportive base.[78] The sense of community, which is created is still fragile and will continue to be so until there is a larger acceptance of homosexuality as a legitimate expression of sexuality.

Notes

[1] This essay is based on a study supported by Sarai/CSDS Short Term Independent Fellowships, 2003. An earlier version of this essay appeared in Arvind Narrain and Gautam Bhan (eds), *Because I Have A Voice: Queer Politics in India* (New Delhi: Yoda Press, 2005). A brief report of this study was presented at the SARAI Fellowships Conference in August 2003. Earlier in the same month, we had an opportunity to present the initial findings in a meeting of the Karnataka Association of Clinical Psychologists (KACP). The responses from practitioners at that meeting ranged from being extremely supportive to a few dissenting voices. We have incorporated some of the responses from that meeting into this report. We also presented the study at a meeting of PRISM, a Delhi-based group working on sexuality rights, in the same month. Encouraged by the positive responses, we presented the study in panel sessions at various conferences including: the second International Conference on Sexuality, Masculinities and Cultures in South Asia, held in Bangalore, in June 2004; the Sexualities, Genders and Rights in Asia Conference, held in Bangkok, in July 2005; and at the 23rd National Conference on Sexology, held in Bangalore in October 2006. A report of this study was also presented, on our behalf, by Gautam Bhan in Delhi in August 2005 at a meeting with mental health professionals, organised by Voices Against 377 (a coalition of organisations and groups campaigning against Section 377 of the Indian Penal Code).

[2] Ariel Shidlo and Michael Schroeder, 'Changing sexual orientation: A

consumer's report', *Professional Psychology: Research and Practice*, Vol. 22, No. 3 (2002), pp. 249–59.

3 Ronald Bayer, *Homosexuality and American Psychiatry: The Politics of Diagnosis* (New York: Basic Books,1981), p. 5.

4 See Michel Foucault, *The History of Sexuality, Vol. I* (Harmondsworth: Penguin Books, 1978).

5 Jeffery Weeks, *Sexuality* (London: Routledge,1986), p. 71.

6 Edward. M. Brecher, 'History of human sexual research and study', in A.M. Freedman, H.L. Kaplan and B.J. Sadock (eds), *Comprehensive Textbook of Psychiatry* (Baltimore: Williams and Wilkins, 1976).

7 Joseph Bristow, *Sexuality* (London: Routledge, 1997), p. 30.

8 S.P. Chaube, *Abnormal Psychology* (Agra: Lakshmi Narain Agarwal, 1995), pp. 438–39.

9 Bayer, *Homosexuality and American Psychiatry*, p. 22.

10 Ibid., p. 27.

11 Ibid.

12 Ibid.

13 Charles Silverstein, 'Psychological and medical treatments of homosexuality', in John C. Gonsiorek and James D. Weinrich (eds), *Homosexuality: Research Implications for Public Policy* (London: Sage,1991), p. 107.

14 Ibid.

15 Michel Hersen et al., 'Historical perspectives in behaviour modification: Introductory comments', in Michel Hersen, Richard M. Eisler, Peter M. Miller (eds), *Progress in Behavior Modification*, Vol. I (New York, Academic Press, 1975), p. 2.

16 Kelly D. Brownell et al., 'The behavioral treatment of sexual deviation', Michel Hersen et al. (eds), *Progress in Behavioral Modification*, p. 613.

17 Brecher, 'History of Human Sexual Research and Study', p. 1356.

18 Cllelan Ford et al., 'Patterns of Sexual Behaviour', cited in Ronald Bayer, Homosexuality and American Psychiatry (New York, Basic Books, 1981), p. 46.

19 For a study similar to Hooker's study conducted in India, See Dr. Bharath Reddy, 'A Comparative Study of Homosexuals and Heterosexual Men With Respect to Quality of Life, Substance Use and Suicidality', this volume.

20 Bayer, *Homosexuality and American Psychiatry*, p. 51. It should also be noted that when Hooker refers to social reaction to homosexuality and its influence on homosexuals, she anticipates what is today described as the experience of 'minority stress'.

21 The Stonewall riots marked the first public demonstration against discrimination of LGBT communities and is often hailed as a historic landmark event that led to the emergence of the worldwide queer rights movement. What was considered as a routine police raid at a gay bar called 'Stonewall'in New York, in mid-1969, led to unprecedented widespread riots and protest marches by the LGBT community against police harassment when the patrons

of the bar resisted police arrest and attacked the police convoy to defend the bar.

22 Bayer, *Homosexuality and American Psychiatry*, p. 93. Also see Martin Duberman, *Stonewall*, (New York: Plume, 1994).

23 Ibid., p. 82.

24 Ibid., p.104.

25 Bayer, *Homosexuality and American Psychiatry*, p. 5.

26 Ibid., p. 54.

27 Arthur Kleinman, *Rethinking Psychiatry* (New York: Macmillan/The Free Press, 1988); and S. Lee, 'Cultures in Psychiatric Nosology: The CCMD-2-R and International Classification of Mental Disorders', *Culture, Medicine and Psychiatry*, Vol. 20, No. 4 (Dec. 1996), pp. 421–76.

28 American Psychiatric Association, 'Homosexuality and Sexual Orientation Disturbance: Proposed Change in DSM- II', [http://www.psych.org/edu/other_res/lib_archives/archives/197308.pdf.]

29 Ibid.

30 Ibid.

31 Bayer, *Homosexuality and American Psychiatry*, p. 148.

32 Ibid., p. 60.

33 Ibid. p. 176.

34 'Previous Editions of DSM', *DSM Library: Psychiatry Online* [http://dsm.psychiatryonline.org/dsmPreviousEditions.aspx].

35 Gerald Davison, 'Construction and Morality in Therapy', in John C. Gonsiorek et al. (eds), *Homosexuality*, p. 138.

36 http://www.psych.org/lib_archives/archives/200417.pdf (accessed Jan 2012).

37 Douglas C. Haldeman, 'Therapeutic antidotes: Helping gay and bisexual men recover from conversion therapies', *Journal of Gay and Lesbian Psychotherapy*, Vol. 5, No. 3/4 (2001), p. 119.

38 Douglas C. Haldeman, 'The practice and ethics for sexual orientation conversion therapy', *Journal of Consulting and Clinical Psychology*, Vol. 62, No. 2 (1994), p. 222.

39 Ibid., p.223.

40 Shidlo and Schroeder, 'Changing sexual orientation: A consumer's report', p. 253.

41 Douglas C. Haldeman, 'Therapeutic Antidotes', pp. 117–30.

42 Ibid., p. 124.

43 Davison, 'Construction and morality in therapy', p. 141.

44 Mark Yarhouse et al., 'Ethical issues in attempts to ban reorientation therapies', *Psychotherapy: Theory/ Research/ Practice/ Training*, Vol. 39, No. 1 (2002), p. 73.

45 David Arnold, *Colonizing the Body: State Medicine and Epidemic Disease in Nineteenth-century India* (Berkley: University of California Press, 1993).

46 Venkoba Rao, 'India', in J.G. Howells (ed.), *World History of Psychiatry* (New York: Brunner, 1975).

47 Bhargavi Davar, *Mental Health of Indian Women: A Feminist Agenda* (New Delhi: Sage, 1999), pp. 44–45.

48 Similarly the Chinese Classification of Mental Diseases (CCMD) is also struggling with the objective of accommodating culturally specific diseases. See Sing Lee, 'Cultures in psychiatric nosology: The CCMD-2R and international classification of mental disorders', *Culture, Medicine and Psychiatry*, Vol. 20 (1996), pp. 421–72.

49 Sudhir Khandelwal, 'Classification of mental disorders: Need for a common language', in R. Srinivas Murthy (ed.), *Mental Health in India* (Bangalore: Peoples Action for Mental Health, 2000).

50 Davar, *Mental Health of Indian Women*, pp. 44–5.

51 Prakash Kothari, *Common Sexual Problems... Solutions* (New Delhi: UBS Publishers, 1999), p. 89.

52 Gene Nakajima, 'The emergence of an international lesbian, gay, and bisexual psychiatric movement', in *Journal of Gay and Lesbian Psychotherapy*, Vol. 7, No. 1/2 (2003), p. 180.

53 P.V. Pradhan, K.S. Ayyar, and V.N. Bagadia, 'Homosexuality: Treatment By behaviour modification', *Indian Journal of Psychiatry*, Vol. 24, No. 2 (1982), pp.182–86.

54 R.C. Jiloha, 'A case of unusual sexual perversion', *Indian Journal of Psychiatry*, Vol. 26, No. 4 (1982), p. 403–4.

55 For an exhaustive survey of the Indian academic literature on the treatment of homosexuality, see Suresh Parekh, 'Homosexuality in India: The light at the end of the tunnel', *Journal of Gay and Lesbian Psychotherapy*, Vol 7, No. 1/2 (2003), pp.145–63.

56 M. Mehta and S. Nimgoanka Deshpande, 'Homosexuality: A study of treatment and outcome', *Indian Journal of Psychiatry*, Vol. 25, No. 3 (1983), pp. 235–58.

57 Bardhan, Ayyar and Bagadia, 'Homosexuality: Treatment by Behavior Modification', pp. 182–86.

58 David Halperin, *Saint Foucault: Towards a Gay Hagiography* (Oxford: Oxford University Press, 1995), p. 47.

59 Foucault, *The History of Sexuality Vol I*, p. 48.

60 Ibid., p. 44.

61 Sheikh, Danish (2013) "The road to decriminalization: Litigating India's anti-sodomy law," Yale Human Rights and Development Journal: Vol. 16: Iss. 1, Article 3.

62 Donald K. Routh, 'Hippocrates meets Democritus: A history of psychiatry and clinical psychology', in Alas S. Bellack et al. (eds), *Comprehensive Clinical Psychology*, Vol. I (New York: Pergamon, 1998), p. 22.

63 See Michael Singer, 'Being gay and mentally ill: The case study of a gay man with schizophrenia treated at a community mental health facility', *Journal of Gay and Lesbian Psychotherapy*, Vol. 9, No. 3/4 (2004), pp. 115–25. As Singer

describes it his work involved, 'disentangling the two issues of the patient's minority status: being gay and mentally ill. At the beginning of treatment, the two categories were undifferentiated for him and the difficulties of being gay were entangled with the difficulties of schizophrenia. Over time, the work to expand and clarify what is meant to be gay helped free the patient to explore the relationship between his sexuality and other components of his core identity.'

[64] Davison, 'Construction and morality in therapy', p. 159.

[65] Foucault, *The History of Sexuality Vol.- I*, p. 101.

[66] See Simon Levay, 'A difference in hypothalamic structure between homosexual and heterosexual Men', in *Science*, New Series, Vol. 253, No. 5023 (Aug. 30 1991), pp. 1034–37.

[67] James Watson, the Noble Prize winner for biology, for example, said that if one does discover the gay gene, the baby should be aborted. See http://www.telegraph.co.uk/htmlContent.jhtml?html=/archive /1997/02/16/nabort16.html

[68] Section 377. Unnatural offences: Whoever voluntarily has carnal intercourse against the order of nature with any man, woman or animal, shall be punished with [imprisonment for life], or with imprisonment of either description for term which may extend to ten years, and shall also be liable to fine. Explanation—Penetration is sufficient to constitute the carnal intercourse necessary to the offence described in this section.

[69] See PUCL, Human Rights Violations Against Sexuality Minorities in India, http://www.pucl.org/Topics/Gender/2003/sexual-minorities.htm

[70] *The Indian Express* (20 May 2001).

[71] See Action Alert by IGLHRC with respect to medical treatment of homosexuality in India, 2001, http://www.iglhrc.org.

[72] *The Pioneer* (2 August 2001).

[73] Nivedita Menon (ed.), *Sexualities*, (New Delhi: Women Unlimited, 2007), p. 306.

[74] Davar, *Mental Health of Indian Women*, p. 113.

[75] PUCL-K, Human Rights Violations Against the Transgender Community, (Bangalore, 2003), p. 51.

[76] See Sanghamitra, Issue 4 (June 2005).

[77] Bhargavi Davar (ed.), *Mental Health from a Gender Perspective*, (New Delhi: Sage Publications, 2001), p. 93.

[78] Ibid.

Medical Students' Attitudes, Knowledge and Perception of Homosexuality[1] in India

DR. BHARATH REDDY

Within the typical secondary school curriculum, homosexuals do not exist. They are 'non-persons' in the finest Stalinist sense. They have fought no battles, held no offices, explored nowhere, written no literature, built nothing, invented nothing and solved no equations. The lesson to the heterosexual student is abundantly clear: *Homosexuals do nothing of consequence.* To the homosexual student, the message has even greater power: *no one who has ever felt as you do has done anything worth mentioning.*

Gerald Unks[2]

Background

There is an emphasis laid by various agencies such as the WHO and documents like *Healthy People 2010* on the elimination of health disparities and to provide equal access to health care to all patients.[3] There is evidence that lesbian, gay, bisexual and transgender (LGBT) patients have felt discomfort with physicians who are insensitive to or have a lack of knowledge about LGBT issues, hence impeding their ability to receive quality health care.[4] However, these studies were conducted by western researchers and significant information regarding the same in India is not available.

The medical community plays an important role in preparing medical students in handling marginalised groups such as LGBT patients and in actively reducing healthcare disparities for these patients. In India, statistics quote that five per cent of the sexually active male population contributes to a core population of 13.5 million homosexual males in India.[5] These males eroticised other males at some time or the other in their lives and had occasional sex with them. Some of these males were behaviourally bisexual or moved up or down the Kinsey scale depending on circumstances. However, the final figure of Indian males practising homosexual behaviour was found to be nearly 50 million by adding up the figures (and this does not include women who have sex with other women, intersex, transgender, *hijra* and other populations). This is considerable and indicates the need for action as soon as possible, in spite of no studies quantifying the likelihood of physicians in India encountering LGBT patients. However, based on the above statistics it is reasonable to infer that most or all doctors will encounter LGBT patients during the course of their careers.

Studies in the United States of America and the United Kingdom reviewed programmes in medical schools that aimed at reducing homophobia during medical training along with teaching about homosexuality in order to improve healthcare of homosexual patients and to improve the learning environment for gay and lesbian physicians-in-training. Homophobic attitudes and heterosexual biases in medical training and clinical interventions were reviewed. Pedagogical approaches that were used to address homosexuality and homophobia in medicine were discussed. Finally, strategies and opportunities to integrate teaching about homosexuality with the needs of homosexual patients throughout the medical school experience were presented. The studies conclude that opportunities for teaching about homosexuality and the clinical needs of homosexual patients are present throughout the medical school curriculum. The studies recommend that impediments to utilising these opportunities need to be overcome so that homosexual patients receive optimal healthcare by physicians trained to understand their clinical needs.[6]

Many organisations across the world advocate the development of curricula on cultural sensitivity and competent healthcare for LGBT patients. LGBT individuals share common social behaviours and choices that influence health-seeking behaviour, vulnerability to disease and preventive health measures taken by them. The distinct experiences of these populations require education of healthcare professionals to effectively assess and manage their health status. In 1996, the American Medical Association recommended that greater educational efforts be directed towards medical students and physicians, focusing on the healthcare needs of LGBT people in the United States. However, no similar attempts have been made in India.

Prior publications in the US have concluded that medical schools do not adequately address healthcare issues relevant to LGBT people. It is assumed that the same scenario (or perhaps something much worse) exists in India. There are only a few publications anywhere in the world that systematically assess medical students' attitudes, knowledge, and clinical skills pertaining to the healthcare of LGBT patients. There is a dire need to assess the attitude and knowledge of medical students in India to effectively implement teaching programmes related to homosexuality and LGBT persons as a part of the curriculum.

This study was done in order to assess such attitudes, knowledge and clinical skills of medical students in India with respect to the LGBT population. The study is envisaged as an initial attempt towards enabling educational interventions regarding LGBT healthcare needs for medical students in India. Further, the study aims to demonstrate vital gaps in medical education in India with regard to handling homosexuality, and also the consequent impact on healthcare needs of LGBT persons in India.

Methodology

Between 26 June 2006 and 13 August 2006, medical students of the third year, fourth year, in their internship and postgraduates attending a large, private, urban medical school were invited to participate in the study to assess their attitudes, knowledge and clinical skills pertaining to the healthcare needs of LGBT patients. Informed consent was taken from the students after explaining the objectives of the study and anonymity of all participants was assured and ensured.

All participants were given questionnaires to answer. The questionnaire consisted of four parts. Part one pertained to demographic characteristics of medical students. Part two consisted of assessing the attitudes of medical students with respect to LGBT communities in general. Part three consisted of questions to assess clinical skills of the participants including communication skills and their reactions on encountering LGBT patients. The questionnaire items in part two were derived from a validated survey of residents and attending physicians' attitudes toward patients with AIDS.[7] This instrument was used because its items were specific to medical trainees, contained items on sexual behaviour and identity, and had been previously approved and implemented at other institutions both in the US and UK. Questions in part three also assessed students' career goals, their desire to care for LGBT patients, attitudes toward physician responsibilities to LGBT patients, their comfort with LGBT clinical encounters, and their opinions about same-sex intimate relationships. Participants indicated their agreement or disagreement with each item along a five-point scale where five indicated strong agreement and one indicated strong disagreement. We also adapted this portion of the instrument from the survey mentioned previously.

Part four consisted of ten true or false questions and 4 multiple-choice knowledge-based questions pertaining to LGBT healthcare. While this portion of the survey has not been used before or validated, the questions were based on health objectives presented in *Healthy People 2010: Companion Document for Lesbian, Gay, Bisexual and Transgender (LGBT) Health.*[8] This document identifies priority areas and inequalities in health that medical professionals are expected to address. These questions assessed ten domains namely, cancer risk, health communication, immunisations, HIV and AIDS, mental health, nutrition, sexually transmitted diseases, substance abuse, tobacco use, and violence prevention. The questionnaire was designed following a pilot study and hence the assessment of knowledge was standardised.

Data analysis

Data were coded for each question and basic descriptive statistics were computed using SPSS.[9] Survey responses were analysed and divided under the following demographic characteristics: medical school class, race, gender, age, sexual orientation, and religious identity. We used analytic statistics, appropriate to data types and distribution. The attitude items were scored for median and frequency to assess the most common score among the attitudes of the medical students.

Further, a qualitative study was conducted by giving students an excerpt about homosexuality from the textbook of forensic medicine that they studied. They were given ample space and time to fill in their responses to two questions. First, what their inference was on reading the passage and second, how the medical education system and/or the book influenced their point of view vis-à-vis homosexuality. Again, responses were grouped under categories as related below and analysed.

The study is limited to one inner-city private medical school and hospital (serving a large urban population) where the medical students obtain their clinical training. Second, non-respondents may have had more negative attitudes and less clinical experience with LGBT patients. Third, students may have been concerned about researchers or school administrators linking their survey responses to their identity, thus discouraging their participation or biasing their responses toward expression of socially desirable answers. Fourth, self-reporting without triangulation does not allow a more objective evaluation of students' true abilities. Last, a mean score of 48 percent on a mostly true or false knowledge test may indicate a result from chance alone

Study results: Part I

A total of 92 students participated in the study. These students volunteered to take part in the study and provided informed consent for the same. Table 1 shows the characteristics of participants.

Part one of the questionnaire contained questions pertaining to the attitude of the subjects toward the LGBT community and the responses noted were as follows:

- 17.39 per cent of the population reported that they have homosexual friends.

TABLE 1
Demographic characteristics of the Survey Population (n=92)

Characteristic		n (%)
Year of Training	Third year students	25 (27.17)
	Fourth year students	55 (59.78)
	Internship/Postgraduates	12 (13.05)
Age (in years)		21.8 (range 19 to 26)
Gender	Male	50 (54.35)
	Female	42 (45.65)
Sexual Orientation	Heterosexual	87 (94.56)
	Homosexual or bisexual	0
	Not disclosed	5 (5.44)
Religious identity	Christian	3 (2.60)
	Hindu	79 (85.87)
	Muslim	3 (3.26)
	Atheist	6 (6.52)
	Others	1 (1.09)

- 43.48 per cent accepted homosexual friends while 36.96 per cent do not wish for homosexual friends.
- 52.17 per cent said that nothing would change in their reaction to friends who they discovered were homosexual. However, 18.48 per cent reported that they would 'pretend to accept them' while 11.96 per cent reported that they would 'run away' from friends they found to be homosexual. When asked for their reactions if they discovered 'close' friends to be homosexual, 22.83 per cent claimed that they would 'pretend to accept them'.
- 79.35 per cent thought that learning and working habits of homosexuals were the same as heterosexuals, whereas 16.3 per cent thought that they would be lower than heterosexuals. Interestingly, all interns claimed that learning and working habits would be the same and it was other batches of students who claimed that they would be lower.
- 33.70 perc ent students believed that homosexuals would affect school reputation negatively.

TABLE 2 Attitudes towards LGBT Patients Scale (n=92)		
Item	Median*	Number of students whose answer corresponded to the median n** (%)
Lesbian and gay patients deserve the same level of quality care from medical institutions as heterosexual patients	5***	64 (69.56)
Gay and lesbian patients should only seek health care from gay and lesbian health clinics	1	48 (52.17)
Physicians in private practice have a responsibility to treat LGBT patients	4	45 (48.91)
I would be comfortable if I became known among my professional peers as a doctor that cares for LGBT patients	4	40 (43.47)
I am concerned that if my heterosexual patients learned that I was treating LGBT patients, they would no longer seek my care	3	31 (33.69)
I would be comfortable telling my intimate partner that I cared for LGBT patients	4	46 (50.00)
Homosexual patients should disclose their orientation to their physicians	4	45 (48.91)
Same-sex sexual ATTRACTION is a natural expression of sexuality in humans	2.5	27 (29.34)
Same-sex sexual BEHAVIOUR is a natural expression of sexuality in humans	2	26 (28.26)

* Unlike averages, calculating the "median" does not depend on either the total or the number of items. A median is obtained by arranging all data in ascending or descending order of magnitude and locating the value of the exact middle.

** 'n' refers to the total number of students taking part in the study. The column shows the number of students (with percentage) who selected the median answer for the corresponding question.

*** Scoring (Likert scale): 5-Strongly agree, 4-Agree, 3-Neutral, 2-Disagree, 1-Strongly disagree.

- 66.30 per cent students thought mass media imposed a negative image of homosexuality in public with 72 per cent of the third year students agreeing with this, compared to 40 per cent of postgraduates.
- 39.13 per cent of subjects thought homosexuals were more promiscuous and 41.30 per cent thought homosexuals had more one night stands.
- 45.65 per cent thought homosexuals were more likely to practise sadism.
- A significant 55.43 per cent thought homosexuality was a psychological disorder and required therapy.

Table 2 summarises responses of students for nine items, assessing students' attitudes towards LGBT patients and the desire and willingness to care for them. The scores are based on a five-point Likert scale, where a score of five was the most positive attitude score and a score of one was the most negative score. It can be seen from the table that *most* students:

- Strongly agreed that lesbian and gay patients deserve the same level of quality care from medical institutions as heterosexual patients (69.56 %).
- Strongly disagreed that gay and lesbian patients should only seek healthcare from gay and lesbian health clinics (52.17 %).
- Agreed that physicians in private practice have a responsibility to treat LGBT patients (48.91%).
- Agreed that they would be comfortable if they became known among professional peers as doctors who cared for LGBT patients (43.47 %).
- Responded that they were neutral towards concerns that heterosexual patients would no longer seek care from them if it was learned that they were treating LGBT patients (33.69 %).
- Agreed that they would be comfortable telling their intimate partner that they cared for LGBT patients (50.0 %).
- Agreed that homosexual patients should disclose their orientation to their physicians (48.91 %).

- Disagreed that same-sex sexual ATTRACTION was a natural expression of sexuality in humans (29.34 %).
- Disagreed that same-sex sexual BEHAVIOUR was a natural expression of sexuality in humans (28.26 %).

Findings indicated that students who reported having LGBT friends were more likely to have a more positive attitude score and this was truer for women and for older students. However, a majority of students shared concerns about challenges they faced discussing sexual identity and sexual behaviour. Further, self-reported comfort alone is not an adequate measure of a student's ability to care for LGBT patients. Although a majority of students reported feeling comfortable providing care to LGBT individuals, they were not likely to elicit comprehensive histories.

But a majority of students held negative opinions about patients who experienced same-sex attraction or patients who engaged in same-sex behaviour and they experienced greater challenges discussing sexuality in clinical encounters. Studies[10] on homophobia have indicated that lack of personal contact with gay and lesbian people is highly correlated with negative attitudes. Studies show that teaching and promoting tolerance by designing discussion forums where students can voice their opinions and feelings about these encounters and listen to others do the same can result in change. Hence, more research needs to be done to identify what interventions are effective in enhancing attitudes toward the care of this population.

Study results: Part II

Part two of the questionnaire considered skills of medical students with respect to taking sexual history and their reactions and application of their skills in history-taking and examination on encountering a patient from the LGBT community.

From Table 3, it can be concluded that:

- When taking sexual history 39.13 per cent students said that they were instructed to ask about sexual orientation of their patients and 33.33 per cent of these said that they rarely asked this.

TABLE 3
Clinical Skills and Attitudes Stratified by Medical Students'
Possible Clinical Encounters

Item	Median (n=92)	Number of students whose answer corresponded to the median (%) n =92
1. When taking a sexual history, are you instructed to ask about the sexual orientation of your patient?	Yes	36 (39.13)
2. If yes, how often do you do it?	2	12 (33.33)
3. Overall, how comfortable are you addressing the health care needs of your LGBT patients?	3	37 (40.21)
4. Compared to heterosexual patients how differently would you treat self-identified LGBT patients with respect to the following:		
a. Less eye contact	1	39 (42.39)
b. Conduct fewer procedures to avoid physical contact	1	43 (46.73)
c. Spend most visits discussing sexual behaviour	1	27 (29.34)
d. Spend most visits screening patients for STDs	4	32 (34.78)
5. During your clinical encounters, how often did the following occur:		
a. Avoided questions about sexual behaviour	4	27 (29.34)
b. Asked patients their sexual history in the chart	3	26 (28.26)
c. Asked if they had an intimate partner	3	27 (29.34)
d. Asked if they had any children in the family	5	44 (47.82)
6. It is more challenging to gather an oral history from homosexual patients than from heterosexual patients.	4	37 (40.21)
7. It is more challenging to conduct a physical examination on homosexual patients than on heterosexual patients.	4	29 (31.52)
8. It is more challenging to conduct a genito-urinary examination on homosexual patients than on heterosexual patients.	2	27 (29.34)
9. It is more challenging to discuss sexual behaviour with homosexual patients than with heterosexual patients.	4	41 (44.56)

*   Scoring for items 1, 2, 4(a-d) and 5(a-d): 1-never, 2-rarely, 3-sometimes, 4-often, 5-always

** Scoring for item 3: 1-very uncomfortable, 2-uncomfortable, 3-neutral, 4-comfortable, 5-very comfortable.

*** Scoring for items 6-9: 1-strongly disagree, 2-disagree, 3-neutral, 4-agree, 5-strongly agree.

- Students were neutral on their level of comfort addressing the healthcare needs of LGBT patients (40.21 per cent).
- Students said that they made eye contact (42.39 per cent), did not conduct procedures that avoided physical contact (46.73 per cent), did not spend more time discussing sexual behaviour (29.34 per cent) and often spent visits screening patients for STDs (34.78 per cent).
- During their clinical encounters participants said that they often avoided questions about sexual behaviour (29.34 per cent), sometimes asked patients about their sexual history in the chart (28.26 per cent), only occasionally asked if patients had an intimate partner (29.34 per cent) and always asked patients if they had any children in the family (47.82 per cent).
- Students (40.21 per cent) agreed that it was more challenging to gather an oral history from homosexual patients than from heterosexual patients.
- A third of the students (31.52 per cent) agreed that it was more challenging to conduct physical examinations on homosexual patients than on heterosexual patients.
- Students disagreed (29.34 per cent) that it was more challenging to conduct genito-urinary examinations on homosexual patients than on heterosexual patients.
- Around half of the students agreed (44.56 per cent) that it was more challenging to discuss sexual behaviour with homosexual patients than with heterosexual patients.

Again, study results revealed that students with LGBT friends demonstrated better knowledge of their health concerns and a more positive attitude. Yet many participants demonstrated a sufficient amount of disagreement and confusion on several LGBT health concerns to merit clarification through curricular modifications. Studies have already shown that reservations in discussing sexual orientation were due to a lack of knowledge regarding LGBT patients' health care needs.[11] More education in the areas of cancer risk, nutrition, HIV risk, and mental health can address these knowledge gaps.

Qualitative responses to pathologisation of LGBT:
Role of medical education

The Medical Council of India (MCI) prescribes a course consisting of three phases with three subjects in the first phase, four subjects in the second phase, three subjects in part one of phase three and four subjects in part two of phase three. This accounts for a four-and-a-half-year course with four university examinations. However, students all over India have no specific text-books prescribed by the council and they read or study both Indian as well as foreign authors. Colleges and students are given the liberty of choosing textbooks of their choice to cover the syllabus prescribed by the University.

As part of their syllabus, students undergo training for one year in forensic medicine and two months of posting in psychiatry along with theory classes (all in the second year of the course). There is, however, no mention of homosexuality made anywhere in the entire course. Issues of sexuality are discussed only in forensic medicine and not psychiatry where mention is made of LGBT only under sexual offences and sexual deviations. This may account for the lack of knowledge regarding the subject as well as the attitude of medical students towards the homosexual community. The lack of exposure to the subject has also created confusion in the minds of medical students who are torn between views of pathologisation and normality vis-à-vis homosexuality. Some popular textbooks label homosexuals as 'abnormal' and present homosexuals not only as requiring treatment, but also as criminals who need to be prosecuted under Section 377 of the Indian Penal Code (IPC).

To assess qualitative responses of students to the pathologisation of LBGT people, participants in the study were given a passage from a popular textbook. The passage, as extracted below, was given to participants so that they could read and write down their responses to two questions regarding the passage and the role of the book and the medical education system in influencing their views on homosexuality. This book is still used widely all over India as a textbook of forensic medicine for studying for the phase II examinations.

Voluntary sexual intercourse against the order of nature with any man, woman or animal is an unnatural sex offence—section 377 IPC. These offences are punishable with imprisonment for life or up to 10 years and also with fine. Homosexuality means persistent emotional and physical attraction to the members of the same sex. As such it is an abnormal personality development.... Sodomy is the anal intercourse between two males or between a male and a female.... It can be heterosexual or homosexual. Any degree of penetration or attempt at penetration is punishable. Proof of emission is not necessary.... Crime is frequent among sailors, prisoners, in hostels, military barracks, etc. or where they are thrown together for long periods.... Many lesbians are masculine, possibly because of endocrine disturbances and are indifferent towards the individuals of the opposite sex. The practice is usually indulged in by women who are mental degenerates or who suffer from nymphomania. It is a result of interactions of biological, psychological, developmental and sociologic factors. It may lead to interference with young girls. Lesbians who are morbidly jealous of one another when rejected may commit homicide, suicide or both.[12]

The responses of the participants to this passage are listed below and classified into three categories:

a. Respondents who saw homosexuality as immoral or pathological.
Out of 56 medical students belonging to the eighth term, 12 shared strong views about homosexuality as an 'unnatural sexual offence', which was 'not culturally or socially acceptable'. Seven of these referred specifically to Section 377 of the IPC as being 'absolutely right'. They believed that those who 'practised' what the 'law prohibited' and those who did not abide by 'legal definitions' and 'rules and regulations made for the humans' needed to be punished severely. One respondent said that 'there is a law which protects sex and wrong acts, violating this should be treated not only psychiatrically but also with punishment'. One respondent quoted the Holy Bible saying 'homosexuality is a sin and God made the female (Eve) to be with man and entertain him'. This respondent believed homosexuality to be an abnormal personality development and considers punishment as the 'only' solution to the 'problem'.

Several students also stated 'sex is wonderful within the institution of marriage with the opposite gender only'.

In speaking about homosexuality, five of these 12 respondents referred to the need for the 'right sex education' as one solution to respond to the 'failure on the part of our system'. One of them said that there is a need for sex education, which 'has to do with strong roots that go deep into the understanding of what is natural and what is not'. Another student asserted, 'Homosexuals are a black mark to the society and can be removed with good sex education at the right time. The concept of sex education needs to be correctly defined among the laymen'. Two other respondents stated that counselling all homosexuals could be another solution for this 'psychiatric disorder' as they tended to stay within 'groups of people having similar behaviour' and that 'their confidence needs to be upgraded and they should be taught how to live like normal people'.

Respondents in this category included psychological and physical mal-development and even emotional disorders that needed to be 'detected early' and given medical help, as causes for homosexuality. These responses came from three of the 11 respondents. Two of the students are strongly against the 'thought of abnormal sexuality' on purely religious, social and cultural grounds. One girl mentioned that she 'cannot believe the extent to which people go to have sex' and goes on to talk about how the book of forensic medicine has influenced her point of view and alerted her to the 'problems of present day which are increasing'.

Out of 56 participants, 12 (21.42 per cent), of whom one-third were women, shared strong opinions against the LGBT community. This is not only attributed to the educational and cultural backgrounds of the students but also the system of education. One student stated that the book by Dr. Narayana Reddy was useful in talking about 'right and wrong sexual practices'. Another student felt grateful to the educational system for highlighting the need to treat the psychological problems of these 'patients'.

In this category, boys stated that they were *for* Section 377 of the IPC since punishment was an important means to 'eliminate the social evil'. However, 27.7 per cent of female participants did not have a stand on the legal aspects of this 'health problem'. Female participants tended to talk about it more as a public health problem that needed to be tackled by healthcare professionals. They felt that it was their responsibility as part of the medical profession to 'treat these patients'.

All participants in this category identified themselves as heterosexual, belonging to upper- to lower-middle-class Indian families, with 'cultural' and 'social acceptability' being vital in their perception of homosexuality as immoral or illegal.

A student of the sixth-term said that 'at least in India' homosexuals needed to be punished or put into a hospital or mental health institution. The sixth-term students talked more about the positive role of the education system and stated that it gave them the 'right picture' on sexual deviations prevalent in our society. They also referred to the 'incomplete' picture given by textbooks and the education system, which caused difficulties in understanding realities associated with these 'perversions'.

Of the pool of respondents, from interns and postgraduates, there were none who considered homosexuality illegal or liable to punishment. Although some of them did consider homosexuality a condition, which needed to be treated psychologically, none of them thought that legal action was warranted. The responses in general were more positive than the responses from the other pool of graduate students.

b. Respondents who thought homosexuality was a natural variant of human sexuality.

In this category, respondents comprised 11 (19.62 per cent) eighth-term students, five (21.73 per cent) sixth-term students, two interns (out of 14) and four postgraduates (out of five). These respondents were positive in their view of homosexuality as 'not an abnormal personality disorder' and as perfectly 'normal'. Around two-thirds (63.6 %) of these students were strongly against Section 377 of the IPC and said 'homosexuality is not an offence'. One respondent said that the law 'does not consider the emotional mindsets' when framing homosexuality as abnormal. Another respondent held strong opinions against the extract from the forensic textbook and said 'the passage has put forward statements as though they define "rules of sex" and "order of nature"'. A sixth-term student raised an important question: 'according to whose interpretation is the order of nature defined?' The student also felt that the judicial system did not consider emotional implications of treating sex between man and a woman as 'natural' and other forms of sex as a crime, which the student felt was 'not right on the part of our legal system'.

There is a reference by many students to 'criminal acts' such as intercourse against the will of the person, indecent behaviour in public places and many forms of sexual violence within heterosexual or homosexual communities, which they felt should be punished with severe action such as 'life imprisonment' or 'hanging till death'. This indicated that they veered strongly against non-consensual sexual acts rather than consensual homosexual behaviour. This point is further enhanced by the numerous mentions of how same-sex attraction is just as natural as heterosexuality.

The respondents also pointed out the negative attitude of the Indian public to homosexuality that is reflected in the passage from the forensic textbook. One student said:

> In spite of the large number of lesbians and gay men in the country, society does not accept the fact that it(homosexuality) even exists; and even if they do, they are treated as outcasts. It is high time laws were relaxed, people realise times are changing and that LGBT are not abnormal or unnatural but just human beings with a difference.

Respondents of the third year refer to the generation gap between the law and the present day as these were 'laws formulated aeons back' and showed the 'orthodox and regressive' views of the Indian judicial system. A young respondent with primary education in the west, studying currently in India said, after reading the excerpt, 'I am appalled. India is the first place I have come across which believes in such nonsense'. Respondents also feel that since homosexuality has existed across the world, and other developing countries have been addressing the issue in a 'mature' way, it is high time that India does so as well. Another respondent spoke about the responsibility of the medical community as part of the public in playing a pivotal role 'in making homosexuals come out and handle their sexual problems and treat them with care trying to make them understand themselves'.

With reference to the book and the medical education system, this group of students classified it as encoding a 'bias against homosexuals', which should be altered in the subsequent editions of the book. The book, and the system, as one student says, tries to 'change your point of view' enforcing discrimination against homosexuals'. Most of them however noted that though the educational system laid stress on the 'abnormality' and the 'offence' of homosexuals, this negative viewpoint does not influence them or change their 'broad-minded' viewpoint. *The medical system still considers sex to be a taboo and this contributes to a very negative perception of homosexuality.* One of the respondents also felt that homosexuals were portrayed to be constantly associated with anal intercourse as a sexual practice and also with STDs and AIDS. The respondent said that this was offensive as neither was anal intercourse restricted to the homosexual community nor was the homosexual community exclusively affected by HIV and AIDS.

One respondent said, 'The system doesn't seem to encompass discussions nor does it impart knowledge on issues such as these'. Students felt that the book strongly emphasised the 'psychological' aspect of homosexuality which they felt had never been scientifically substantiated. They also felt that the legal aspects opined in the passage were not sufficient arguments considering the book catered to a large population of medical students. Hence, most of the respondents focused their voices on the fact that the information was insufficient and lacked scientific references. Some of the interns and postgraduates said that it was through 'personal experience', and not from reading their textbooks, that they concluded that homosexuality was just as 'normal' as heterosexuality. This group had not only encountered patients who were LGBT but also had friends who were open about their sexuality.

A few of the respondents were strongly against the paragraph in the passage that referred to lesbians as masculine, mental degenerates and nymphomaniacs, and stated that this was highly derogatory. Some respondents asserted that this was not based on any scientific knowledge and hence should not be taught in medical colleges as part of the curriculum. They maintained that, 'The books and medical system should instead lay more stress on how homosexuals can be given the right to be treated on par with heterosexuals'. Another respondent said 'they should be given equal importance in all aspects of life (education/career/adoption/marriage) and medical professionals should help them in overcoming depression and other problems due to social stigma which could instigate them to commit offences'. This group also expressed the opinion that there needs to be a change in the way homosexuality is perceived and treated by the medical education system, which needs to be implemented soon.

In this group, a certain trend can be seen with respect to gender and the point of view held by the students. Seven (out of 11) students (63.6 per cent) of the eighth term were females. In the sixth term, all students were female. Generally female students seemed more open about homosexuality than male students. Additionally, male students were against referring to lesbianism as abnormal, while only one male student referred to 'sex' as a natural expression of emotion both in homosexuals and in heterosexuals. Female respondents were also stronger in their view against discrimination of homosexuals and the role of the medical fraternity in ensuring non-discrimination. These students seemed to have had adequate exposure and education, which influenced their opinion even before joining the medical course. Hence the influence of the medical education system has not been significant. The other important factor, mentioned earlier, which determined a positive response was if respondents had homosexual friends. More than one-third of eighth-term students (36.3 per cent) and all the sixth-term students in this group had homosexual friends. This, however, did not seem to influence their opinion strongly, as these were students who reacted with statements of 'shock' and 'disgust' at several things including the excerpt, the opinions of the homophobic general population and the 'lack of concern' of the medical fraternity.

c. Respondents who believed homosexuality was a medical condition that needed treatment.

This group of students stood by the view that homosexuality was a medical condition requiring treatment. The group believed that owing to the pathological basis of the 'disease', homosexuals needed to be handled by the medical fraternity and healthcare system of the country and not through law. This opinion was held by nearly 25.2 per cent of all students comprising nearly an equal male and female population.

There was a strong suggestion by many students that homosexuality was attributed to various pathological reasons such as psychiatric conditions, endocrine disorders, abnormal upbringing and some even said that homosexuals were just 'helpless and had no role to play in choosing their sexuality'. Most of these students stated that 'rather than considering it a punishable offence, LGBT patients need to be guided, helped and supported to lead a more normal and better life'. Statements were made with regard to the cause of homosexuality being 'organic disorders of the nervous system not diagnosed on routine investigations' and possibly due to 'psychiatric *or* endocrine disturbances'. One respondent referred to it as 'aetiology yet to be identified'. A few responded that this was a 'psychiatric disorder' credited to 'past incidents in life and the absence of action by medical practitioners to identify them and counsel them at the right time'. Phrases such as 'perversion significant to the emotional requirements' were used in the responses, indicative of the misconceptions held by this group about the therapeutic aspects of homosexuality.

There is a constant association of homosexuality with the word 'disorder' along with reference to 'solutions to the problem' as a responsibility of all medical practitioners who need to help in 'identifying' homosexuals and 'counselling' them. The respondents also referred specifically to the 'psychological' approach being the best treatment option. One student spoke about 'teaching the general public through the use of mass media to not look down upon homosexuals as abnormal but sexual inclination influenced and caused due to many factors and being multi-factorial in aetiology'. Another student claimed, 'Occurrence of homosexuality can be reduced by means of education to public and counselling of susceptible people'. Terminologies like 'social support' and 'education' to 'become heterosexual' was used time and again in this group. Most of the students considered that among all the possibilities counselling was the best solution to 'help out these people from their abnormal behaviour'. An interesting view held by this group was the role of physicians and medical students in counselling and education. They strongly felt that it was their responsibility as part of the medical fraternity to handle these 'patients' without discrimination and hence the book from which the extract was drawn is seen to provide 'essential guidelines in a doctor's practice'.

With reference to the medical education system and the book, most students felt the book just talks about the legal aspects and the various sexual deviations existent in societies helping students to 'refer' them to psychiatrists on encountering them in clinical practice. Some interns expressed their opinion that the book portrayed what was largely acceptable to society. One of the respondents also felt that the book expressed a person's viewpoint, which was by definition subjective and relative, since the author justified his opinion, and hence the passage concerned was in a sense fair. Another respondent felt that the passage had 'increased awareness' on the subject and helped to deal with situations appropriately by communicating the pathological background of homosexuality. Some students also said that the book and the medical system collectively helped them understand the 'psychological and physiological changes' in life and helped modify attitudes in life toward sexual perversions.

All students in this population held the opinion that homosexuality was a treatable disease and there were increased chances of transforming a homosexual into a heterosexual by appropriate therapeutic measures. They sympathised with the community but did not criticise Section 377 of the IPC at all. On the question regarding the role of the educational system in influencing their view, students were divided, with half of them considering the medical system favourable in changing their views positively whereas the other half considered the topic not adequately communicated to medical students. One student raised a point that the opinions of students were influenced by 'cultural and peer influences' more than the education system or the textbook. Male respondents in this group agreed with the pathologisation of the issue and with the law, which prohibits sodomy. Female respondents, on the other hand, had a more sympathetic opinion on the issue. This population reflected the lack of adequate scientific knowledge of students and a fallacy of the medical education system which has left the students confused and ill informed.

Conclusion

Students with LGBT friends showed better understanding towards healthcare needs of the LGBT community. On a qualitative analysis, 21.42 per cent of students expressed a strong opinion against homosexuality stating that it needed to be criminalised and treated hence reflecting homophobic attitudes prevalent among many medical students. A little less than a quarter (nearly 24.5 per cent) of students felt homosexuality is absolutely pathological and attributed it to psychological, genetic and endocrine causes and hence it should be treated by counselling and early screening. Between 37 and 39 per cent of students considered homosexuality pathological but felt discrimination against the community was derogatory and hence sympathised with the need for decriminalisation of the same. Only between 19 and 21 per cent of students did not consider homosexuality pathological or in need of any therapeutic measures.

It is probably important to note that social factors such as peer opinion, parenting, educational background, etc., do play a role in influencing the view of medical students even before joining medical college. However, it is imperative that the medical education system instil opinions and inculcate an attitude in the students which is based not on personal opinions but what is scientific and backed by serious research studies.

The textbook of forensic medicine used by the students correctly explains section 377 of the IPC. However, the textbook contains unempirical attitudes and perceptions. The medical explanations in it are not research-derived. These attitudes are propagated among students, restricting them from treating patients ethically and in medically sound ways. There is a great need to expose students to discussion of non-normative sexuality and on gender, influencing the ways in which students understand these issues. These attitudes adversely affect the treatment of LGBT patients, the treatment of STDs, HIV and AIDS and also increase the taboos and restrictions around talking about sexuality, thus disabling discussions about safer sex practices and consensual sex practices.

The qualitative study does show a stark difference of opinion held by students of different religions. For example, students of the Hindu community did have a more open point of view in comparison to students of other communities. More research needs to be done with regards to the influence of religion as a factor in the opinion held by medical students on homosexuality.

Educational interventions should be instituted for medical students providing accurate information on normality of homosexuality, history of the LGBT movement and the removal of homosexuality as a disorder from the DSM and ICD, sexual history-taking and clinical skills when dealing with patients of the LGBT community, STDs, HIV and AIDS and other healthcare needs of the LGBT community, ethical issues and need for non-discrimination among the medical fraternity and finally legal issues of homosexuality and implications.

Acknowledgements

The author thanks Dr. Padmini Prasad, Bangalore; Vinay Chandran, Director, SWABHAVA Trust, Bangalore; Arvind Narrain, Alternate Law Forum, Bangalore and all the participants of this study.

Notes

[1] This paper was presented at the National Conference of Sexology and Reproductive Health 2006, conducted in Ambedkar Bhavan, Bangalore and received the third place among research paper presentations in October 2006.

[2] Gerald Unks, 'Thinking About the Homosexual Adolescent', in *The High School Journal*, Vol. 77, Nos. 1 and 2 (Oct.–Nov. 1993, Dec.–Jan. 1994) pp. 1–6.

[3] Gay and Lesbian Medical Association and LGBT health experts, *Healthy People 2010: Companion document for lesbian, gay, bisexual, and transgender (LGBT) health* (San Francisco: Gay and Lesbian Medical Association, 2001).

[4] See Anonymous. 'Health care needs of gay men and lesbians in the United States', Council on Scientific Affairs, American Medical Association. JAMA 1996; 275(17): 1354–9 and A *Provider's Handbook on Culturally Competent Care: Lesbian, Gay, Bisexual and Transgendered Population.* Oakland, CA: National Diversity Council, Kaiser Permanente; 2000.

[5] This figure was obtained from the 1991 census by calculating the sexually active male populations as 60% of the population (males falling between the ages of 15 and 60 years) and then computing 5% of that figure. Another 37.5 million males fell in ranges between numbers 3 to 5 on the Kinsey scale. See www.gaybombay.org

[6] See C.M. Tesar, S.L.Rovi, 'Survey of curriculum on homosexuality / bisexuality in departments of family medicine'. *Family Medicine,* Vol.30, no.4 (1998), pp. 283–7 and M.M. Wallick, K.M. Cambre, M.H. Townsend. 'How the topic of homosexuality is taught at US medical schools'. *Academic Medicine,* Vol. 67, no. 9 (1992), pp. 601–3.

[7] J.A. East. 'Pediatricians' approach to the health care of lesbians'. *Journal of Adolescent Health,* Vol. 23 (1998), pp. 191–3.

[8] Gay and Lesbian Medical Association and LGBT health experts, *Healthy People 2010: companion document for lesbian, gay, bisexual, and transgender (LGBT) health* (San Francisco: Gay and Lesbian Medical Association, 2001).

[9] SPSS, 2005, SPSS is a computer program used for statistical analysis and is also the name of the company (SPSS Inc.) that sells it.(www.spss.com)

[10] See C.J. Skinner, P.C. Henshaw, J.A. Petrak, 'Attitudes to lesbians and homosexual men: Medical students care' in *Sexually Transmitted Infections,* Vol. 77 (2001), pp. 147–8 and M.M. Wallick, K.M. Cambre, M.H. Townsend, 'Influence of a freshman-year panel presentation on medical students attitudes toward homosexuality' in *Academic Medicine* Vol. 70 (1995) pp. 839–41.

[11] S.M. Lena, T. Wiebe, S. Ingram, M. Jabbour. 'Pediatricians' Knowledge, Perceptions, and Attitudes Toward Providing Health Care for Lesbian, Gay, and Bisexual Adolescents', in *Annals of the Royal College of Physicians and Surgeons of Canada,* Vol. 35, no. 7 (2002), pp. 406–10.

[12] Dr. K.S. Narayana Reddy, *Essentials of Forensic Medicine and Toxicology,* (New Delhi: Jain Book Depot, 23rd edition, 2004).

Further References

A. Shidlo, 'Assessing heterosexuals' attitudes toward lesbian and gay men' in B. Greene and G.M. Herek (eds), *Lesbian and gay psychology: Theory, research, and clinical applications,* Vol. 1 of *Psychological perspectives on lesbian and gay issues,* (Thousand Oaks, California: Sage, 1994), pp. 176–205.

C.J. Skinner, P.C. Henshaw, J.A. Petrak, 'Attitudes to lesbians and homosexual men: medical students' care', *Sexually Transmitted Infections,* Vol. 77, no. 2 (2001).

D. Bhugra, 'Doctors' Attitudes to Male Homosexuality: A survey', *Sexual & Marital Therapy*, Vol. 5 (1990), pp. 167–74.

G.A. Chaimowitz, 'Homophobia among psychiatric residents, family practice residents and psychiatric faculty', *Canadian Journal of Psychiatry*, Vol. 36 (1991), pp. 206–9.

G. Rubinstein, 'The decision to remove homosexuality from the DSM: Twenty years later', *American Journal of Psychotherapy*, Vol. 49, pp. 416–27.

J.A. Kelly, J.S. St. Lawrence, S. Smith S Jr., H.V. Hood, D.J. Cook, 'Medical students' attitudes toward AIDS and homosexual patients', *Journal of Medical Education*, Vol. 62 (1987), pp. 549–56.

R. Bayer and R.L. Spitzer, 'Edited correspondence on the status of homosexuality in DSM–III', *Journal of the History of the Behavioural Sciences*, Vol. 18 (1982), pp. 32–52.

R.M. Epstein, D.S. Morse, R.M. Frankel, 'Awkward moments in patient-physician communication about HIV risk', *Annals of Internal Medicine*, Vol. 128, no. 6 (1988), pp. 435–42.

S.M. Lena, T. Wiebe, S. Ingram, M. Jabbour, 'Pediatricians' knowledge, perceptions, and attitudes toward providing health care for lesbian, gay, and bisexual adolescents', *Annals of the Royal College of Physicians and Surgeons of Canada*, Vol. 35, no. 7 (2002), pp. 406–10.

S.R. Leiblum, 'Sexual attitudes and behavior of a cross-sectional sample of United States medical students: Effects of gender, age, and year of study', *Journal of Sex Education and Therapy*, Vol. 62 (1993), pp. 235–45.

M.H. Townsend, M.M. Wallick, R.R. Pleak, K.M. Cambre, 'Gay and lesbian issues in child and adolescent psychiatry training as reported by training directors', *Journal of the American Academy of Child & Adolescent Psychiatry*, Vol. 36, pp. 764–68.

M.M. Wallick, K.M. Cambre, M.H. Townsend, 'Influence of a freshmen-year panel presentation on medical students' attitudes toward homosexuality', *Academic Medicine*, Vol. 70 (1995), pp. 939–41.

Stroller RJ, Marmor J, Beiber I, Gold R, Socarides CW, Green R, Spitzer RL, 'A symposium: Should homosexuality be in the APA nomenclature?', *American Journal of Psychiatry*, Vol.130, (1973), pp. 1207–16.

W.C. Mathews, M.W. Booth, J.D. Turner, L. Kessler, 'Physicians' Attitudes Toward Homosexuality: Survey of a California county medical society', *Western Journal of Medicine*, Vol. 144 (1986), pp. 106–10.

WHO, 2003. The Mental and Behavioural Disorders—International Classification of Diseases, 10th ed. Available at http://www3.who.int/icd/vol1html2003/fr-icd.htm

Medical Response to Male Same-sex Sexuality in Western India

An Exploration of 'Conversion Treatments' for Homosexuality

KETKI RANADE

Introduction

Until the mid-1950s, sexual orientation hardly qualified as a subject of scientific study. Homosexuality was listed as a mental disorder by the American Psychiatric Association (APA) in their *Diagnostic and Statistical Manual of Psychiatric Disorders* (DSM), branded a sexual deviation by mental health professionals, and condemned by religion and society as 'immoral' and 'abnormal'. Consequently, homosexuals were, by and large, invisible.

In 1957, Evelyn Hooker's pioneering study, challenging the prevalent belief that homosexuality is an illness and deviancy, led to the accumulation of a large body of empirical evidence. As a result, the past three decades have witnessed a remarkable transformation in the status of homosexuality. In 1973, the APA declassified homosexuality as a mental disorder from the DSM and in 1987 also deleted its clinical sub-variant, 'ego-dystonic homosexuality', from the DSM (DSM-III-R) and from American textbooks of psychiatry. Subsequently, in 1992, the World Health Organisation (WHO) removed homosexuality from its list of mental illnesses ICD-10 (International Classification of Diseases).

Prior to the declassification of homosexuality, Western literature is replete with the attempts of medical, psychotherapeutic and religious practitioners to alter same-sex orientation. Referred to as 'conversion therapy', such attempts include a variety of methods intended to change a homosexual orientation to a heterosexual one. Following the APA decision, however, mainstream medical organisations no longer endorse conversion therapy, though it continues to be supported by some major religious organisations and professionals.

By contrast, Indian scholars of psychiatry and psychology have 'preserved an almost complete silence on the subject of homosexuality'. There has been very little debate or theorising on sexual orientation and the shift of homosexuality from abnormality to normality has been passively accepted by the medical community. In fact, neither the inclusion of homosexuality or ego-dystonic homosexuality as mental disorders in the APA classification nor their subsequent deletion has provoked any dialogue on the cultural relevance of these diagnoses.

Unfortunately, apart from a few sporadic reports or articles in the print media, there is very little systematic study or documentation of the views of Indian health care professionals regarding homosexuality or the use and outcomes of conversion treatments. Given that conversion as a form of therapy for homosexuality is used by many practitioners in India and also taking into account the paucity of scientific data on conversion therapy, this report aims at exploring its use by health care providers in Western India to treat homosexuals, the criteria used for selecting clients for conversion therapy, the types of therapies employed, and perceived outcomes of such therapies. Finally, it suggests recommendations for enabling health care providers to employ mainstream thinking in their treatment of homosexual individuals in India.

What do we know about conversion therapy?

The use of conversion techniques presupposes that homosexuality is pathological or problematic and warrants treatment or repair. The APA defines conversion therapy as 'psychiatric treatment ... which is based upon the assumption that homosexuality per se is a mental disorder or based upon the a priori assumption that a patient should change his/her sexual homosexual orientation' while the *American Psychological Association* (American Psychological Association, 2008) defines it as therapy aimed at changing sexual orientation. Both these organisations also use the term 'reparative therapy' introduced by Nicolosi in 1991 as a synonym for conversion therapy in general.

The evolution of conversion therapy can roughly be traced through three periods: an early Freudian period, a period of mainstream approval of conversion therapy, and a period following the declassification of homosexuality as a mental illness when the mainstream medical profession disowned it. Conversion therapy subsumes a wide variety of psychoanalytical, behavioural, biological and religious methods. During the early Freudian period, measures such as castration, sterilisation and hypnosis were the methods of choice. The three decades between Freud's death in 1939 and the birth of the gay rights movement in 1969, a period during which conversion therapy was approved by most of the psychiatric establishment in the US, witnessed a diversity of approaches. The interventions included psychoanalysis, prayer and spiritual interventions, electric shock, nausea-inducing drugs/aversion therapy, hormone therapy, surgery, and various adjunctive behavioural interventions including masturbatory reconditioning, rest, visits to prostitutes, and so on. However, by the mid-1970s, subsequent to the depathologisation of homosexuality, these methods were largely abandoned by the mainstream health establishment. Despite this, some professionals offer 'a possibility of change' for homosexuals who are unsatisfied with their sexual orientation rather than promoting cures; often emphasising the reduction of the individual's homosexual desires rather than eliminating them completely.

Conversion therapists have different views on what constitutes effective treatment. While religious groups often encourage celibacy for their 'ex-gay' followers, interpreting lack of sexual contact as successful treatment, many behaviour-change techniques define 'success' as suppression of homoerotic response (reducing or eliminating homosexual behaviour rather than in creating or increasing heterosexual attractions) or mere display of physiological ability to engage in heterosexual intercourse. Neither outcome adopts the complex set of attractions and feelings that constitute sexual orientation. Even so, if some individuals eventually do make such a change, there is no evidence for a cause-and-effect relationship and such therapies would remain ethically questionable.

Conversion therapy has been discredited on several grounds. Almost all medical organisations maintain that there is little or no empirical evidence supporting the efficacy of these treatments. Most studies that claim success often have serious limitations and/or study-design flaws, including sampling biases, absence of comparison groups, exclusive reliance on self-reported or therapist-reported outcome data, low success rates, varying definitions of success, and limited follow-up data. Besides, most of the studies define sexual orientation only in behavioural terms ignoring the biological, gender-based, social and emotional components integral to sexual orientation. The fundamental objection to conversion therapy that if human desire is seen as being diverse, varied and plural, the notion of converting back to something does not arise, has been aptly summarised by Halpert in the title of his review: 'If it ain't broke, don't fix it'.

Thus, while numerous researchers and clinicians have claimed to re-orient homosexual individuals, the critical methodological problems mentioned above cast much doubt on the authenticity of their conclusions. The APA has stated that success and harm stories are anecdotal and that 'there are no scientifically rigorous outcome studies to determine either the actual efficacy or harm of "reparative" treatments'.

In addition to the scepticism over efficacy, serious concerns have been expressed over the safety and ethics of conversion therapy and harmful effects such as increased guilt, anxiety, low self-esteem, sense of personal failure, suicidal ideation, and temporary or long-term sexual dysfunction have been reported.

Concerns have also been expressed over its unethical practice and potential for reinforcing societal prejudices and pathological views of homosexuality. Consequently, in 1998, through a resolution, the APA opposed any psychiatric treatment including conversion therapy which is 'based upon the assumption that homosexuality per se is a mental disorder or based upon the a priori assumption that a patient should change his/her homosexual orientation'. Furthermore, respecting the client's right to self-determination, most mainstream health organisations including the APA have issued ethics guidelines or statements warning of possible harm and the potential of serious safety risks resulting from participation in conversion therapies. In 2000, the APA called for more scientific research to determine the risks and benefits involved and until such research is available, recommended that 'ethical practitioners refrain from attempts to change individuals' sexual orientation'.

In view of the mainstream consensus regarding the efficacy, safety and ethical concerns of conversion therapy, traditional conversion approaches have been replaced by more 'affirmative' approaches to help the individual overcome societal prejudices against homosexuality and lead a satisfying life as a homosexual.

The Indian context

In India, most medical practitioners consider ego-dystonic homosexuality a condition warranting treatment. In this clinical sub-variant of homosexuality, the sexual preference of the individual is not in doubt but the individual wishes it were different and seeks treatment. In such a case, treatment is warranted. By contrast, in ego-syntonic homosexuality, the individual is comfortable with his or her sexual preference or gender identity and treatment is not warranted.

The People's Union for Civil Liberties (PUCL) reports that doctors will often diagnose the patient as ego-dystonic even if the patient is ego-syntonic. The PUCL further reports that though it is claimed that a person's ego-syntonicity or dystonicity is determined clinically, a reputed doctor at a prominent Bangalore hospital has conceded that a person's distress with his homosexuality may be due to different factors like the pressure to get married or the need to conform to culturally appropriate sexual practices.

Due to lack of adequate research, data regarding the number of people treated by and the outcomes of conversion therapy are sorely lacking. In fact, the first reported case was a complaint filed before the National Human Rights Commission in 2001 by the Naz Foundation (India) Trust on the grounds that it violated the fundamental rights of a patient who was being treated for homosexuality with counselling and drugs over a four-year period at the All India Institute for Medical Sciences, New Delhi. A scan of academic literature indicates that there is only one paper on the use of behavioural modification techniques which reports that eight out of 13 male homosexuals showed a shift to heterosexual adaptation that was maintained during a six-month and one-year follow-up.

Thus, in the context of a society where there is scant information about same-sex desires and relationships, and little dialogue among the medical community or research on the subject, homosexuals continue to be subjected to a wide range of conversion treatments. There is no evidence either that these practitioners follow prescribed norms for treating homosexuality or use standard treatment protocols and prescribed ethics guidelines. Likewise, there is no documentation of the 'cures' for homosexuality offered by practitioners of the traditional and informal systems of medicine who cater to the health problems, including sexual problems, of a substantial population.

Study design

The study was conducted in the metropolitan cities of Mumbai and Pune in Maharashtra between April 2007 and January 2008. An exploratory, descriptive and qualitative research design was used.

The health care providers originally selected for the study comprised psychiatrists, sexologists, gynaecologists, dermatologists, urologists and counsellors who had been consulted by homosexual clients. Based on its objectives and literature review, the research design initially intended to target only psychiatrists, sexologists and gynaecologists. Psychiatrists were selected because psychiatry, as a branch of medicine, has been historically engaged with the question of homosexuality as a perversion or normal variation and thereby its treatment or acceptance; sexologists by dint of their being medical professionals specialising in sex and sex therapy; and gynaecologists because literature suggests that lesbian and bisexual (LB) women are likely to seek their services. However, subsequently the study was extended to other health care providers such as dermatologists, urologists and counsellors because early field experience and key informant interviews indicated that a substantial number of homosexual men also consult these categories of caregivers.

The health care providers were identified by purposive selection. The sample was derived by sending out 525 letters soliciting participation to the membership of professional bodies of psychiatrists, gynaecologists and obstetricians in Mumbai and Pune. The poor response to the letters was followed up by telephone calls as a result of which 30 psychiatrists, gynaecologists and dermatologists were enrolled. Sexologists and urologists were contacted through information received from key informants while counsellors who had treated homosexual individuals joined the study in response to a call posted on e-groups such as the 'Counselors Association of India', a group of mental health professionals in India. Finally, 40 health care providers from the two cities emerged as participants.

A semi-structured interview schedule was designed, consisting of both open- and closed-ended questions. It comprised sections on the background of the health care providers, practice-related information, their knowledge of sexuality in general and homosexuality in particular, and their attitudes towards homosexuality.

Data were collected by way of a one-time, 45 to 90 minute interview. Oral consent was sought from each health care provider prior to the interview. The interview team consisted of an interviewer and a note-taker. Field notes were expanded and computerised on the day of the interview itself. Data analysis of coded text segments was performed with the computer software package MAX QDA version 2k1 R030801 (© 1995–2001UdoKuckartz Berlin).

Limitations

The sample comprised 40 practitioners across six categories of health care providers in the two cities. Thus, a small sample is one of the limitations of the study. Moreover, since the sample was drawn by purposive sampling, the findings are representative of the health care providers interviewed and cannot be generalised to the larger health care community in these cities or in other parts of India. A further weakness of the study is that the limited time available for data collection did not permit follow-up interviews which would have provided richer descriptions of the treatments and experiences of respondents.

Profile of study participants

As seen in Table 1, the health care providers were more or less equally distributed between the two cities both by number (Mumbai: 19 and Pune: 21) and profession. Together they comprised 19 psychiatrists, four sexologists, eight dermatologists, three gynaecologists, five counsellors and one urologist.

The category 'sexologist' included medical practitioners who had graduated in medicine (MBBS degree) and held a postgraduate qualification in dermatology, psychiatry, radiology or a course in sexual medicine from an overseas university. Irrespective of their educational background, all the health care providers had listed themselves as 'currently practising sexologists' or 'clinicians working with sexual medicine'.

Of the 40 health care providers, 28 were male and 12 were female. They were between 24 and 86 years of age and had an experience range of nine months to 50 years. Most (N=32) of the health care providers were associated with private hospitals apart from having a private practice; 14 were also attached to public hospitals and NGOs engaged in mental health activities (including

TABLE 1		
Profession and location of study participants (N=40)		
Specialist	*Pune*	*Mumbai*
Psychiatrist	10	9
Sexologist	2	2
Dermatologist	4	4
Gynaecologist	2	1
Counsellor	2	3
Urologist	1	0
Total	21	19

running a rehabilitation centre, day care centre and/or halfway home). Four of the five counsellors worked with NGOs providing services to lesbian, gay, bisexual and transgender persons.

The treatment approaches employed by the health care providers can be broadly categorised into two main groups: (1) conversion therapy for homosexuality, and (2) other therapies for symptoms presented by the client, either linked or unrelated to the client's homosexuality. In keeping with its objectives, this report explores only the first approach in detail that is, the treatment attempts of health care providers who used conversion therapy.

The majority (N=34) of the health care providers reported that their clients were predominantly male homosexuals. In fact, when asked whether they had been consulted by homosexual clients, they associated the word 'homosexual' only with 'male homosexuals' and passed over descriptions of female homosexuals. Eliciting information about lesbian clients required special probing. It is important to note, therefore, that this report describes the use of conversion therapies administered to male homosexuals alone, except in one instance where information about lesbian clients was available.

Table 2 shows that close to half (N=18) of the 40 health care providers were using some form of conversion therapy to help a homosexual person convert to a heterosexual one. Three others reported that they no longer practised it because they doubted its efficacy; two of them also said that they would not consider it 'right to treat homosexuality *per se*'. For instance, a 43-year-old female psychiatrist from Mumbai said:

> There was this guy ... this must be years ago, maybe at least 10 years ago. He was a doctor's son. The doctor told me that he is gay and he wanted his son to be converted. So, at that time, I gave him some behaviour therapy. He even got married after that. But it obviously did not work out... I always give this example to parents who come and ask me to convert their children. The idea is to support your children, not convert them. It would be a shock to you. It may not be acceptable to you. I can help you cope with those difficulties. But I just can't convert the child, it would simply not be right.

TABLE 2 Therapeutic approaches used by health care providers (N=40)			
Type of therapy	*Conversion*		*Other than*
	Ever users	*Current users*	*conversion*
Number of health care providers	21	18	19

The remaining (19) health care providers claimed that they focussed on the psychological symptoms for which the client sought help; 11 of them reported working with the client or the client's family to help enhance acceptance of homosexual orientation.

Interestingly, the 18 health care providers who used conversion methods, administered supportive treatments for some of their clients. It appears then that these health care providers employed specific criteria to decide which of their clients needed conversion therapy as distinct from those who required some form of supportive therapy.

Also of interest is the finding that five of the 19 health care providers did not consider homosexuality a disorder. They responded to the question of the probable cause of homosexuality with statements or counter questions such as:

Looking for a cause for homosexuality is irrelevant.

Asking what causes homosexuality is like asking what causes the colour of one's eyes.

Why do I like to wear earrings?

Looking for a cause implies abnormality; do we ask what causes life?

How often do we ask what causes heterosexuality? We just accept it.

Table 3 presents a profession-wise distribution of the health care providers who used conversion therapy.

As can be seen from Table 3, psychiatrists, gynaecologists and sexologists were more likely to use conversion techniques than those who practised other specialities. Thus, a majority of the psychiatrists (12 out of 19, three reporting discontinuation of conversion therapy since), gynaecologists (two of the three), and sexologists (three of the four) offered conversion therapy while fewer dermatologists

TABLE 3 Profession of health care providers using conversion methods (N=21)		
Profession of health care provider	Total number of health care providers	Number of health care providers who used conversion
Psychiatrist	19	12*
Sexologist	4	3
Dermatologist	8	3
Gynaecologist	3	2
Counsellor	5	0
Urologist	1	1
Total	40	21

* 3 psychiatrists reported having discontinued the practice of conversion therapy.

(only three of the eight) and none of the five counsellors did so. The following sections of this report are confined to the 18 health care providers who were practising conversion therapy at the time of the interview.

Most of the psychiatrists and sexologists among the 18 health care providers reported the use of several techniques, often behavioural, to change their patient's sexual orientation. The interventions included the use of heterosexual imagery, fantasy building, creative visualisation and cognitive behaviour therapy. On the other hand, the remaining six health care providers employed methods such as 'advice' and information-giving, suggesting thereby that these categories of caregivers lacked training in specific conversion techniques.

What determines the use of conversion therapy?

Interestingly, as was seen from Table 2 above, the health care providers appeared to be able to determine whether a client would 'benefit from' conversion therapy or from supportive (non-conversion) therapy and/or counselling of her/his family members. Clients can be grouped under four broad categories of criteria reported by the health care providers to decide who warranted conversion therapy—those who were diagnosed as ego-dystonic, those whose homosexuality was perceived to have been caused largely by environmental factors, those who were diagnosed as 'superficially' homosexual, and those who possessed adequate motivation to change their sexual orientation.

Ego-dystonic homosexuality

Six of the nine psychiatrists cited the distinction between ego-syntonic homosexuality and ego-dystonic homosexuality as a criterion for determining the eligibility of a client for conversion therapy. Thus, the health care providers viewed ego-dystonic homosexuality, that is, homosexuality associated with feelings of alienation from or distress about one's sexual identity to be indicative of conversion therapy while ego-syntonic homosexuality, wherein the individual is comfortable with his homosexual identity did not require a change in orientation. These views are reflected in the following:

> There was this one person who was very distressed with his homosexuality and he came and told me, 'I don't want it. I want to be able to live like any other normal person and get married, have a family and so on. He was what we call a case of ego-dystonic homosexuality. (50 years, male, Psychiatrist, Pune).

> I first ask the patient if he wants to continue as a homosexual. If he says, 'yes', then I tell him about the consequences like social pressure and stress, and I tell the parents that it's [homosexuality] not an illness it's just an attraction. I also tell them that it doesn't exist in our diagnostic category. It has been removed from the DSM-IV [classification of mental disorders]; so homosexuality is not a 'diagnosis'. [But] if he doesn't want to continue with it [homosexuality], I tell him about my treatment. I personally don't treat it if it's not ego-dystonic, and because of family and societal pressure...(38 years, male, Psychiatrist, Pune).

> ... there are two types of homosexuals, ego-alien and ego-syntonic. Those who are ego-alien require treatment but those who are ego-syntonic are as fine as what we call 'normal sexuality'. They are

comfortable with it [homosexuality]. So what can anyone do about it? (57 years, male, Psychiatrist, Mumbai).

I try to assess if it [homosexuality] is dystonic or syntonic. In syntonic cases, there is no point in giving treatment, but if the patient is dystonic, he looks around in trains, urinals and places like that. For syntonics, there are groups they can go to and ... if it is ego-syntonic, what is there to treat? It is very difficult to treat... (45 years, male, Psychiatrist, Mumbai).

The health care providers believed that some homosexual individuals are comfortable with their sexual orientation while others are not. Furthermore, they considered individuals who are not comfortable with their sexual identity, for whatever reason, as likely candidates for conversion therapy while those who were comfortable were considered to possess 'normal sexuality', not warranting a change in sexual orientation. Conspicuously, the health care providers did not seem to see a role for themselves in helping individuals understand the source of their discomfort/dystonicity, that is, whether the distress was an inherent discomfort with one's sexuality or was located outside the individual as a problem of social prejudice. Equally, health care providers did not mention the need to help clients to achieve comfort with their sexuality or to develop an integrated identity as part of the care and treatment model.

Perceived environmental cause of homosexuality

The perceived cause of homosexuality or why the individual turned to homosexuality was another criterion that was used to identify clients requiring conversion therapy. As can be seen from Table 4, the most cited cause (by eight of the 18 health care providers) of homosexuality focussed on experiences in 'male only' environments such as prisons, military sites and boys' boarding schools along with the non-availability of opposite-sex partners.

A second category of perceived causes mentioned by an almost equal number of healthcare providers (N=7) involved environmental factors such as childhood same-sex exploration, sexual abuse experienced in childhood and past aversive sexual experiences.

That homosexuality ascribed to environmental factors was used to justify the administration of conversion therapy is reflected in the following:

> I check if it [homosexuality] is because of obsession or compulsion, or because they never had any experience [of heterosexual contacts]. I ask them not to be prejudiced about heterosexual relationships. I ask them to be more comfortable with heterosexual contacts. Is it that they don't want it [heterosexual contact] because they have found their comfort zone? One hears that the first sexual encounter with a man is always painful; so, could it be because they are afraid of childbearing? We don't know if they have such fears or whether they are really not attracted to men. People who have had stern fathers or...they refuse to get attached to men. In that case, is it because they are afraid of men?... When they come for counselling, we need to confirm what it [homosexuality] is due to... (60 years, female, Sexologist, Pune).

> I try to find out how homosexuality began—was it always there, was it through play, was it some aversive experience/s, etc...? I try to analyse how it started and how it was nurtured. Then, I concentrate on the painful and more aversive experiences. I look for pointers that lead to aversion or non-availability of a partner (38 years, male, Psychiatrist, Pune).

> If I have a client whose father is a much older man and has married a young woman (the boy's mother), and if they do not have a good marriage and the boy has a lot of pity and sympathy for the mother and disgust for the father and, therefore, turns towards men, then I would try to create ambivalence. I would tilt him to feeling positive towards his father and help him identify with his father. Also, if there is a heterosexual relationship in this person's life or such a relationship has been attempted, I would try to strengthen it. (50 years, male, Psychiatrist, Pune).

All the health care providers seemed to think that environmental factors were responsiblefor homosexuality; only two attributed it to both biological and environmental factors. Those who viewed same-sex orientations as resulting from environmental factors such as abuse and exploitation were inclined to believe that homosexuality

TABLE 4
Perceived causes of homosexuality as reported by health care providers
(N=18)

Causes	Number of respondents	
Environmental Factors		
Early exposure	7	• Accidental sexual exposure/sexual exploration/sexual abuse by person of the same-sex was the first sexual experience, which was pleasurable • Habit formation of same-sex attraction
Same-sex spaces	8	• Hostels • Army/Navy • Truck drivers • Prison • Culturally not allowed to mingle with the opposite sex • Lack of choice or exploration • Peer pressure or incidents of ragging.
Negative feelings towards the opposite sex	2	• Negative attitudes towards heterosexuality • Negative feelings or a deep-rooted conflict with the opposite sex
Early childhood	1	• Upbringing among/along with several girls experiences (*specifically mentioned in the context of a male homosexual*)
Other environmental factors	4	• Lack of sex education • Same-sex act under the influence of alcohol • Same-sex act for buying drugs or for money • To try out something new • Poverty • Lack of emotionally nurturing environment in the family
Biological factors	2	• Genetic/inborn • Hormonal

Note: *The number of responses is > n due to multiple responses.*

or same-sex desire could not be a 'choice' and was often, 'learnt' behaviour which could be 'unlearnt' through therapy.

While these statements indicate the acceptance of homosexuality as a normal variant of sexuality and not an abnormality, these heath care providers (as we shall see later, in the section on 'Enhancing heterosexual sexual performance') mainly used sex therapy to treat the client's clinical symptoms of sexual dysfunction, in the context of his marital relationship, ignoring thereby, his concerns with regard to his sexual identity and related issues.

'Superficial' homosexuality

Four health care providers based their decision to administer conversion therapy on what they termed as 'superficial' homosexuality. They stated that these individuals had come to 'believe' that they were homosexual though in reality they were not. Hence, the providers were of the opinion that if adequately motivated, such 'superficial' homosexuals could overcome their homosexual behaviour. Conversely, five health care providers spoke of a concept variously labelled as a *true* homosexual, *classic* homosexual or *pakka* [fixed] homosexual. Such individuals, they claimed, did not warrant conversion therapy.

> Actually, I have seen 10–15 people but they are not all classic homosexuals. If the person has not had intercourse and it's only attraction, then he is not a classic homosexual .... Classic homosexuality is not a disorder, it's normal. The other kind or person who thinks he is homosexual and has a typical history. Every patient of this kind that I have seen has had some kind of experience in childhood. I mean an elder brother or an uncle or a cousin has done something sexually to the person who has not been oriented since and has come to believe that this [homosexual behaviour] is the right thing and continued with it. He is not homosexual but he has been doing the same thing since childhood ... like he would have masturbated his brother or something like that.... But there is no anal intercourse, only superficial acts have been performed and the person thinks he is homosexual. But actually, he can be shifted to normal sexuality. I would tell him

how a homosexual is ... theoretically. Then I would tell him that a homosexual does such-and-such a thing; you don't have those traits and so, you are not a homosexual. Therefore, you can change... (32 years, male, Psychiatrist, Pune).

This health care provider seemed to believe that 'classic' homosexual behaviour was characterised by anal intercourse alone, and could not be cured. According to him, any other form of sexual expression implied 'superficial homosexuality' which was amenable to treatment and hence an indication for using conversion therapy.

Another health care provider, however, perceived that having multiple partners in a homosexual relationship suggested that the person can be easily converted to heterosexuality. He explained that such a client was unlikely to be emotionally attached to any one partner and, therefore, his multiple partners could be readily replaced by a woman.

There are a lot of them [homosexuals] where it is only one-to-one like a love affair between a man and a woman. In such a case, it becomes very difficult for the person to get out of it. If the attachment is with one guy/friend only, it can be difficult, but if there are already many partners, they can easily be substituted by a woman. (32 years, male, Psychiatrist, Pune).

Adequate motivation to change

That the motivation possessed by the client to change his/her sexual orientation contributes significantly to the success of conversion therapy was a view shared by the majority of the health care providers (15 of the 18 respondents who were interviewed) and was, therefore, an important criterion used to select clients for conversion therapy.

For example:

I first check for the person's motivation. Only if he wants to stop this then it can work... I have both pre-marital and post-marital cases such as cases wherein a homosexual wants to get married and when he is already married. I tell the patient as well as the family that this may work only if he is motivated and determined [to change]... (52 years, male, Sexologist).

Well, I tell them that I am ready to give it a try. But, it would require your determination. It may take years together and for all you know, it may never happen... (60 years, female, Sexologist, Pune).

One of the health care providers who was involved in a study aimed at helping young priests to give up homosexual behaviour corroborated their views:

I was working on this study with young priests who had homosexual behaviour and wanted to get rid of it because their profession didn't allow it. Basically, their urge to give it up was very strong because they were priests and their homosexual behaviour had resulted from a few instances of sexual abuse. What we largely used for behaviour change was the concept that homosexuality is not parallel to their profession. This worked for them and they came out of it! (34 years, male, Psychiatrist, Mumbai)

Ten health care providers reported that they informed both the patient and his/her family members that a change toward heterosexuality is possible if the person possesses sufficient motivation to change. They also cautioned that it could take a long time and may not necessarily occur.

Overall then, all the 18 health care providers affirmed that conversion therapy was warranted in those individuals who were diagnosed as ego-dystonic, those whose homosexuality was diagnosed to have been caused mainly by environmental factors, those who were diagnosed as *superficially* and not *really* homosexual, and those who possessed adequate motivation to change their sexual orientation.

What are the methods used?

Several methods to change the sexual orientation of homosexual persons emerged from the interviews. Psychiatrists, by and large, reported the use of interventions such as heterosexual imagery, fantasy building, creative visualisation and cognitive behaviour therapy. On the other hand, most of the other health care providers employed methods such as 'giving advice' on how to curtail 'such behaviour'. The treatment administered by a small number of health care providers (five) was limited to treating the symptoms of sexual dysfunction presented by the client in the context of his marital relationship and improving heterosexual behaviour and sexual performance.

Fantasy building

Techniques of imagery, fantasy building and creative visualisation are based on learning theories that have been widely used in behaviour therapy. The primary assumption of these techniques is that homosexuality is a learnt or acquired behaviour wherein the person has learnt to associate pleasure, specifically sexual pleasure, with a person of the same sex. This may have occurred due to the person having experienced same-sex sexual contact and finding it pleasurable. Different health care providers described various techniques such as creative visualisation, fantasy building, and imagery to help the person to break this pleasurable association with same-sex contact and form a new association between sexual pleasure and opposite-sex contact.

In addition to these techniques, these health care providers prescribed certain ground rules that the patient was expected to follow during the course of the therapy such as, not fantasising about the same sex, not keeping in touch with past lovers' and complete cessation of same-sex sexual acts. Narratives describe the exercises of fantasy building and creative visualisation used by the health care providers:

> 'I use imagery wherein a homosexual image is shown and the person is asked to masturbate. Then, during masturbation, just before ejaculation, when there is ejaculatory inevitability, the image is replaced with a heterosexual image. It can either be done in the mind or on screen. If the person has any heterosexual relationship in his life, I try to make it healthier. I would use her [the heterosexual partner] as a co-therapist. I would try to find out why the person has developed this alienation ... this disgust for the other sex...' (50 years, male, Psychiatrist, Pune).

'... I believe that [in normal circumstances] there is libido which flows [in a certain direction]; for homosexuals, it flows in the wrong direction. So, the first step is to make the patient stop everything that has to do with his sexual life. Basically, his libido has to stop flowing in that [homosexual] direction. Therefore, I make him abstain from all activities that have anything to do with homosexuality; even fantasising about homosexual sex has to stop. As a result, the patient is deprived [of homosexual contact/fantasy], his libido builds up to a point when it seeks release. At that point, the patient is shown heterosexual images or arousal stimuli. Then, he can be changed to a heterosexual... (38 years, male, Psychiatrist, Pune).

Another thing that I do is ask the person to buy a magazine and whenever he sees a man's photo, to just ignore it and go ahead. Then, find a woman's photo... look at it. Do you like her? If you like her, what do you like about her? Oh, her figure is wow! OK, cut it out and keep it aside. Go to the next picture—what do you like in this woman? Her lips? OK. Cut it out and keep it. I ask him to repeat this till he has cut out 30 pictures and then come back to see me. So, in this way, I have already made him begin to focus on females, I have started making him look for beauty in females.... Then, I will ask him to pick out three top women from those pictures and put them into a fantasy theme. For example, if he has liked the picture of Madhuri Dixit [a famous film actress in India] because she is pretty, I will start off by saying, 'Imagine it's a Sunday and you are alone at home. OK? You are totally relaxed and the bell rings. You open the door and see Madhuri Dixit standing there smiling at you. You are shocked! She tells you that till tomorrow morning she is going to be with you and you can do whatever you want with her ... you can take her to the movies, you can sleep with her, you can touch her wherever you want...So, basically, you have 24 hours with her. Now, tell me, what will you do in these 24 hours?' Then the patient starts imagining and talking, and I keep nudging him to make it [his narrative] more erotic. Then, I ask the patient to repeat this every day and then, eventually, to start masturbating. Keep practising this exercise... (48years, male, Sexologist, Mumbai).

I use creative visualisation in which the person gets very intimate with a woman, and tape it so that he can hear it all the time. Basically, fantasy life is very short; therefore, we use visualisation. When he begins to feel very comfortable, you begin to build a story [about the patient and the woman] saying, 'You are holding hands and you are aroused by the touch.' You have to create a Mills and Boon story for him. This takes time and he has to walk with you. The results are uncertain... (53 years, male, Psychiatrist, Mumbai).

Advice giving

Six of the 18 health care providers offered advice about what the client should or should not do in lieu of conversion techniques in order to effect a change. For example, 'avoid thoughts [of same-sex]' or 'think of the same-sex person you are attracted to as your brother or sister' or merely telling the person that 'this is not acceptable and is causing problems like STDs; so change your habits'.

I ask them: 'Why do you need to do it? What do you feel? You have the same [implies body parts] as they have, so what is attracting you?' I always tell them to try and avoid [such behaviour], to divert the mind. I say, 'If you are attracted to a person, you should think of the person as your brother or sister, whoever the person may be.' We say: 'No... Keep control!...' I tell them that it [homosexuality] is still not accepted here.... I don't give any medication, just tranquilisers to calm the mind because they keep thinking about this thing only... (28 years, male, Dermatologist, Pune).

The purpose of therapy as reflected in these two quotes is to enhance heterosexual behaviour and the tool for doing so is 'advice'. Most dermatologists and gynaecologists who were interviewed reported that they practised such advice-giving as a method of conversion possibly because they were not trained in the specific behavioural techniques used by psychiatrists and sexologists. Nonetheless, the extracts reflect provider opinions endorsing the deviancy view of homosexuality.

Another psychiatrist who used imagery during masturbation also reported that he advised his clients thus:

If the patient is bisexual, he finds both acts pleasurable. So I tell him to try and increase attraction towards the opposite sex and reduce same-sex attraction. I know it can't be zero per cent, but at least to try and make it 75–25, 75% towards the opposite sex and 25% towards the same sex. I tell him to increase attraction towards his wife. This is the ideal situation but if it is not possible, to enjoy both! But he should keep a partition between the two; that is the practical way to be. In the case of a bisexual person, there is a very good chance of increasing libido to increase attraction for the opposite sex... (32 years, male, Psychiatrist, Pune).

Although this provider did not advise the complete cessation of homosexual behaviour, he did give a message about the desirability of enhancing heterosexual contact and relationships in the client's life and the reduction of homosexual attraction.

Enhancing heterosexual sexual performance

Five of the 18 health care providers who practised conversion therapy spoke about helping the homosexual client to deal more effectively with problems related to sexual performance in a heterosexual relationship. In some cases, the reason for consultation was the client's desire to be able to marry, though more often, it occurred when the homosexual person attained marriageable age or if he/she had a marital problem. For example, a sexologist from Pune who gives many public lectures and writes about marital sex had this to say about his experience with homosexual clients:

In premarital cases, many have got involved and are engaged in homosexual activities. They need to dissociate themselves from that before marriage and learn to develop heterosexual fantasies and techniques which I teach them. In post-marital cases, the objective is to make the person comfortable with the idea of foreplay and postures during intercourse. I would guide him in developing and being comfortable with the idea of heterosexual sex (52 years, male, Sexologist, Pune).

For married homosexual men, the treatment of sexual dysfunction involved the use of various therapeutic measures such as hormones, drugs and surgery to induce artificial erection so that the client could consummate his marriage or perform the procreative function, or to improve the quality of sexual performance as the following quotes indicate:

> Sometimes, people have to get married under pressure.... They come to me asking for help so that they can have sex just once with their wife. Just so that they can have a child. They literally beg me to do something, just once. In such a case, I provide hormonal therapy. Maybe create an artificial erection by giving a papaverine injection in the penis. I would tell the person to imagine that he is having anal sex with his partner so that he can have sex [with his wife].... Many of them return to show me their children... (smiles) (49 years, male, Psychiatrist, Mumbai).

> We do counselling, we give medication, hormonal injections— sildenafil, trimix and papaverine injections, and tadanafil in severe cases. These are used for artificial erection. I have also given implants to two of my patients... (46 years, male, Urologist, Pune).

A health care provider in Mumbai spoke about married homosexual men approaching him for treatment of sexual impotence in the marital context:

> If the person is married ... basically, early in the morning, when you get up, there is a fine, good quality erection because of hormonal cycles. So, we ask him to have sex at that time, if it is possible. (45 years, male, Psychiatrist, Mumbai).

Although these practitioners did not actively seek to convert the sexual orientation of their clients through the use of conversion techniques, the basic framework of the treatment they administered remained the same in that, they used sex therapy to combat sexual dysfunction in their clients and help them to achieve successful heterosexual performance.

The above extracts indicate that these health care providers, including psychiatrists and sexologists, restricted the focus of their therapy to the clinical symptom of sexual dysfunction within the framework of a conventional marriage, while completely ignoring sexual identity and related issues. However, in helping both unmarried and married clients to improve their heterosexual expression, issues such as dealing with the pressure to marry or finding out whether or why a homosexual person wanted to get into a heterosexual marriage were not addressed. Likewise, other health or mental health needs of married homosexual men, their spouses or same-sex partner/s apparently remained unaddressed.

What defines successful therapy?

While conversion, by definition, aims at changing homosexual orientation, most of the health care providers interviewed focussed on 'conversion of behaviours' and, in many cases, their aim was not really conversion but the 'learning of new/heterosexual behaviours' by their clients.

Many homosexuals claimed to have been cured by 13 of the 18 health care providers. Most of them defined 'success' or 'cure' in terms of the client getting married or reporting a happy marriage or returning to show them his/her baby. Thus, the treatment was deemed successful if the client was able to have heterosexual sex, get married and procreate (if already married) thereby reflecting the cultural emphasis on male sexual performance. Significantly, their assessment of successful conversion from homosexuality to heterosexuality did not touch on homosexual desires or behaviours and/or their reduction nor cessation following therapy.

> Many of them return saying that I am happy. They say things like they do not have those [homosexual] thoughts anymore and are able to enjoy with their wives. But, I don't believe that they have stopped anything. They must be continuing with whatever they were doing. It's just that they are not anxious and they are happy. Anyway, they have got the concept. They become more or less bisexual. They start enjoying both the sides... (45 years, male, Psychiatrist, Mumbai).

> Success is difficult to measure.... See, basically, they are deviants and then they get married and these are success stories. Once the treatment is successful, they stop coming to me. And, even if it is unsuccessful,

> they stop coming; they may go elsewhere… so one really can't say…
> (60 years, female, Psychiatrist, Pune).

In both these extracts, the health care providers while describing successful conversion of same-sex sexual orientation have limited their definition to the occurrence of heterosexual contact/s or marital status and not the cessation of homosexual behaviours. In fact, as one of the health care providers (male psychiatrist from Mumbai) stated, homosexual activity may be going on furtively and may not be reported by the client during follow-up visits.

Three of the health care providers also talked about treatment failures that they had encountered and possible reasons for such failures.

> I have had almost 100% success with very few exceptions…. In the bisexual group, people come with motivation. Only three cases failed even after counselling. He had some psychological block. Such cases were referred to a psychiatrist. He was obsessed with his homosexuality. He was repeatedly getting involved in homosexual activity. I couldn't help two or three cases. Their motivation [to change] was not adequate… (52 years, male, Sexologist, Pune).

> Perhaps with counselling and psychiatric help, you can control it, but I haven't seen anyone who has been successfully treated. It is like any other mental problem. There is no total cure. Lifelong treatment and regular follow-up is needed… (25 years, male, Dermatologist, Mumbai).

The health care providers' responses to the question of failures encountered in the course of their efforts to convert their clients underscore the point that the client's motivation to change is the key to successful conversion. Thus, treatment success or failure is dependent to a large extent on the patient's own will. Furthermore, the two extracts above equate homosexuality with psychiatric disorder, the first describing homosexual preference/desire as *obsessive* and the second equating homosexuality with chronic mental disorders that require lifelong treatment. Overall, it seemed that the health care providers neither followed any clear-cut guidelines or criteria for treatment success or efficacy nor did they mention any specific tool or measure for ascertaining success.

Discussion

This study has shown that despite the fact that international psychiatric circles no longer consider homosexuality as a mental illness or an abnormality, almost half of the healthcare providers we interviewed in Mumbai and Pune often treat it as a deviation or mental health problem that should be changed to a heterosexual orientation. By subscribing to this view, these practitioners do not appear to deal with the issues of stigmatisation, discrimination and other stressful social experiences that may be important contributors to the individual's health or mental problems. On the other hand, three health care providers who had used conversion therapy reported a change in their practice with homosexual clients in that they completely gave up conversion therapy because they had reservations about its efficacy and did not consider it 'right to treat homosexuality per se'. The other half of our respondents, however, took a different approach to dealing with homosexuality in that they treated the symptoms for which the individual had approached them and/or supported the individual and his/her family to accept his/her homosexuality. Interestingly, five of them stated that looking for a cause for homosexuality was irrelevant as homosexuality was as natural as any other sexual orientation or behaviour.

Among the health care providers we interviewed, an almost equal number of those who practised conversion therapy attributed the 'condition' of homosexuality to child sexual abuse or early sexual initiation and exploration (N=7) or to a lack of exposure to the opposite sex while living in 'male-only' environments (N=8). Thus, it appears that these health care providers considered same-sex sexual orientation to be partially or wholly 'caused' by or 'learnt' through adverse environmental factors and hence amenable to change. A similar perspective can be seen in older psychoanalytic literature in which homosexuality was considered to be pathological sexualisation and therefore in need of 'repair'.

While the rationale for treating homosexuality was 'environmental causation', the treatment focused on 'individual behaviour', thus locating the problem within the 'homosexual client' and placing the responsibility of assuming a heterosexual orientation also on the individual 'homosexual client'. Several of the health care providers communicated to the homosexual client as well as family members that the success of their interventions was dependent on the client's motivation to change and that there was no guarantee of success. This implies that the onus of the success or failure of the therapy lies entirely on the homosexual client. Further, the client also faces pressure from both his/her family and health care provider to change and to report the success of the treatment. This makes self-reporting of the success of conversion therapy—which according to the health care providers was the only criterion of measuring the efficacy of their treatment—a questionable proposition.

Half of the health care providers we interviewed continued to use conversion therapy, the theoretical foundations as well as effectiveness of which are questionable. A recently published systematic review of 28 empirically-based, peer-reviewed, full length articles and brief reports addressing the efficacy of reparative therapies shows that most of these studies are methodologically flawed. The limitations include the lack of a theoretical base to the interventions carried out, inconsistent definitions and measurement of sexual orientation, restricted samples and lack of follow-up. In terms of what constitutes change, most of these research studies focused on sexual acts or behaviours. Even in the current study, many health care providers defined success of treatment in terms of heterosexual performance, including getting married plus successful procreation. However, same-sex sexual orientation/preference does not imply sexual impotence or a complete inability to engage in peno-vaginal sex. Moreover, sexual orientation goes beyond sexual behaviours and consists of several dimensions including sexual desire, sexual preference, and affectional and relational components. Therefore, such criteria of 'success' of treatment for 'homosexual orientation' are debatable.

Some studies like Haldeman's have described negative outcomes of the use of conversion therapies, including chronic depression, low self-esteem, difficulty in sustaining relationships and sexual dysfunction. Shidlo and Schroeder noted that a majority of those who sought reparative therapy perceived psychological harm in the form of depression, suicidal ideation and attempts, social and interpersonal harm, loss of social support, and spiritual harm as a direct result of the interventions. In a study conducted in the United Kingdom, 29 individuals and two relatives of former patients who had received therapy for their homosexuality from the1960s to the 1980s were interviewed to understand the circumstances in which people sought therapy, referral pathways, the process and aftermath of the therapies. No participant thought he/she had benefited from the therapy and for many it increased their sense of social isolation and shame, and lowered their sense of self-worth. The study concluded by cautioning against the use of mental health services to change aspects of human behaviour that are disapproved of on social, political, moral or religious grounds.

Mental health practitioners such as Haldeman have also reported that the practice of sexual reorientation therapy socially devalues homosexuality and bisexuality. Moreover, many of these conversion therapies approach the whole issue of homosexuality in a vacuum with no regard to the homophobic social attitudes in which individuals with same-sex desires live out their lives. Thus, the use of conversion therapy for changing sexual orientation is fraught with several problems.

Some of the other issues raised by the health care providers' responses in the sections on 'What defines successful therapy?' and 'Enhancing heterosexual sexual performance' concern the 'compulsory' nature of heterosexual marriage in Indian society and the cultural links of masculinity and manhood with the man's ability to procreate. Some of them also seemed to subscribe to this normative thinking and hence provided various medical solutions for consummation of marriage and procreation to the married homosexual. Interestingly, some responses of the health care providers in these same sections also hint at the acceptability of sex 'outside marriage' for married homosexual men as long as the duties of heterosexual marriage and procreation are fulfilled.

Thus, it seems that despite conversion therapy falling short both on standards of efficacy as well as ethics, in reality, there would always be people who would seek help for 'unwanted' same-sex attractions. The reasons for such help-seeking may include social and familial factors such as pressures to marry or the individual's own desire for socio-legal recognition through heterosexual marriage or embracing an overtly heterosexual lifestyle. Reasons for seeking change in orientation may also include such factors as internalised homophobia, shame, fear, anxiety, confusion and so on. In fact, literature on lesbian / gay identity development indicates that most lesbian / gay individuals go through several stages of identity development before they reach identity synthesis, wherein they are at peace with themselves. Some of these stages include identity confusion, identity comparison, tolerance, acceptance, pride and synthesis. The stage of identity confusion, for instance, is especially relevant here as it is characterised by internal conflict, attitudes that homosexuality is incorrect and undesirable, wishing away same-sex attraction and so on. An individual struggling through this stage may often be presented in clinical situations as an 'ego-dystonic homosexual' and if this developmental struggle is not seen in the context of peer, familial or social pressures then he / she may get diagnosed as an 'ego-alien' or 'ego-dystonic' homosexual. The need to understand the concerns of young homosexual individuals in the Indian socio-cultural context with strong familial bonds and rather rigid ideas of 'compulsory' marriage is being highlighted here. Under these circumstances, continuing to treat clients with a perspective of 'reparation' and 'conversion' to heterosexuality raises serious ethical concerns.

In the Western countries, increased efforts are being made to draw linkages between the social marginalisation of sexual minorities and its impact on health outcomes. Lesbian and gay affirmative therapy is one such outcome. Here, the emphasis of therapy is to understand the client's discomfort with his / her sexual orientation as resulting from internalised and external homophobia. Thus, the social and psychological context of discomfort assumes more importance than the clinician's theoretical perspective on sexual orientation or either type of sexual reorientation therapy. The American Psychological Association, the National Association of Social Workers, and the American Counseling Association have specific, detailed guidelines for psychotherapy with gay, lesbian and bisexual clients. These guidelines broadly state that clinicians should understand that homosexuality or bisexuality is not a mental illness and that the clinician's attitude towards homosexuality could easily reflect in his or her therapy. Therefore, they need to be free of prejudice and judgement. The guidelines also mention that the stigmatisation that a gay or lesbian person faces, poses a risk to his or her mental health and well-being and that it must be taken into consideration during diagnosis and therapy. Regardless of the treatment focus, anything less than an affirmative stance in which individuals are treated with positive regard can further undermine their self-esteem.

Summing up and recommendations

Summing up

In contrast to most international guidelines for treatment of homosexuality, conversion therapy for homosexuality still seems to be practised by many health care providers in India. Findings suggest that health care providers' attitudes, understanding and assumptions regarding normative and non-normative sexuality, homosexuality, marriage, procreation and change or cure of homosexual sexual orientation makes up a complex belief system that has not incorporated some of the latest international health and human rights perspectives. Findings also suggest that a few health care providers reported a change in their practice with respect to homosexuality as a response to changes in the social and medical understanding of same-sex desires over time. The social, political and legal contexts of same-sex desires in India intersecting with the realities of class, caste, gender and other factors makes the lived experiences of individuals with same-sex desires extremely complex.

Recommendations

Given the ambiguities in provider perceptions and experiences regarding conversion therapy that emerge from the findings of this report, there is an urgent need to integrate some of the guidelines and models of 'affirmative therapy' used in the West into clinical practice in India. Findings suggest the need:

- To help professionals to be alert to the complexities of

homosexual sexual orientation and not respond out of personal prejudices or lack of knowledge;
- To dialogue with national and international medical training institutes as well as medical professional bodies;
- To review the existing medical curriculum, of both graduate and postgraduate training, in different branches of medicine to understand current levels of knowledge and approaches concerning 'homosexuality';
- To incorporate a multidimensional understanding of homosexuality and associated health/mental health issues;
- To set up consultations of various health professionals to review the guidelines for 'affirmative therapy' available in international literature and adapt them (where appropriate) to the Indian context;
- To include representations of researchers, academicians and activists working on issues relating to sexual minorities to be a part of the above-mentioned review processes.

Acknowledgements

Several people provided valuable assistance during the course of this study. I would like to thank Yogita Hastak and Sudeep J. Joseph, who worked dedicatedly as research assistants on this study and Mira Oke for training the research team. I am grateful to Pertti J. Pelto for providing valuable guidance throughout the study. I would like to place on record my appreciation to the study respondents who generously gave their time and shared their experiences. I am thankful to Bapu Trust, Pune for enabling me to undertake this research and housing the project within their premises.

I would like to thank Shireen Jejeebhoy, K.G. Santhya, Shveta Kalyanwala and Komal Saxena at the Population Council for their guidance throughout the study and on previous versions of this report. I am grateful to Pertti J. Pelto and Radhika Chandiramani for reviewing the report and to Jyoti Moodbidri for editorial contributions and careful attention to detail which have made the report more readable and clear.

References

American Psychiatric Association (APA). 1952. Diagnostic and Statistical Manual of Psychiatric Disorders (DSM). Washington, APA.
American Psychiatric Association (APA). 1973. "Position Statement on

Homosexuality" in Comprehensive Textbook of Psychiatry, Volume I (7th Edition), ed. B.J. Sadock and V.A. Kaplan. Lippincott Williams & Wilkins.

American Psychiatric Association (APA). 1987. Diagnostic and Statistical Manual of Mental Disorders—DSM III-R. Washington, APA.

American Psychiatric Association (APA). 1998. "Position Statement on psychiatric treatment and sexual orientation," American Journal of Psychiatry (APA). 1999; 156:1131, www.psych.org/edu/other_res/ lib_archives/archives/ 980020.pdf

American Psychiatric Association (APA). 2000. "Position Statement on Therapies Focused on Attempts to Change Sexual Orientation (Reparative or Conversion Therapies)". APA, May, <http://archive.psych.org/edu/other_res/ lib_ archives/archives/200001.pdf> accessed on 28 August 2007.

American Psychological Association (APA). 2008. "Answers to Your Questions: For a Better Understanding of Sexual Orientation and Homosexuality," Washington, DC: <www.apa.org/topics/sorientation.pdf>.

Cass, V.C. 1979. "Homosexual identity formation: A theoretical model." Journal of Homosexuality, 4:219-235.

Chandran, V. 2006. "Prayer, punishment or therapy? Being a homosexual in India," InfoChange News & Features, February. http://www.infochangeindia.org/ agenda4_24.jsp accessed on 28 August 2007.

Drescher, J. 1998. "I'm your handyman: A history of reparataive therapies." Journal of Homosexuality 36 (1): 19–42. <DOI: 10.1300/J082v36n01_02> accessed on 25 June 2008.

Economic and Political Weekly. 2008. "Section 377 and Denial of Rights to Sexual Minorities." 25 October. South Asia Citizens Web. 30 October 2008. <http:// www.sacw.net/article198.html>

Haldeman, D.C. 1994. "The practice and ethics of sexual orientation conversion therapy," Journal of Consulting and Clinical Psychology, 62(2): 221–227.

Haldeman, D.C. 2002. "Gay rights, patient rights: The implications of sexual orientation conversion therapy," Professional Psychology: Research and Practice, 33(3): 260–264.

Halpert, S. 2000. "If it ain't broken, don't fix it: Ethical considerations regarding conversion therapies," International Journal of Sexuality and Gender Studies, 5(1): 19–35.

Herek, G.M. 1996. "Heterosexism and homophobia," in Textbook of Homosexuality and Mental Health, ed. R.P. Cabaj and T.S. Stein. Washington, DC: American Psychiatric Press, pp. 101–113.

Herek, G. 1999. "Reparative Therapy" and other attempts to alter sexual orientation: A background paper." 5 November, http://psychology.ucdavis.edu/rainbow/ html/ facts_changing.html

Hooker, E. 1957. "The adjustment of the male overt homosexual," Journal of Projective Techniques, 21(1): 18-31.

International Commission of Jurists (ICJ). 2007. "Yogyakarta Principles—

Principles on the application of international human rights law in relation to sexual orientation and gender identity." Available at: http://www.yogyakartaprinciples.org/

Joseph, S. 1996. "Gay and lesbian movement in India," Economic and Political Weekly, 31: 2228–2233, August 17.

Katz, J. 1976. Gay American History: Lesbians and Gay Men in the U.S.A.: A Documentary Anthology. New York: Crowell, p. 129.

Morrow, S.L. and A.L. Beckstead. 2004. "Conversion therapies for same-sex attracted clients in religious conflict: Context, predisposing factors, experiences, and implications for therapy," The Counseling Psychologist, 32:641–650.

Murphy, T. 1992. "Redirecting sexual orientation: Techniques and justifications." Journal of Sex Research, 29: 501–523.

Narrain, A. 2002. "Medicalisation of homosexuality." Available online <http://www.combatlaw.org/information.php? Article_id21&issue_id=1> accessed on 10 March 2008 [Vol.1, Issue 1, Mar-April 2002].

Nicolosi, J. 1991. Reparative Therapy of Male Homosexuality: A New Clinical Approach. Northvale, NJ: J. Aronson.

Nicolosi, J., A.D. Byrd and R.W. Potts. 2000. "Retrospective self-reports of changes in sexual orientation: A consumer survey of conversion therapy clients," Psychological Reports, 86:1071–1088.

Parekh, S. 2003. "Homosexuality in India: The light at the end of the tunnel," Journal of Gay & Lesbian Psychotherapy, 7 (1/2): 153.

People's Union for Civil Liberties-Karnataka Chapter (PUCL-K). 2001. Human Rights Violations Against Sexuality Minorities in India. A Fact-finding Report about Bangalore. A Report of PUCL-Karnataka, February.

Pradhan, P.V., K.S. Ayyar, and V.N. Bagadia. 1982. "Homosexuality: Treatment by behavior modification," Indian Journal of Psychiatry, 24(1): 80-83.

Ranade, K. 2003. "Stigma, stress and coping among gay, lesbian, bisexual individuals—A qualitative study." Dissertation submitted in partial fulfilment for MPhil in Psychiatric Social Work, NIMHANS (Unpublished).

Serovich, J.M., S.M. Craft, P. Toviessi et al. 2008. "A systematic review of the research base on sexual reorientation therapies." Journal of Marital and Family Therapy, 34(2): 227–238.

Shidlo, A. and M. Schroeder. 2002. "Changing sexual orientation: A consumers' report," Professional Psychology: Research and Practice, 33: 249–259.

Smith, G., A. Bartlett and M. King. 2004. "Treatments of homosexuality in Britain since 1950s—An oral history: The experience of patients," British Medical Journal, 328:427–9.

The Times of India. 2006. "Govt's AIDS cell pushes to legalise homosexuality." Delhi Edition. TNN, 20 July. http://times of india.indiatimes.com/articleshow/msid-1779097, prt page-1.cms

Throckmorton, W. 1998. "Efforts to modify sexual orientation: A review of outcome literature and ethical issues," Journal of Mental Health Counseling, 20: 283–305.

Throckmorton, W. 2003–2004. "What is reparative therapy?" accessed on 21 March, 2007.http://www.drthrockmarton.com/article.aspid=4

Tozer, E.E. and M.K. McClanahan. 1999. "Treating the purple menace: Ethical considerations of conversion therapy and affirmative alternatives," The Counseling Psychologist, 27: 722–742.

Vanita, R. and S. Kidwai. 2000. Same-Sex Love in India: Readings from Literature and History. Macmillan India Ltd.: Delhi.

Voices Against 377. 2005. Rights for All: Ending Discrimination against Queer Desire under Section 377. A compilation by Voices Against 377, Delhi.

Whitman, J.S., H.L. Glosoff, M.M. Kocet et al. 2006. Ethical issues related to conversion or reparative therapy. Cited in Serovich, J.M., S.M. Craft, P. Toviessi et al. 2008. "A systematic review of the research base on sexual reorientation therapies." Journal of Marital and Family Therapy 34(2): 227–238.

World Health Organization (WHO). 2002. ICD-10 Classification of Mental and Behavioural Disorders. Geneva: WHO.

Yoshino, K. 2002. "Covering." Yale Law Journal 111: 769, 772–73.

Mental Health Professionals' Perspectives about Lesbian Women[1]

BINA FERNANDEZ

The data presented in this chapter is based on interviews with 22 mental health professionals (MHPs). It is organised in three sections. In the first we discuss the lesbian client profiles; in the second we present the views and therapeutic interventions of the MHPs with an analytic comment in the final section.

Lesbian client profiles

Almost all the MHPs had at least one lesbian client and the median number of clients was five.[2] Client histories for 70 women were recorded. Two of the MHPs who were affiliated to specific counselling services for lesbians/gays had a comparatively high percentage of lesbian clients—both reported that they had about two new clients per month. However, three to five clients over the entire span of the average MHP's career is a relatively low number of clients. Some MHPs commented on the fact that the incidence of lesbian clients was lower than the incidence of gay male clients.

Client concerns

Several striking features emerged from the lesbian client profiles. The single most disturbing feature in the client histories was the number of women who were forced to visit the MHP. About 15 women (21%) were compelled in this manner. Out of these, 12 young women had been brought by parents who found out they were lesbian. The remaining three women had been taken for therapy by their husbands.

Second, none of the women had come to the MHPs requesting to 'become heterosexual'. That is, although four or five women were exploring their sexual orientation and were consequently confused, guilty or anxious, there was no distress expressed about their lesbian sexuality per se.[3] They reported distress, grief, anxiety and/or depression about a range of other issues such as break-up of relationships, pressure to marry, bad marriages, etc. As three of the MHPs observed, this is in marked contrast to some of their gay male clients who approach them specifically to 'become heterosexual'. The explanation offered was that although both men and women faced pressure for marriage, the pressure on men to 'perform' sexually was far greater.

As mentioned earlier, several MHPs observed that lesbian clients were generally more comfortable with their sexual identity than male homosexual clients. From among the self-referred clients, the typology of client concerns described by the MHPs included:

- Young women who were exploring their sexuality with other women ('teenage crushes') and who had questions about whether it was 'normal', 'right', etc. They would express feelings of confusion and guilt.
- Women who were married into large joint families, have conjugal relations with their husbands and are in a relationship with another woman in the family. Most of these women perceive the relationship as peripheral to their reasons for consultation (career, children, etc.).
- Bisexual women who were involved with both a man and a woman and wanted to sort out their confusions regarding relationships.
- Women with concerns due to separation, break-up or dysfunctional relationships with their female partners.
- Women who are survivors of child sexual abuse and had, according to the MHP, 'learnt' homosexuality.
- Women who wanted sex re-assignment surgery (SRS).

Third, the incidence of depression is predictably high at 21% of the total sample. Four of these women were clinically depressed and had taken depression medication for some duration. Six women had suicidal ideation or had attempted suicide. Four women had problems of drug or alcohol abuse, and three women had problems of poor scholastic performance.

Another significant feature of the client histories is that none of the 10 women (7% of the sample) who had approached MHPs because they wanted SRS were evaluated as meeting the criteria. These were typically 'masculine' women (wearing men's clothes and hairstyles), who were in relationships with other women. Three of them had been referred by plastic surgeons for psychiatric assessments. Often, these women wanted to undergo SRS not because of gender identity disorder (feeling like they were men trapped in women's bodies), but because they felt that they would be able to get married and live as a heterosexual couple with their women partners once the surgery was carried out. Most of these women did not have a clear understanding of the physical and emotional implications of SRS for themselves and any partner they were currently with. They were also unaware of the time and expense involved in SRS operations.

Violence faced by lesbian clients

Many of the client histories recorded incidents of both physical and emotional violence and aggression experienced within the families. Nine women had experienced familial pressure to get married.

Among other instances of violence, one woman had been physically confined to the house by her parents, one woman had been evicted from her parental home and one woman was forced to undergo aversive therapy.

Only five of the MHPs noted that they had not observed any violence in the lives of their lesbian clients. This was partly due to the fact that many clients had not disclosed their sexual orientation to others. As three MHPs observed, the incidence of violence and discrimination is predicated on disclosure, that is, clients did not report experiences of ostracisation, because most of the self-referred clients had not told anyone other than their partners.

Almost all the MHPs recognised, to varying degrees, familial and social violence faced by lesbian women. The degree of recognition depended on the definition of the violence used. The interviewer clarified that the definition of violence being used was both physical and emotional abuse. However, while some of the MHPs recognised that lesbians faced social stigma and ostracisation, they said that they would not necessarily label it as 'violence'. Further, as one MHP pointed out, some of the women came from dysfunctional families, therefore it was difficult to distinguish if the aggression or violence was because of sexual orientation *per se*, or existing familial dysfunctionality.

Some significant observations were made by MHPs regarding violence. The first was on the double-bind women faced, 'If they choose not to hide, then they face the ostracism that's there. If they hide, then there's the whole shame of that relationship, they can't tell other people, they can't hold hands in public…'. This double-bind of silent shame vs. ostracisation produced situations where if women disclosed their sexual identity, they ran the risk of violent reactions from family and society. And if they chose to keep their sexuality a secret, then they were likely to internalise the social stigma in the form of shame, guilt or taken to the extreme—in forms of self-abuse (suicide or addiction).

The second significant observation is that while there was comparatively less physical abuse reported, the incidence of emotional violence was high, mostly within the family. One possible explanation for this was 'because, if the family wants to hide it… [they would not] start beating and shouting…the whole society will come to know about it.'

Views and therapeutic interventions of MHPs

Views about homosexuality

There was a clear awareness among all of the MHPs that homosexuality is no longer considered a mental or sexual disorder. Almost all of the MHPs unambiguously expressed the opinion that homosexuality was 'normal'. They described it variously as a sexual 'preference, 'practice', 'inclination', 'identity', 'way of life', or 'routine behavioural pattern'. Three of the MHPs cited statistics from studies indicating that homosexuals were a small minority in society. A discussion on whether homosexuality was 'learnt' or 'genetic' was engaged in by five of the MHPs, with some saying it was inborn and others arguing that it was a combination. There was also an articulation by four among the sample that there needs to be greater awareness and acceptance of homosexuality in society.

Four MHPs' discomfort with the topic indicated that they implicitly did *not* think homosexuality was 'normal', although they did not explicitly say they considered it 'abnormal'. All four were MHPs who had been practising for 20 years and over, so their ambiguity and discomfort may be explained by the fact that 20 years ago homosexuality was classified as an abnormality. Underlying their comments was a perception that the *source* of homosexuality was in some aberrant situation such as a dysfunctional father-son relationship or childhood sexual abuse. Situational homosexuality (of the 'passing phase' variety, found in hostels or among adolescent boys) was also viewed as more acceptable than long-term, confirmed homosexuality—'Many of them are normal individuals; it is circumstances which push them into this.'

A subtle extension of this perception was expressed by two other MHPs who, while they categorically stated that homosexuality was normal, thought that homosexuality resulted in 'not-normal' or 'problematic' behaviour. This was illustrated by the following comments:

> I have seen many people who have had some psychiatric problems because of this behaviour. If it is not exactly psychiatric problems, then para-psychiatric…problems with their relationships in the family, some personal problems, some sort of an adjustment problem does come in these people.
>
> … that commitment which a heterosexual couple would give, that commitment which is expected, which naturally comes through—is somehow not very much there in a homosexual relationship. That's the reason why many of these people have problems.

Views about lesbian sexuality

The distinctions MHPs made when specifically talking about lesbian sexuality were related to the perception of women as tending to get more emotionally than physically involved, compared with homosexual men. Another observation made was that lesbian women have space in the private arena for greater freedom of physical intimacies—such as grooming hair, bathing together, massages, and shared confidences. This was contrasted to the public arena that homosexual men inhabit.

Several of the MHPs spoke of lesbian clients typically in terms of 'dominant' and 'passive' partners—the former being the one who wore 'masculine' clothing and hair styles, and the latter being the 'feminine homemaker'.

Again, there was a common perception that childhood sexual abuse resulted in lesbian behaviour. For example, one MHP located the source of lesbian sexuality in dysfunctional families. Her observation about four of her clients was that:

> Somewhere they had a very confusing identity about their fathers.... It is very important that you have a parent of your own sex who is very strong. And at the same time, you also need the opposite sex to be strong to develop a role model.... OK, so this is how I behave like a woman, and this is what I would want a man to be. So when I don't see those roles being fulfilled, somewhere it could develop a change in my own sexuality.

However, there were also points of view that were a departure from the usual stereotypes:

> If sexual abuse made women lesbians, a lot of women would be lesbians.

> Just because you are lesbian doesn't mean you can't be a good mother. I'm sure many of them would like to adopt a child.

Knowledge of diagnostic classifications

Significantly, all of the MHPs knew that homosexuality was no longer classified as a sexual or mental disorder in the ICD-10 or the DSM-4. Depending on which system they followed, there was varying degree of knowledge about the precise classification of homosexuality in that system. Three MHPs mentioned how the gay and lesbian lobby in the US was actively campaigning for the declassification of homosexuality as a sexual disorder in the DSM-3. Two knew that ICD-10 had declassified homosexuality only as recently as 1993.

More generally, four of the MHPs expressed scepticism about the system of diagnostic classifications. Their reasons varied—from believing that such classifications were reductionist, and, therefore, not useful for diagnosis and therapy; to believing that they were structured to benefit profit-making by pharmaceutical companies.

Views on classification of ego-dystonic homosexuality

Only two of the MHPs had a completely clear understanding of the differences between the ICD-10 and DSM-4 classifications of homosexuality with regard to ego-dystonic homosexuality.[3]

With the exception of four MHPs, the others (81%) believed that it was necessary to retain a classification of 'ego-dystonic homosexuality'. Two of the four who advocated removal of the classification, also did not believe in classifications in general. All four were of the view that 'how many would be naturally very happy being homosexual? Not many, because the environment is such that it is not very encouraging for homosexuals.'

A detailed examination of the different rationales offered for retaining the classification of ego-dystonic homosexuality revealed a variety of opinions. In the first rationale, two of the MHPs drew a comparison between ego-dystonic homosexuality and alcoholism.

> You know it's sort of equivalent to an alcoholic saying I feel excited when I see a glass of rum ... there are so many people who have one drink and stop.... So alcohol per se is not bad, it is when people are attracted to it against their will.

The second perspective focussed on the use of the phrase ego-dystonic. 'The word to emphasise is ego-dystonic, not homosexuality. Anything to do with ego-dystonic would be abnormal'. To illustrate his point, he said that even scratching would be 'abnormal', if the person was very distressed with the behaviour. One MHP articulated this in his statement saying, 'A person may be unhappy with their heterosexuality—with sexuality totally, and go in for asceticism. We have to cover all possibilities.' That is, if one were to accept that people could be unhappy with themselves because of any behaviour, or any sexual orientation, the classification should be ego-dystonic behaviour, or ego-dystonic sexuality rather than only ego-dystonic homosexuality. In such a categorisation, even a heterosexual person could experience ego-dystonicity about their sexuality and would want to become homosexual.

The third, emic perspective, was more client-centered. 'Client is boss... I would not impose and say, you are biologically attracted, you jolly well stay a lesbian....' This perspective would ostensibly support the woman to change her sexual identity if she was unhappy about being lesbian, particularly if the level of the client's distress was extremely high. 'If she is so disturbed that she wants to go and kill herself, then definitely I would help her out of it.'

Two MHPs recognised that the existence of distress in a lesbian client did not equal dystonicity about homosexuality. The causative factors for distress are externally induced, as one MHP pointed out, 'There are people who call up and say they want to change, but they always give a reason—they're lonely, there are more advantages being heterosexual, the security of marriage—and that's why they want to change.' This MHP recognised that it was not being attracted to women per se which was distressing; it was the *impact* of such an attraction which produced distress. Further, that in situations when fear of factors inducing distress were internalised the client experienced self-hatred or was self-abusive.

Finally, as one MHP pointed out, 'We have to start thinking about the classifications. What is thought to be ego-dystonic might be social expectations. In India, a gay woman would want to have a child and husband. So what component of ego-dystonicity is because of social norms?'

Views of classification of Gender Identity Disorder
MHPs were divided almost equally into those who were adequately informed about the exclusion criteria for Gender Identity Disorder (GID) and those who did not have any clarity on these criteria.

Again, only three had total clarity on the exclusion criteria for GID. Of these three, one MHP (along with other psychiatrists) had conducted a study on transsexuals while she was at K.E.M. Hospital in the 1970s.[4]

Assessment tools

The majority of the MHPs used the clinical interview and the clients' self-reporting as their assessment tool. Two psychologists reported using other assessment methods such as Rorschach, MMPI and TAT battery of tests. However, these evaluation methods were not routine procedure for them, but were used only in instances where such evaluation was specifically requested (for e.g., to assess a client for SRS). Two of the MHPs observed that such screening instruments were more usefully for research purposes where exclusion criteria had to be maintained. According to them, these tools are less useful for diagnosis and counselling practice.

Therapeutic interventions

Confusion, self-esteem, anxiety, depression, grief, non-acceptance, turmoil, anger, guilt, fear of sexuality, fear of rejection, worry about future, addictions, drop in scholastic performance—these were some of the main problems that the lesbian clients came to MHPs with. Most of the MHPs clearly expressed that their priority in therapeutic interventions would be to address the presenting symptoms of anxiety, depression, grief, etc. One MHP reflected on building the client's trust in the MHPs, she observed that some of her clients initially checked out what she looked like and whether they thought she would be likely to accept or reject them on the basis of sexual orientation. Counselling, psychotherapy and rational-emotive therapy were the primary techniques used by the MHPs. In cases of clinical depression, this was combined with depression medication.

Four of the MHPs unambiguously spoke about helping clients suffering from confusion and guilt to come to terms with their sexual orientation:

Reduce the guilt, try to make them more accepting ... that it's o.k.

to be in a same-sex relationship. Trying to help them see the family's perspective ... help them reduce their anxiety.... Then I just counsel them like how one would counsel someone who has any other problems. Be more supportive.

Two of the MHPs also spoke about the importance of family counselling. The purpose of this was to help the parents (who may have forced their daughter to visit the MHP) come to terms with her sexual orientation.

Services and resources for lesbians

Over 50 per cent of the MHPs (13) had heard about the Humsafar Trust[5] and mentioned it when asked about services/resources for lesbians in Mumbai or India. Only four MHPs however had heard of a lesbian organisation, and only two of them were aware of the name of the organisation (Stree Sangam).

Similarly, two MHPs knew that a book for lesbians in India had been published, but did not know the details.[6] Psychology text books and booklets on sexuality was the other reading material that four of the MHPs said they would offer if clients asked for information on sexual orientation.

One MHP actively advocated bibliotherapy as a means of a client educating herself about lesbian sexuality. She and three other MHPs reported that they would also refer clients to the Internet and websites with information for lesbians.

Analytic comment

Comment on lesbian client profiles

The data on these women is second-generation, having passed through the filters of the MHPs' perceptions and memories. Nevertheless, it is valuable because it is the only data on the larger population of lesbian women (compared to the questionnaire and interview samples). Second, it is useful for triangulation of key concerns with the other two smaller data sets (quantitative and narrative) on lesbian women.

When we examine the question of why there are so few lesbian clients, the immediate inference that could be drawn would be that lesbian clients have fewer problems. Conjectures that are more realistic are: first, in general women are less likely to seek mental health services than men. Gender bias as well as the fear of the stigma of being labelled 'mentally ill' may dissuade them. Further, the pervading social stigma attached to homosexuality as an abnormality and their apprehensions about the attitudes of the MHP (as the MHP above pointed out) would be a reason why such few lesbian clients voluntarily meet MHPs. It is also interesting to note that the incidence of depression in this sample (21%) is comparable to the figure for women in an urban population.

Given the heteronormativity in society, it is remarkable that none of these women wanted to change their behaviour and 'become heterosexual'. However, it is perhaps too simple to imply (as some MHPs have) that the reason for this is less pressure on women to sexually perform in a marriage. We need to view this finding against the fact that all of the women who wanted SRS were evaluated as not meeting the criteria. This may lead to the conjecture that, rather than change their behaviour (or the desire for women), women may be more likely to consider changing their *bodies* in order to meet heterosexual social norms.

The low level of reporting on violence could be, as pointed out, due to the double-bind of silent shame and ostracisation. However, it could also be in part due to the MHPs, differing perceptions about emotional violence and their lack of awareness of the emotional pressures faced by lesbian clients. In such a situation of silence around violence therefore, communication with women who are undergoing these experiences and support of them becomes difficult.

Comment on MHP views and interventions

Despite their overt proclamations about the normality of homosexuality, a nuanced reading of the MHP statements uncovers other ambiguities and persistent stereotypes. For instance, the perception of some MHPs that homosexuality *causes* maladjusted or 'abnormal' behaviour problematises homosexuality and fails to examine society's non-acceptance of homosexuality as the cause of adjustment problems. Second, when discussing the source of homosexuality or lesbian sexuality, several MHPs, points of view reflect variations on the classic Freudian psychoanalytic perspective of it being the result of 'arrested development' or 'dysfunctional family history.

Further, the perception of lesbian clients in terms of 'dominant' and 'passive' partners shows the MHPs, underlying assumption of heterosexual and gender stereotypes as determining lesbian relationships. This is more disturbing in the context of Gender Identity Disorder, where MHPs' lack of clarity on the exclusion criteria for GID could mean that lesbian women who consider SRS as an option in order to live in a hetero-normative world may not receive the support they require to adjust to a lesbian identity.

Although all the MHPs knew that homosexuality is no longer classified as a disorder, it is in the understanding of the diagnostic classifications of ego-dystonic homosexuality that the maximum ambiguities surfaced. Implicit in the comparison between ego-dystonic homosexuality and alcoholism is the equation of homosexuality with a negative behaviour such as addiction, something that has to be resisted. The potential danger is also that from this point, it would be an easy transition to view homosexuality as a sexually obsessive behaviour.

Notes

[1] This chapter is taken from the study: Bina Fernandez, *The Nature of Violence Faced by Lesbian Women in India* (Mumbai: Research Centre on Violence Against Women, Tata Institute of Social Sciences, 2003).

[2] Since it is a sample drawn from MHP clients, rather than the general population.

[3] Ego-dystonic sexual orientation is a classification retained within the ICD-10. The DSM-III had this category, but the DSM-IV dropped the classification of ego-dystonic sexual orientation in 1986.

[4] See Doongaji et al. (1978). The study was of 12 transsexual clients (both FTM and MTF); only 6 of whom were finally assessed as being genuinely suffering from Gender Identity Disorder. The others were excluded either because they were adjudged to be not 'true transsexuals'—i.e., either they were homosexual, or they exhibited some psychosis.

⁵ In 1990, Mumbai-based gay activist Ashok Row Kavi established the Humsafar Trust, India's first organisation for gays and lesbians.

⁶ Ashwini Sukhtankar (ed.), *Facing the Mirror: Lesbian Writing from India* (New Delhi: Penguin India, 1999).

Sex Change Operation and Feminising Procedures for Transgender Women in India

Current Scenario and Way Forward

VENKATESAN CHAKRAPANI, M.D.

Since we cannot change the mind to fit the body we change the body to fit the mind.

Dr. Harry Benjamin, Pioneer in Gender Dysphoria Research

One's own surgeon

'*He* is the one who cut *it* off by *himself*', my senior told me as he pointed to a person sitting on a bed in the male inpatient ward. That was in 1998, when I had just enrolled in Madras Medical College, Tamil Nadu, to pursue my post-graduation in sexually-transmitted infections. I saw a fragile figure in a saree in the direction he pointed at and instantly recognised that the person in the saree was an *ali* (I later learned that 'ali' was a derogatory term and one has to use the term '*aravani*' which is equivalent to the pan-Indian term *hijras,* not a widely-known or used term in Tamil Nadu at that time).[1] I was surprised as well as ashamed; surprised, because here was a person who was bold enough to cut one's own genitalia despite how horrifying it might seem to others; ashamed, because, although I knew about 'gender identity disorder' and also about aravanis, I failed to equate aravanis with biological males who identify as women. I thought they were hermaphrodites[2]—a common misconception found among most doctors even today.

During the ward 'rounds', when I approached her, she said her name was Kumudha (name changed). I looked at her inpatient case-sheet and it showed a male name. She casually asked whether

I was new. The conversation that followed changed my ideas and misconceptions about aravanis and Kumudha literally became my teacher, teaching me about the aravani community. I came to know that they are born biologically as males, but as they grow up they begin to feel they are more like women, and hence want to dress and behave like them.[3] Medically, I learnt that if these feelings start at an early age, it is called 'Gender Identity Disorder of Childhood' and if it occurs around puberty or later, it is called 'Gender Identity Disorder of Adolescence' or 'Gender Identity Disorder of Adulthood'.[4] The World Professional Association for Transgender Health's (WPATH) *Standards of Care for Gender Identity Disorders*[5] clearly states that:

> The designation of gender identity disorders as mental disorders is not a license for stigmatization or for the deprivation of gender patients' civil rights. The use of a formal diagnosis is often important in offering relief, providing health insurance coverage, and guiding research to provide more effective future treatments.

Though it is still listed as a psychiatric disorder, recent evidence suggests that it is more likely to be a neuro-developmental condition—a condition that results from the change in the structure (and thus function) of the foetal brain because of hormonal or other causes.[6] Also, even the aim of the psychiatric 'treatments' of Gender Identity Disorder (GID) is not to 'cure' persons with GID from 'disorder' but to decrease the stressful aspects related to their gender identity issues and to help them in leading satisfactory lives.

Not all aravanis choose to get their male genitalia removed. Kumudha was unique in that she carried out the surgery by herself, and the way she did it—at midnight, in the male inpatient ward—ultimately led to police enquiries directed towards the doctors in charge of the ward. She was known to be HIV-positive, so none of the other patients in the male ward wanted to help her while she lay in a pool of blood. And she might have died were it not for some sympathetic doctors and nurses who helped her get through those testing times.

When I first met Kumudha, it was several months after her self-surgical removal of male external genitalia. She was having problems urinating and was referred to the urology department where they diagnosed her with a 'urethral stricture' (blockage of the urethral canal), a complication that arose from the self-surgery. Urologists made a hole in the lower abdominal area and inserted a urethral catheter (supra-pubic cystotomy) and said they would do the urethral reconstruction surgery later, which was necessary for her to pass urine naturally. Weeks and years passed and even after the completion of my post-graduation, the surgery was not done. The reason—Kumudha's HIV-positive status.

I once asked Kumudha what accounted for her extraordinary courage that led to performing a self-surgery. She told me that for emasculation[7], aravanis usually go to unqualified medical practitioners in a nearby town in Andhra Pradesh and some go to a *thaiamma* (a senior aravani). This removal of external genitalia is referred to, as '*doctor-kai*' if done by a doctor or as '*thaiamma-kai*' if performed by a thaiamma. Irrespective of who is conducting the emasculation, aravanis are usually tested for HIV. Kumudha tested positive and therefore was denied the operation'. She told me that having the male genitalia kept reminding her that she was born a male and so one day she decided to remove it by herself—freedom from the tyranny of the phenotype sex that made her feel bad about herself.

Ackwa and Nirvan

Not all aravanis would take the extreme step as Kumudha did. Some may never want to get operated and some may be in a dilemma whether or not to undergo the operation for personal or other reasons. Aravanis call those who have not had the operation, 'ackwa' and those who have, 'nirvan'. The term 'zenana' that was once used to denote those who did not want to get operated[8] is not used commonly anymore and may mean different things to different aravanis. The English equivalent for ackwa would be 'pre-operative/ non-operative transsexual/transgender woman' and for 'nirvan' it would be 'post-operative transsexual/transgender woman'.[9]

Emasculation by 'Thaiamma'

It is not known how many aravanis in Tamil Nadu have undergone emasculation and how many of them have undergone sex reassignment surgery (SRS) by qualified surgeons. However, one usually hears of emasculation by quacks or by thaiammas. Emasculation by thaiammas is conducted as a ritual. Early in the morning (by about 4 am), the aravani who is going to undergo the emasculation takes a bath and gets ready. After worshipping *Bahuchara Matha*, the deity of aravanis, she is made to stand with her legs apart and both hands tied or held by another aravani called *pin-thaiamma* (means 'thaiamma who stands in the back') or sometimes even by the 'husband' of the thaiamma. Using a thin but strong rope, the base of the male organ is tied. Then using a knife, in a fraction of a second, the male organ is cut off—with a nick above and a nick below. No anesthesia is given for this. Some mentioned having taken alcohol but most others denied having had any alcohol before this procedure. As the blood pours out of the cut genital area, the aravani is made to lie on the floor in a prone position with the genital area compressed over a bed of sand. (Some mentioned a variant of this where the aravani is made to lie over a cot beneath which a pot filled with sand is kept to collect the blood coming out of the cut area.) Then, betel leaves and some herbal medicine along with compression bandages are applied over the bleeding area. Until sunrise, she is kept awake by other aravanis by constantly slapping her face. Some aravanis have allegedly died during such emasculation procedures by thaiammas. Some of these cases were reported to be followed-up by the police.

But why would an aravani take such a risk that might cost her life? It shows the determination of aravanis to get rid of male genitalia in an effort to become woman-like and the respect they have for the centuries-old method of emasculation. There could be one other reason as well. In a qualitative study conducted among hijras, some expressed that there is a belief among hijras that if emasculation is done by a *thaiamma* rather than a qualified doctor, then all the 'masculine blood' will be drained from that hijra's body and thus she would become more feminine.[10]

Post-emasculation ritual

After emasculation, often it is the responsibility of the *guru* (master), a senior aravani, to take care of her *chela* (disciple) who has undergone emasculation. She may follow the customs that have been traditionally passed on from generation to generation of aravanis. Some of these include: giving *kalachaya* (black-tea) and 'goat-leg soup' to drink, producing smoke by dropping *omam* and garlic peels over hot charcoal, and striking the pubic area with a jet of water from a distance so that unhealthy tissue gets separated (in an attempt to facilitate rapid healing). This procedure goes on for 39 days.

On the 40th day, the emasculated aravanis undergo a ritual called *paaloothuthal* (literally, 'pouring milk'). Among Hindus, a ritual is conducted on a particular day after the death of a person called *karumaathi* in Tamil; a similar ritual is followed in the aravani community after emasculation symbolising the death of the male soul/body of the aravani and the birth of the new female soul/body.

Emasculation by 'quacks'

Many aravanis go to a small town in Andhra Pradesh or a couple of small towns in Tamil Nadu for undergoing emasculation. In these places emasculation is done by unqualified medical practitioners. These practitioners are often those persons who have previously worked with a qualified medical practitioner and later set up their own clinic to perform illegal abortions and emasculation operations. Often, these unqualified persons perform emasculation in a clinic setting where privacy cannot be ensured.

One of my aravani patients told me that in one such clinic, only a cloth screen acted as a barrier to separate her aravani friend (who was undergoing emasculation) from a female who was undergoing an illegal abortion. Thus, in addition to the lack of privacy, there is also a risk of 'hospital-acquired' infections. These unqualified practitioners, however, either give spinal anesthesia (themselves, without a qualified anaesthetist) or give 'local anaesthesia' (i.e., anesthesia injection given locally around the male genitalia).

In contrast to *thaiamma's* operation, however, the operated site is sutured. After the operation, catheterisation is done and the catheter is removed only after four to seven days. But often, many aravanis want to leave the clinic as early as the second or third day for a variety of reasons—one being the money spent on inpatient admission charges.

Some aravanis, however, do not want to undergo complete emasculation. They want to remove the testes to get rid of male hormones (testosterone). They retain the penis even though they do not identify as men so that when they can afford a 'vaginoplasty' or 'neovagina creation', they can use the outer skin of the penis as the inner-lining of the neovagina. For some, however, the fear of post-operative urethral complications prevents them from removing the penis, even if they otherwise wish to remove it.

Emasculation and sex change operation by qualified medical practitioners

Some qualified general practitioners and surgeons might also perform emasculation operations for a fee which may be regarded by aravanis as 'reasonable' but still not 'affordable'. The operation costs around INR 10,000 but the legality of the operation is uncertain. This leads doctors to be cautious and get written consent forms signed by the aravanis undergoing the operation stating that they are undergoing emasculation because their biopsy shows 'cancer of the male genitalia' or stating in the form that they wish to become 'full' women. One problem with this is that in the future if the legal status of those aravanis who have undergone emasculation is to be considered as 'female' then the consent form stating the reason for emasculation as 'cancer of the male genitalia' may prove to be a problem.

I have heard of as well as met a number of aravanis who have undergone SRS following proper procedures, that is, those who have undergone pre-operative psychiatric assessment, surgery performed by a proper surgical team, and also had proper post-operative follow-up. In the Government General Hospital in Chennai, about 15 years ago, emasculation along with neovagina ('new vagina') construction was known to have been conducted. These days, aravanis do not approach government hospitals because SRS is no longer conducted there (at the time of writing this essay). This might be because of the lack of interest or expertise or possibly because of its ambiguous legal status.

An aravani told me that she had undergone SRS by a plastic surgeon in Bangalore. However, no female hormones were prescribed and also no effort towards breast construction was made. She also mentioned that the depth of the neovagina was not sufficient and she never had (neo)vaginal sex with anyone because of the loss of libido and also fear of (neo)vaginal tear. This shows the lack of appropriate post-operative counselling and lack of post-operative medical care of the operated site.

Complications following emasculation

In 2001, I opened a free clinic for men who have sex with men and aravanis in a community-based organisation called Social Welfare Association for Men (SWAM) in Chennai. I came across a lot of aravanis who were asking for information about sex change operations and hormonal therapy. Also, many aravanis who have undergone operations by unqualified practitioners came with many post-operative complications—inability to urinate (acute urinary tract obstruction), difficulty in passing urine because of narrowed external urethral opening (meatalstenosis or stricture), and multiple openings in the pubic area (fistulas).[11] While I could only clean the wounds and administer antibiotics for healing them, I referred them to urology departments in government hospitals for treatment of the surgical complications in urethra.

Sometimes, the complications following emasculation may occur after many years. There was an aravani who had chronic kidney failure due to prostate gland enlargement and meatalstenosis. The prostate gland is located at the base of the urinary bladder and usually left untouched in traditional emasculation operations conducted by unqualified or qualified medical practitioners. In some aravanis this gland might enlarge as one ages and in the presence of urethral stenosis or stricture, a common complication in emasculation done by unqualified medical practitioners, it can ultimately lead to chronic kidney failure.

These urethral complications are seen more often among those aravanis who undergo emasculation by unqualified medical practitioners than by 'regular doctors' (that is, by certified allopathic medical practitioners). Complications are mainly because of the faulty surgical procedure as well as infections due to contamination from the operating room.

Though, even 'quacks' often give spinal anaesthesia before performing emasculation, I have been told that sometimes they just use a local anaesthetic injection, blocking the nerves serving the pubic area. After emasculation, many aravanis usually complain of back-pain even months after the operation, in addition to the major post-surgical complications. This back-pain may be due to administration of spinal anaesthesia or just psychogenic.

After emasculation, usually a catheter is placed in the urethra for three to seven days so that the person does not have any problems as long as it remains. Once removed, however, problems might arise— especially if the operation was conducted by quacks. I have seen some aravanis who come after three days of emasculation with infections at the operated site and sudden blockage of urine. Sometimes it requires puncturing the lowermost part of the abdomen with a needle/catheter (suprapubic puncture) to release the accumulated urine in the urinary bladder. If the sudden blockage is only due to infections and inflammation, the blockage might go away only to come back after a few weeks if it leads to the formation of a scar within the urethra (urethral stenosis or stricture).

'Jalli': Indigenous urethral dilator of hijras

Once I was taking the clinical history of an aravani who complained of problems in passing urine about three months after emasculation. She just asked me to excuse her for some minutes as she wanted to use the restroom. When she came back she showed me a 'jalli' (also called 'saliya'—usually custom-made in silver) that she used as a dilator to widen the urethra when she felt the urge to urinate. Sometimes a 'jalli' is left in the urethra for some time since it is supposed to widen the urethral opening. Thus, by function, a 'jalli' is closer to a 'urethral dilator' used by urologists to temporarily widen the constricted part of the urethra. Aravanis have become their own urologists since they are denied treatment or cannot afford treatment by urologists.

Emasculation and HIV-positive hijras

Almost all the practitioners, whether unqualified or qualified, screen aravanis for HIV before emasculation. But what happens if they are found to be HIV-positive? Often, the HIV-positive aravanis are asked to pay more money (about 3,000 Indian Rupees or 75 USD more) than the money charged for HIV-negative aravanis. Some aravanis learn of their HIV-positive status for the first time while being screened before the emasculation. Often there is no pre-test HIV counselling. Sometimes, in spite of being HIV-positive, some aravanis want to go ahead with the emasculation. While in a focus group discussion some senior aravanis opined that it could be because of the misconception that the blood coming out during operation might wash away HIV from their body,[12] it is also possible that it may not be the sole reason since those HIV-positive aravanis might have even otherwise undergone emasculation because they came specifically for it. While HIV-positive status alone should not preclude hijras from undergoing emasculation or a sex change operation, HIV-positive hijras should be offered adequate information and non-directive counselling to make informed choices about whether or not to undergo surgery.

Female hormones and other feminising procedures adopted by hijras

Aravanis undergo a range of procedures to make their body more in line with biological females. One of the important feminising procedures is breast enlargement. In line with some notions of feminine beauty, aravanis may desire larger breasts so as to conform to their own ideas of who a desirable woman is. Whatever the reasons are, the desire to have well-developed breasts makes some aravanis self-administer female hormonal tablets or injections. Often the names of the female hormonal tablets (such as Ovral-G, Mala-N and Mala-D), which are usually female oral contraceptive pills, are passed on from one aravani to another.

Some aravanis have told me that sometimes they have taken 5, 10, or even more number of female hormonal tablets in one go since they cannot wait to see their breasts develop. Such overzealous self-treatment can result in side effects such as liver damage. Some aravanis go to pharmacies to buy oral contraceptive pills and pharmacists may even give them some tips regarding tablets that might work well. But some pharmacists do not want to give those tablets without prescription or even if they do, they overcharge aravanis. Thus, the absence of qualified medical practitioners who can or want to assess the medical condition of aravanis and determine their eligibility for female hormonal therapy forces many aravanis towards self-treatment or to rely upon pharmacists or unqualified medical practitioners. Sometimes, ignorance among even qualified practitioners may lead to wrong hormonal prescriptions for breast development. For instance, one aravani from Bangalore told me that a 'qualified' medical practitioner prescribed her growth hormone injections for breast development.

Some aravanis may even self-inject themselves with female hormones. I know of an aravani who acts as an 'injector'—providing hormonal injections to other aravanis who believe that breast growth will be rapid if hormones are given through injections. However, I have not heard about sharing of hormonal injections among aravanis though such sharing has been reported as an HIV-related risk behaviour among transgender women in western countries.[13]

After emasculation, because of substantial decrease in male hormones, facial hair growth might be comparatively less. However, one may continue to have facial hair growth because of the production of male hormones from the adrenal glands, a pair of glands on the top of each kidney. Taking female hormones may help in decreasing the rate of facial hair growth. Aravanis may use a *chimta*, a traditional hair tweezer used by the aravani community. These days, some aravanis might prefer to undergo electrolysis or even laser treatment, if they can afford it. A community organisation working with aravanis in Chennai supported a group of aravanis to be trained as beauticians through a three-month course so that they could provide the services to their own community.

Many aravanis complain of lack of affordable procedures to change their voice, which is often masculine or has a distinct tone that can make others recognise that they are aravanis. Adam's apple reduction or laser treatment of vocal cords, however, is not available at an affordable cost to aravanis.

Sex change operations and transwomen from middle/upper economic class

Several cases of both male-to-female and female-to-male sex change operations[14] have made headlines in national and local newspapers[15] and have been reported from many major cities from different parts of India. These operations have been done by both government and private medical doctors—especially by plastic surgeons. Some biological males (whose gender identity is 'woman') from middle and upper economic classes do not want to join hijra/aravani communities and might like to undergo sex change operation by qualified medical practitioners with or without their family's support.

While I was posted for undergoing short-term training in the Psychiatry Department of the Chennai Government Hospital, an 18-year-old boy from a middle class family who came in a woman's attire, was scanned for the presence of a uterus, tested for the presence of abnormal chromosomes, and finally presented as a case of 'gender identity disorder' (GID) in the clinical meeting of psychiatrists. This person with GID diagnosis was seen as a rare case, worthy of presentation in a clinical meeting. This is understandable since the otherwise highly visible hijra/aravani communities are not seen as people with GID. Doctors, including many psychiatrists, usually think biological males diagnosed with GID are different from hijras. A national newspaper quotes a psychiatrist saying: 'Till around 10 years ago, I had seen no case of GID. I saw 20 [people with GID] in the last decade. Not all of them go on to get the surgery done.... People with GID at least have the confidence today to seek medical opinion'.[16] If hijras are also assessed and diagnosed to have GID then psychiatrists might probably help them in getting the necessary surgical and endocrinological interventions from qualified medical practitioners.

Legal status of surgical sex reassignment in India

Is sex change operation legal in India? The Indian legal system is silent on this issue. The presumably illegal nature of sex change operation or voluntary emasculation arguably influences the attitude of health care providers towards hijras. But it also, understandably, makes hijras seek help from quacks since it is not available in government hospitals.Quacks do it with no questions asked and without showing any obvious prejudice against hijras.

According to Section 320 of the Indian Penal Code (IPC), 'emasculating' someone (the term is ambiguous here, but may refer to 'castration', i.e., removal of testes) is causing him 'grievous hurt' for which one can be punished under Section 325 of the IPC. Thus, technically speaking even if one voluntarily chooses to be 'emasculated', the person who performs emasculation is liable for punishment under this provision and the person undergoing emasculation could also be punished for 'abetting' this offence. However, under Section 88 of IPC an exception is made in case an action is undertaken in good faith and the person gives consent to suffer that harm. That section reads:

> Nothing which is not intended to cause death is an offence by reason of any harm which it may cause or intended by the doer to cause any person whose benefit it is done in good faith, and who has given consent...to suffer that harm, or to take the risk of that harm.[17]

In reality, the legal process is activated by someone filing either a first information report (FIR) in a police station or by filing a private complaint. This does not happen in the case of sex change operation (or emasculation) of hijras as both the medical practitioner (quacks or qualified practitioners) and patient have given their consent to this procedure and it is extremely unlikely that they will activate the criminal law process. Thus there is no documented case in India of doctors and patients having been prosecuted for causing 'grievous hurt' or 'abetting the causing of grievous hurt' through voluntary emasculation or sex change operation. In the unlikely case that such a process is activated, a qualified doctor who does sex change operation would be protected by the general exception under the Section 88 of the IPC. The legal status of voluntary emasculation and sex change operation should be clarified and this surgery should be offered in government hospitals so that hijras do not need to go to unqualified medical practitioners for having their male external genitalia removed. This can prevent post-operative complications that often arise due to bad surgical procedures followed by quacks.

Legal sex recognition in Indian identity documents

Some hijras received certificates from qualified doctors who did the sex change operation stating that they have now become women and need to be treated as such. These medical certificates have been used by some hijras to apply for new passports as 'female' or even change the sex in the previous passport from 'male' to 'female'.[18] The latter can be done if hijras submit a sworn affidavit and a medical certificate from the hospital where the person has undergone the sex change operation.[19] The form to be filled is titled application form No. 2 (Application for Miscellaneous Services on Indian passports) and it is available online.[20] This shows the importance of getting a proper certificate from a qualified doctor who performs a sex change operation or emasculation. Also, it indirectly shows that a sex change operation is not considered illegal by the government of India. Those hijras who have not undergone sex change operation can choose the box marked 'others' from the three boxes (male, female and others) in the 'sex' column.[21] Some ackwa hijras (who have not undergone emasculation or sex change operation) have received passports with their sex marked as 'E' (to refer to 'eunuch'—possibly by ticking in 'others' box in 'sex' column). However, many hijra activists do not like the label 'E' or the term 'eunuch' since it is technically incorrect to call hijras eunuchs (castrated males) and also as it is seen as a derogatory term.[22]

Only the Indian Ministry of External Affairs seems to have recognised the need to include an 'others' box in addition to 'male' and 'female' boxes when asking for an applicant's sex. But application forms for other identity cards (such as voter's card, ration card, and driving license) do not have this additional box thus denying the right of hijras to get an identity card as 'female' or 'other [gender]'. Hopefully, other government departments will also soon adopt the system followed by the Indian Ministry of External Affairs or possibly even come out with a better system.

Relevance of 'western' guidelines on diagnosis and treatment of transsexualism

Usually Indian psychiatrists follow either ICD-10 or DSM-IV guidelines. The former is used more often. These are diagnostic, and not treatment, guidelines. Though many textbooks in psychiatry discuss the treatment of GID, none of them is as comprehensive as that of the *Standards of Care* (sixth version) from the World Professional Association for Transgender Health (WPATH), formerly known as the Harry Benjamin International Gender Dysphoria Association. It discusses in detail confirmation of the diagnosis—'gender identity disorder' or 'transsexualism'—by two qualified mental health practitioners; ruling out other similar conditions ('differential diagnosis'); 'Real Life Test'—asking the person to be in 'women's attire' full-time and to go to educational institutions or workplace for a minimum of one year; pre-operative counselling; involving multidisciplinary team; and post-operative counselling and follow-up.

However, as the commonly used diagnostic (ICD-10 or DSM-IV) and treatment (WPATH) guidelines are primarily 'western', cross-cultural issues need to be taken into account and hence we might need India-specific and hijra-relevant diagnostic and treatment guidelines for GID. For example, if a psychiatrist sees a *kothi*-identified, feminine, same-sex attracted male who occasionally cross-dresses but who does not desire a sex change operation, then there might be confusion whether this person has GID or not.[23] In several areas in Tamil Nadu, *kothi*-identified feminine same-sex oriented males have strong connections with the aravani community because according to them, both are 'feminine' and both are attracted to masculine males (whom they call *panthi*). Also, it is believed by both *kothis* and aravanis that those who now identify as *kothis* might eventually become hijras. Thus, these perspectives of *kothi* and aravani communities about their sexuality and the overlap of persons belonging to these communities might easily confuse a psychiatrist in diagnosing whether a person from one of these communities has GID or not.

Similarly, some of the WPATH treatment guidelines may not be relevant to the Indian context especially for hijras. For example, since most of the hijras live in the hijra community full-time in women's attire, it is not relevant to insist on 'Real Life Test' when a hijra comes for a sex change operation to a qualified practitioner. Also, some hijras may just want a removal of testes and penis, and may not want to undergo any feminising procedures like taking female hormones. I have also seen some *kothi*-identified males who have undergone emasculation but who wanted be in 'men's dress' (shirt and *vesti/lungi)* and who do not want to join hijra communities. Had these persons been seen by psychiatrists they would not have recommended the sex change operation since there was no 'Real Life Test' (because those persons were not or did not want to be in women's attire full-time nor did they want to take female hormones) and they did not identify as hijra or aravani. These difficulties in diagnosis and treatment clearly point out that one needs to adapt the 'western' guidelines to suit the Indian context. However, the rationale and advantages of having an India-specific diagnostic and treatment guidelines for GID need to be discussed, and developed if its need is justified.

Positive steps by the Tamil Nadu state government

In a progressive and rights-based approach, a government order titled Rehabilitation of Aravanis[24] released by the Tamil Nadu state government's Health and Family Welfare Department in February 2007,[25] states that sex change operation needs to be provided to aravanis in government hospitals. That order even has a strong condemnation of any discrimination against aravanis in schools and colleges. However, there are some obvious misunderstandings in the government order. While the relatively minor error is that the order refers to aravanis as eunuchs, the major error is related to the lack of understanding about the difference between MSM (men who have sex with men)[26] and aravanis, as well as the otherwise apparently well-intended attitude to prevent sex change operation to the greatest possible extent. The latter attitude is obvious when one reads the following two sentences taken verbatim from the Tamil Nadu government order:

1. Identify MSM cases and counsel them as far as possible to prevent them from going into Sex Re-construction [sic] surgery.
2. [Provide] legalized Sex Re-construction [sic] surgery in Government Hospitals who are willing to take up the surgery *even after counseling* [emphasis added].

This means that the 'counselling' that is referred to is not about helping aravanis in exploring the various options available to them but instead to 'counsel' them against undergoing a sex change operation. Apart from these errors or misunderstandings, the efforts of the Tamil Nadu government in legalising and providing sex change operation facilities in government hospitals are laudable. Indeed, the Tamil Nadu government has shown a way for other state governments in India to follow.

Initiatives and 'best practices' of community-based organisations

Subsidised sex change operation in a government hospital in Gujarat
In some other states, the community-based organisations working with MSM and hijra communities have taken some initiatives themselves without waiting for the government to act. For example, a community-based organisation in Gujarat has negotiated with the local government hospital in Vadodara to provide sex change operations at a subsidised rate for hijras who are eligible for the operation.[27]

'Gender clinic' in Chennai

In Tamil Nadu, with funding support from the Indian Network for People living with HIV (INP+) and the National AIDS Control Organisation (NACO), the South India Positive People Network (SIP) has started a 'gender clinic' for aravanis. In this clinic, a professional counsellor provides counselling for sex change operations and feminising procedures, and referral services to government hospitals for aravanis with post-operative urological complications. The clinician provides proper medical and surgical care for the healing of post-operative wounds, in addition to providing treatment for sexually transmitted infections (STI) or general illness among aravanis. Thus, this 'gender clinic' differs from other clinics for aravanis in Tamil Nadu, which primarily serve as 'STI treatment clinics'. More such 'gender clinics' for hijras are needed in various parts of India—both in the government hospitals as well as in the clinics run by civil society organisations.

Temporary shelter in Chennai for aravanis recuperating after emasculation

Those aravanis who live with their parents may not be able to talk about sex change operations with them. In such circumstances, after undergoing the operation, these aravanis are in need of a place where they can stay until their wound heals and the post-emasculation rituals are conducted. In Chennai, Social Welfare Association for Men (SWAM), a community organisation working with same-sex attracted men and aravanis offers temporary shelter for homeless aravanis and for those aravanis who require accommodation after emasculation. Other aravanis come to this temporary shelter and take care of the aravanis recuperating after emasculation.

Advocacy efforts of community organisations in Tamil Nadu

The Tamil Nadu government's landmark order legalising provision of free sex change operations for aravanis was due to ongoing advocacy and long-term partnerships developed between the community organisations working with aravanis and the Tamil Nadu Health Secretary and Health Minister since 2004. I remember assisting Priya

Babu, an aravani activist, in drafting a letter to the then Tamil Nadu Health Secretary, Ms. Sheela Rani Sungath, about the need to provide free sex change operations in Tamil Nadu government hospitals. We submitted the necessary documents including our article that documented the stigma and discrimination against aravanis in health care settings.[28] In 2006, following a big rally in Chennai organised by various community organisations, a memorandum was submitted to the Tamil Nadu government that asked for the provision of free sex change operations in government hospitals among other recommendations.[29] In subsequent interactions with the Tamil Nadu government, various community organisations such as the Tamil Nadu Aravanigal Association (THAA), Suder Foundation, and SWAM were instrumental in advocating for providing free sex change operations in government hospitals that ultimately resulted in that Tamil Nadu government order to provide 'legalised' sex change operations in government hospitals. However, community organisations need to follow-up and monitor proper implementation of this initiative, and the government also needs to train health care providers to provide sensitive and competent care for trans-women who want to undergo sex change operations.

Way forward

A lot needs to be changed. The changes need to be reflected in policies and laws; the attitude of the government, general public and health care providers; and health care systems and practice.

Need for supportive policies and laws

There is a need for clarification of the legal sex of transgender women who have not undergone emasculation and who have undergone emasculation/sex change operation. Whether the system followed by the Indian Ministry of External Affairs—considering non-operated or emasculated hijras as 'other(s)' sex and considering those hijras with a medical certificate as 'female'—is acceptable to hijras and other transwomen communities is not clear. A nation-wide community consultation on this issue is urgently required to develop better understanding of the legal implications of legal sex recognition of transwomen and what kind of impact it might have on their civil rights.[30]

Sex change operation (but not emasculation/castration) seems to have never been illegal in India. However, following the positive initiative by the Tamil Nadu government, the other Indian state governments also need to provide legalised and free sex change operations in government hospitals.

Need for positive attitude and better understanding of transwomen

Correct information about transgender people needs to be available and provided to the general public as well as health care providers so that the negative attitude and misconceptions about transwomen change. Since one of the basic reasons for hijras being treated badly is misogyny (considering women as inferior), one of the long-term strategies should be changing the condescending attitude of the general public towards women (or femininity) in general.

Need for non-discriminatory and competent health care systems and providers

Health care systems need to be competent and friendly towards transgender people who access government and private health care settings. These include: welcoming and non-discriminatory environment; trained competent health care staff; and free- or low-cost health care services for health issues specific to transwomen including sex change operations and feminising procedures. Also, there is a crucial need to develop India-specific guidelines for the treatment of transsexualism. Those doctors who perform sex change operations also have the obligation to provide proper pre- and post-operative counselling, post-operative follow-up, and ongoing psychological care, if needed. They also need to provide a proper medical certificate to assist transwomen to correct their birth sex in their identity documents. Health care providers need to have accurate knowledge and understanding about transgender people. For example, in government hospitals, multidisciplinary teams comprised of a psychiatrist, clinical psychologist, general surgeon, plastic surgeon, urologist, endocrinologist and professional health counsellor need to be set up since the treatment of transgender people requires such team work.

Transwomen require the understanding and support of the government, health care professionals, general public as well as their family members. We need to understand and accept that humans are diverse. People have the right to be what they are and what they want to be. For transgender people, the same holds true.

Acknowledgements

I thank the following individuals for their critical review and helpful comments on an earlier version of this essay: Murali Shunmugam, Indian Network for People living with HIV, Chennai; Dr. Jaikumar Velayudham, M.D., Institute of Mental Health, Chennai; Samuel Lurie, Transgender Training and Advocacy, USA; Rose V, Trans Media, Chennai; and Priya Babu, Suder Foundation, Chennai.

Further References

K. Wylie, 'Gender Related Disorders', *ABC of Sexual Health, BMJ*, Vol. 329 (2004), pp. 615–17.

M. Besser, S. Carr, P.T. Cohen-Kettenis, P. Connolly, P. De Sutter, M. Diamond, D. Di Ceglie, Y. Higashi, L. Jones, F.P.M. Kruijver, J. Martin, Z.J. Playdon, D. Ralph, T. Reed, R. Reid, W.G. Reiner, D. Swaab, T. Terry, P. Wilson, K. Wylie, 'Atypical Gender Development: A Review', *International Journal of Transgenderism*, Vol. 9, No. 1, pp. 29–44.

People's Union for Civil Liberties, Karnataka (PUCL-K), 'Human Rights Violations Against the Transgender Community: A Study of Kothi and Hijra Sex Workers in Bangalore, India', *PUCL-K* (2003), http://www.pucl.org/Topics/Gender/2004/transgender.htm (accessed 5 March 2005). http://www.altlawforum.org/PUBLICATIONS/PUCL%20REPORT%20 2003 (accessed 5 March 2005)

V. Chakrapani, A.R. Kavi, R.L. Ramakrishnan, et al., *HIV Prevention Among Men Who Have Sex with Men (MSM) in India: Review of Current Scenario and Recommendations* (2002). [http://indianglbthealth.info/Authors/Downloads/MSM_HIV_IndiaFin.pdf]

V. Chakrapani, P.A. Newman, H. Mhaprolkar, and A.R. Kavi, *Sexual and Social Networks of MSM and Hijras in India: A Qualitative Study* (Report submitted to the Department for International Development (DFID), India), (Mumbai: The Humsafar Trust, 2007).

V. Chakrapani, P. Babu, T. Ebenezer, 'Hijras in Sex Work Face Discrimination in the Indian Health-Care System', *Research for Sex Work*, Vol. 7 (2004), pp. 12–14.

Walter Meyer III, Walter O. Bockting, Peggy Cohen-Kettenis, Eli Coleman , Domenico DiCeglie, Holly Devor, Louis Gooren, J. Joris Hage, Sheila Kirk, Bram Kuiper, Donald Laub, Anne Lawrence, Yvon Menard, Stan Monstrey, Jude Patton, Leah Schaefer, Alice Webb, Connie Christine Wheeler 'The Harry Benjamin International Gender Dysphoria Association's Standards of Care for Gender Identity Disorders' (6th version, 2001) [http://www.wpath.org/documents2/socv6.pdf].

Box-1: Sex Change Operation and Feminising procedures for transwomen

- Removal of penis (penectomy) and testes (orchidectomy)
- Construction of vagina (neovagina or vaginoplasty)
- Construction of labial lip around neovagina (labioplasty)
- Construction of clitoris (clitoroplasty)
- Breast enlargement (augmentation) surgery
- Facial feminisation
- Adam's apple shave (Thyroid chondroplasty)
- Administration of female (oestrogen/progesterone) and anti-male (anti-androgen) hormones
- Facial hair removal treatments (electrolysis or laser treatment)
- Scalp hair transplants

Notes

[1] I have used the terms hijras and aravanis interchangeably. The term 'aravani' is coined in Tamil Nadu to refer to those who would be called as 'hijra' in other states of India. However, this term has been adopted by Tamil-speaking hijras in other states also.

[2] Intersex persons (Formerly called as '*hermaphrodites*'): 'Intersex' is a general term used for a variety of conditions in which a person is born with a reproductive or sexual anatomy that does not seem to fit the typical definitions of female or male. For example, a person might be born appearing to be female on the outside, but having mostly male-typical anatomy on the inside. Or a person may be born with genitals that seem to be in-between the usual male and female types. For example, a girl may be born with a noticeably large clitoris, or lacking a vaginal opening (From http://www.isna.org/faq)

[3] Gender identity: Refers to one's psychological sense of being a man or a woman.

[4] The Diagnostic and Statistical Manual of Mental Disorders—Fourth Edition (DSM-IV) classifies 'Gender Identity Disorder' (GID) as the Gender Identity Disorder of Childhood (302.6), Adolescence, or Adulthood (302.85), and Gender Identity Disorder Not Otherwise Specified (GIDNOS) (302.6). The International Classification of Diseases-10 (ICD-10) provides five diagnoses

for the gender identity disorders (F64): Transsexualism (F64.0); Dual-role Transvestism (F64.1); Gender Identity Disorder of Childhood (64.2); Other Gender Identity Disorders (F64.8); and Gender Identity Disorder, Unspecified.
[6] Gires et al. 2006; Wylie 2004.
[7] I use the term 'emasculation' to refer to the complete removal of the male external genitalia (both testes and penis) since technically the term 'castration' refers to only the removal of testes. Technically speaking 'emasculation' alone cannot be considered as 'sex change operation' or 'sex reassignment surgery' since there is no active construction of vagina or female external genital parts. However, sometimes I have used the terms 'sex change operation' and 'emasculation' as though they are synonymous since the legal status of 'sex change operation' as well as 'voluntary emasculation' remains unarticulated and ambiguous. In some areas, I have distinguished between these two terms.
[8] Chakrapani et al. 2002.
[9] *Transsexual:* Individual whose gender identity is that of the opposite gender (sex). There are male-to-female and female-to-male transsexuals. A transsexual may or may not have had sex reassignment surgery and thus could be 'pre-operative' transsexual, 'post-operative' transsexual and 'non-operative' transsexual. A male-to-female transsexual person is referred to as '*transsexual woman*' and a female-to-male transsexual person is referred to as '*transsexual man*'.

Transgender person: A term used to describe those who transgress social gender norms; often used as an umbrella term to mean those who defy rigid, binary gender constructions, and who express or present a breaking and/or blurring of culturally prevalent/stereotypical gender roles. Transgender persons usually live full or part time in the gender role opposite the one in which they were born. In contemporary usage, 'transgender' has become an umbrella term that is used to describe a wide range of identities and experiences, including but not limited to: pre-operative, post-operative and non-operative transsexual people; and male or female cross-dressers (sometimes referred to as 'transvestites', 'drag queens', or 'drag kings'). A male-to-female transgender person is referred to as '*transgender woman*' or '*trans woman*' and a female-to-male transgender person is referred to as '*transgender man*' or '*trans man*'.
[10] Chakrapani et al. 2007.
[11] Chakrapani et al. 2004.
[12] Chakrapani et al. 2007.
[13] http://www.symposion.com/ijt/hiv_risk/preface.htm
[14] In many sentences, I have used the following terms in an interchangeable manner—'sex change operation', 'sex reassignment surgery' and 'surgical sex reassignment'.
[15] http://www.indianexpress.com/res/web/pIe/ie/daily/19981026/29951504.html; http://ai.eecs.umich.edu/people/conway/TSsuccesses/Tista/Tista.html#News; http://www.telegraphindia.com/1051211/asp/look/story_

5579950.asp; http://timesofindia.indiatimes.com/articleshow/1300633.cms

[16] http://timesofindia.indiatimes.com/NEWS/India/Sex_change_ops_no_longer_uncommon/articleshow/1028001.cms

[17] PUCL, K 2003.

[18] In India, it is not mandatory or necessary that biological males should have undergone sex change operation or emasculation to change their male name to a female name.

[19] http://www.echarcha.com/forum/showthread.php?t=19428

[20] http://passport.gov.in/cpv/miscell.pdf

[21] http://passport.gov.in/cpv/ppapp1.pdf

[22] In India, the term 'eunuch' is often, incorrectly, used to denote hijras (who come under transgender/transsexual category). Originally, this term is supposed to have referred to males who have undergone castration not by choice, but by accident, coercion or as a punishment. Hence it is not technically correct to refer to hijras as 'eunuchs'. E.g., In ancient times, some males were castrated to serve as guards in royal harems. Hijras voluntarily remove their male external genitalia (emasculation)—both testes and penis.

[23] *Kothis* are a heterogeneous group. *Kothis* can be described as males who show varying degrees of 'femininity' (which may be situational) and who are involved mainly, if not only, in receptive anal/oral sex with men. Some proportion of *kothis* have bisexual behaviour and many may also get married to women. Also, many hijra-identified persons may also identify themselves as 'kothis'.

[24] http://www.infosem.org/iNDIAN%20express%20publication.pdf

[25] Health and Family Welfare Department, Letter No. 675/EAPI/2/2007–1, Dated 27.2. 2007, from a Deputy Secretary to [Tamil Nadu] Government.

[26] The term 'MSM' is used to denote all men who have sex with other men, regardless of their sexual identity or sexual orientation. This is because a man may have sex with other men but still consider himself to be heterosexual or may not have any particular sexual identity at all. This, basically an epidemiological term, coined by public health experts, focusses exclusively on sexual behaviour for the purpose of HIV/STD prevention.

[27] Chakrapani et al. 2007.

[28] Chakrapani et al. 2004.

[29] http://www.infosem.org/news.htm#chennairally

[30] Hijra/transwomen communities are divided on whether they should be recognised as 'third gender' (or transgender) or just as 'woman'. Some want to be legally recognised as 'woman' or 'female'. But some others want transwomen to be recognised separately from the biological females in order to get some benefits for transwomen from the government.

Pendulous Penises and Couture Clitorises

What Medical Men do to Intersex Infants

MAYUR SURESH

Raja was born in 1974. At birth, Raja had both a penis and a urethra, and the scrotum was only partially descended. Due to this ambiguity with respect to the sex of the child, the doctor was of the opinion that one should wait a bit before assigning a sex to the child and maybe even consider performing surgery to resolve the sexual ambiguity. However, the parents were anxious that Raja begin schooling and also felt that since anyway they had no money for any kind of operation, a sex be assigned to the child. The doctor then assigned the sex of female to the child and the child was given the name of Rajamma.[1]

What makes us 'men' or 'women'? What distinguishes women from men? Is it the way one walks or the length of one's hair? Is it the pitch of one's voice? Does the presence of testicles mean that the body is that of a male and not that of a female?

Categories of male and female are fundamental to the ways in which we read the world. Without the pronouns of 'he' and 'she', we would barely be able to make sense and speak of the world around us. Intersex individuals pose a fundamental problem to the way we look at bodies and the division of the world into male and female since their sex is ambiguous and their sexual or reproductive anatomy does not correspond to what the medical establishment deems as a normal sexual anatomy. The bodies of intersexed persons do not conform to the social expectation that all human beings belong to one of two clearly marked sex categories, male or female, and are hence culturally unintelligible.[2]

In order to render these bodies readable, they must be changed in some way—made 'normal'. Thus, when confronted with such disorderly bodies, the medical establishment treats these bodies as pathologised, suffering or as a body that needs to be normalised to prevent future embarrassment and hence in need of immediate medical attention; very often this means surgery while the individual is still an infant. The surgery is performed in order to materialise notions of the perfect male or female body. For example, a medical textbook justifies surgery on intersex infants:

> Whatever the aetiology, however, the sex of the infant is uncertain. Rapid diagnostic analysis must be carried out to assign a gender appropriate to the sex of rearing that will give the child the most satisfying eventual functional result. Gender assignment and surgical correction must be done as early as possible to avoid subtle rejection of the child by the family, particularly if the patient's appearance is grossly discordant with the chromosomal or expected sex.[3]

Like the doctor in Raja 's case, the medical community tries to determine who is truly male and who is truly female. And in doing so, conjures certain markers of male-ness or female-ness, be it based on the appearance of genitals, or the presence or absence of certain hormones, or based on the chromosomes of the individual. If, however, the lines are blurred as in the case of intersex infants, then the medical establishment intervenes to physically construct what it considers the true sex of the child. The surgical intervention to create true and natural male or female bodies is done without questioning. If the distinctiveness of 'male' and 'female' bodies is so natural, then why is surgery required to create and preserve these categories? Despite the fact that children are born with both 'male' and 'female' reproductive and sexual traits, the medical profession continues to cling to the idea that being either male or female are the only two 'natural' options.

For the purposes of this essay, intersex is used provisionally to describe a range of anatomical and genetic variations, which result in a certain ambivalence in assigning either a male or female sex to an individual. I use this definition provisionally as there is much debate as to what constitutes an intersex condition, and the definition of an intersex condition, as we shall see, is often dictated by socio-cultural concerns of what a 'proper male' or 'proper female' should look like.

In this essay I argue that intersexuality, while it may be statistically uncommon, is not a disease or disorder that needs medical attention, and that intersex infants present a socio-cultural emergency, not a medical one. Following this, I argue that medical intervention on intersex infants should be deferred till a point at which the individuals can decide for themselves if they want surgery and what gender they want to live as, and that any surgery that is to be performed on infants should be medically necessary and not for cosmetic purposes, or to fix the infants, biological sex. I further argue that doing such surgery that fixes the biological sex of the infant violates certain human rights principles.

What is intersex?

There is considerable ambivalence on what defines the word intersex, because it refers to a wide variety of conditions. Definitions of intersex vary depending on what one considers the marker of one sex. For example, intersex was once referred to as a condition where an individual had both male and female genitalia and approximated the meaning of hermaphrodite. French historian and philosopher, Michel Foucault argues that prior to the 1800s a hermaphrodite was looked upon as a monster, which violated the laws both of nature and of man.[4] By the 1800s, through the rise of gynaecological sciences and military medical examinations in the West, doctors began to document persons with ambiguous genitalia. Biomedical specialists devised a system that would label everyone as having a true sex, either that of male or female, and any ambiguity was considered the consequence of biological eccentricities, imperfections or errors of nature.[5] Therefore, while the hermaphrodite had genitalia of both sexes, the intersex individual of the 1800s had a 'true sex' but whose genitals did not reflect this 'true sex'.

Medical doctors created a test for true sex based on gonadal tissue. A person with non-standard sex anatomy and ovaries is seen as a 'female pseudo-hermaphrodite'; a person with non-standard sex anatomy and testes is seen as a 'male pseudo-hermaphrodite'; and if a person has ovarian and testicular tissue, she or he is seen as a 'true hermaphrodite'.[6] Given the technological limitations of the time, Victorian doctors appeared to like this system because they could not easily diagnose 'true hermaphroditism' in living people; as a consequence, for the most part, the only 'true hermaphrodites' were dead and dissected people.[7]

With the expansion of the domains of biomedical knowledge, the markers of one's sex could no longer be solely located at one's genitalia but came to be also located in genes or hormones. Hence for example, a 'genetic' male will have two different sex chromosomes (X and Y) and a female will have two same sex chromosomes (X and X). Sex can also be located in the hormones and hence, as we are taught in standard X biology, males have androgen and testosterone, and females have oestrogen and cortisone. Hence more recently, the medical community, in the West at least, has begun to refer to intersex conditions as 'defined by congenital conditions in which development of chromosomal, gonadal or anatomic sex is atypical'.[8]

Intersex conditions, however, are not solely medical problems. Two common intersex conditions are micropenis and clitoromegaly; the former referring to a small 'inadequately sized' penis, and the latter referring to an atypically large clitoris. While these may be caused by hormonal changes during the development of the foetus, they do not necessarily indicate medical problems. Instead, the problem posed by these two conditions is cosmetic. Male infants with small penises do not look male enough, and female infants with large clitorises are too far removed from being comfortably feminine. Intersex, thus also refers to what the medical profession considers 'cosmetically unacceptable genitalia'.[9] Another instance of cosmetically unacceptable genitalia is the case of hyposadias, a common male genital anomaly where the urinary outlet is located somewhere other than at the tip of the penis. Largely, this is a minor anatomical variant with no functional consequence. In some cases, however, the displacement of the urinary outlet causes the male genitals to appear feminine in form. In certain chromosomal anomalies such as Kleinfelter syndrome[10] or Turner syndrome,[11] there are commonly genital anomalies, but not genital sex ambiguity. Intersex therefore, also refers to instances where the genitals do not look 'proper' but where there is little ambiguity with regard to the sex of the infant.

Intersex activists in the United States have tended to include a wide spectrum of congenital, atypical genitalia because many of those affected share common psychological effects of early genital examination and surgery.

Hence, the Intersex Society of North America (ISNA) defines intersex as:

> A general term used for a variety of conditions in which a person is born with reproductive or sexual anatomy doesn't seem to fit the typical definitions of female or male. For example, a person may be born appearing to be female on the outside, but having mostly male typical anatomy on the inside, or a person may be born with genitals that seem to be in-between the usual male and female types—for example, a girl may be born with a noticeable large clitoris or lacking a vaginal opening or a boy may be born with a notably small penis or with a scrotum that is divided so that it has formed more like a labia. Or a person may be born with mosaic genetics, so that some of her cells have XX chromosomes and some of them have XY. Though we speak of intersex, as an in born condition, intersex anatomy doesn't always show up at birth. Sometimes a person isn't found to have intersex anatomy until she or he reaches the age of puberty or finds himself an infertile adult or dies of old age and is autopsied. Some people live and die with intersex anatomy without anyone (including themselves) ever knowing.[12]

The problem that intersex conditions pose is that in any attempt to identify them, one runs into the problem of defining they key or essential feminine or masculine anatomy. But as we have seen, the markers of one's sex can be variously located, on the gonadal tissue, the size of genitals, chromosomes and hormones. But if the markers of male and female bodies are varied, shifting, and themselves ambiguous, then intersex conditions not only call into question the naturalness and binary nature of male and female, but since the biomedical markers of sex are also shifting and variable, intersex conditions also throw doubt on the medical establishment's claim to be the authoritative voice in the discovery of 'true' sex.

What happens when intersex infants meet medical men? Dominant treatment protocols for the treatment of intersex conditions

Contemporary treatment of intersex infants is based on a psychosocial theory of gender identity which argues that gender identity arises primarily as a result of psycho social rearing or nurture, and is not directly endowed from nature. The theory, initially propagated by John Money, argues that all children must have their gender identity fixed very early in life for a consistent gender identity to form, and that from very early in life, before the age of eighteen months, the child's anatomy must match the standard anatomy of his or her gender and thus, for gender identity to form properly, male infants must have properly sized penises and no vagina, and girls primarily require a vagina, with no noticeable phallus.[13]

The creation of a male or female gender identity, the theory argues, is based on several conditions. The doctors must ensure that the parents have no doubt about whether their child is male or female and that the parents must constantly affirm the assigned gender of the child. Second, the genitals must be made to match the assigned gender as soon as possible. Third, gender-appropriate hormones must be administered at puberty and intersexed children must be kept informed about their condition with age-appropriate explanations. The theory proposes that the intersex child will develop a gender identity in accordance with gender assignment, regardless of chromosomal sex and will not question his or her gender assignment, if all these conditions are met.[14]

Arguing for the early surgical 'correction' of intersex conditions, the American Academy of Pediatrics in 1996 argued that:

> In large part, the body image of a child is derived from the social interaction with the primary care givers and peers.... Given the early development of body image and the importance of parental response the implication for repair...is that the earlier the repair can be achieved, the more likely the child will achieve a psychologically healthy perspective of body image.... Research on children with ambiguous genitalia has shown that sexual identity is a function of social learning through differential responses of multiple individuals

in the environment. For example, children whose genetic sexes are not clearly reflected in external genitalia (i.e. hermaphroditism) can be raised successfully as members of either sex if the process begins before the age of 2 years. Therefore a person's sexual body image is largely a function of socialization.[15]

When an infant is born, one of the first things that a doctor will do is to announce the sex of the child. According to Dr. SB, if there is no apparent genital abnormality, (which does not mean that there is no intersex condition) usually no further tests will be done on the child to determine if it is a male or a female. Thus, somewhat anachronistically, the first determination of the sex of the child is not determined by karyotyping or by hormone testing, but by simply looking at the genitals of the infant.

If there is ambiguity in determining the sex of the child based on the genitalia, then karyotyping and hormone testing is done on the infant, in order to determine the 'true' sex of the infant. According to Dr. SB, parents of such infants are told that their child does have a true and proper sex, but that there are some anomalies in the development of the genitalia of the child, or that the development of the genitalia is not complete or somewhat 'off-track'. Parents and other care givers of the infant must be convinced of their child's sex and that the ambiguity was just a temporary hurdle in discovering the true sex of the infant. Doctors tell the parents that once the 'true' sex of the infant is determined through karyotyping and hormone testing, corrections can be made so that the body of the infant matches the determined 'true' sex.

This mode of telling parents of the processes of determining the sex of the infant contributes to the impression that the 'true' sex of the infant has been discovered and that something that was there all along has been found.[16] The message conveyed is that the trouble lies in the doctor's ability to determine the gender, not in the baby's gender per se.[17] The 'true sex' of the child will be revealed by testing and the malformed and confusing genitals will merely be repaired by the doctor. Given that 'discovering' the true sex of the child is only done by the medical profession, such 'discovery' of the true sex of the infant serves to maintain the credibility of the medical profession and its authority over the knowledge of the body. Moreover, the idea that the genitals will merely be repaired serves to create the impression that they are merely reconstructing the genitals rather than constructing the gender of the child. If a child has a true sex, then surgery is performed only to physically manifest that true sex. This mode of telling the true sex of the infant, and the consequent 'repair' of its genitals serves to mask the medical profession's attempt at constructing gender for the infant.

The second condition for the successful creation of a gender identity is that the surgery must be done as soon as possible. If the infant is assigned to the male gender, the initial stage of penis repair is done by the first birthday and further surgery is completed before the child enters school. If the child is assigned to the female gender, clitoral reduction and vulva repair is usually begun by three months of age. The initial propagator of the theory, John Money, argues that if reduction of phallic tissue were delayed beyond the neonatal period, the infant would have traumatic memories of being castrated.[18] Similarly, according to Dr. SB, the surgery must be performed early in children, since if the surgery is performed after puberty, the child would not only have to go through the trauma of surgery, but would also know that his or her body was not fully developed or was abnormal, leading, in her opinion, to feelings of shame and embarrassment. The surgery must also be performed early in her opinion so that the body of the infant can develop properly and will be amenable to subsequent hormone treatment.

The diagnosis of intersex conditions, as we have seen, includes assessing the chromosomal sex and the syndrome that produced the genital ambiguity, and may include procedures such as cytologic screening,[19] chromosomal analysis, hormone, gonadotropin and steroid evaluation,[20] digital examination and radiographic genitography.

In any intersexed condition, if the infant is determined to be a genetic female, having XX chromosome make-up, then the treatment—surgery and hormonal treatment resulting in clitoral recession and the creation of a vagina—can proceed quickly, satisfying presumed psychological and cultural demands. If, on the other hand, the infant is determined to have at least one Y chromosome, then surgery may be considerably delayed. A decision must be made whether to test the ability of the phallic tissue to respond to androgen treatment which is intended to enlarge the microphallus adequately in order to become a penis. This androgen is intended to stimulate the production of testosterone which will then lead to phallic development. In infants with a microphallus, either the infant lacks the ability to produce testosterone upon being stimulated by androgen or the tissue lacks the ability to read the testosterone that is produced. As Dr. SB explains, it can take upto three months to see if the phallus responds to this hormone treatment. If the Y-chromosome infant cannot make testosterone or cannot respond to the testosterone that it makes, then the phallus will not develop and the Y-chromosome child will be considered female. If the phallus is less than two cm long at birth and does not respond to the androgen treatment, then the male infant is made into a female. In order to do this, the penis needs to be surgically reduced to an average sized clitoris (meaning that it should not be visible when the child is standing), a vaginoplasty is performed, and the testes are removed. The person must be put on hormones during puberty so that she can develop 'normally'.

If the infant's phallus does respond, the gender assignment problem is taken care of, but the penis will not grow again at puberty when the rest of the body develops. According to Money, while it may be detrimental for an adult male to have a much smaller than average penis, it is very detrimental to the morale of the young boy to have a micropenis. In the former case, Money states, the male's manliness might be at stake, but in the latter case his essential maleness might be. Money suggests that both these problems might be avoided if a female gender is assigned and surgery performed at infancy, suggesting that for Money, chromosomes are less relevant in determining gender than penis size, that is 'male' is not defined by the presence of one X and one Y chromosome, but instead by the aesthetic condition of having an appropriately sized penis.

Thus, despite the many different technologies in determining sex, sex assignment is primarily based on the anatomy of the infant:

The choice of gender should be based on the infant's anatomy.

Often it is wiser to rear a genetic male as female. It is relatively easy to create a vagina if one is absent, but it is not possible to create a really satisfactory penis if the phallus is absent or rudimentary. Only those males with a phallus of adequate size which will respond to testosterone at adolescence should be considered for male rearing. Otherwise, the baby should be reared as a female.[21]

In other words, this means that the decision whether the child should be surgically 'corrected' to be a male or female depends on the appearance of the genitals.

Similarly, the aesthetic appearance of female genitalia, cultural compulsions and presumed psychological ills predominate the treatment of ambiguous genitalia in females. Take for example, congenital adrenal hyperplasia, where the adrenal glands in genetic females cannot make cortisone, and while trying to make cortisone, they instead make an unusually high level of virilising hormones. That is, they can make XX embryos have larger than average clitorises or even a clitoris that looks like a penis and labia that looks like a scrotum.

According to Dr. SB, clitoral recession by cortisone treatment or by surgery is necessary because the clitoris in such females will look abnormally large if left alone. Not only is this aesthetically unpleasing but according to Dr. SB, such large clitorises are physically uncomfortable for women, and may lead to too much libido or excessive sensation during sexual intercourse.

Hence, in these virilised females or genetic males who are assigned a female sex, the genitalia is reconstructed using a piece of the colon to create a vagina, and the large phallus is carved down to an average sized clitoris. Vaginas are built or lengthened in order to make them big enough to accept average-sized penises. Joined labia are separated and various other surgical and hormonal treatments are directed at producing a girl who fulfils the anatomical criterion of being female.

The assumption that all persons need to be assigned one particular gender and that gender is fixed and invariable, lies at the heart of medical treatment of intersex conditions. The medical protocols dealing with intersex are premised on the assumption that children must be either male or female and that once assigned, gender is unchangeable. But Raja seems to belie this assumption. Raja was born as Rajamma—a girl—and lived the first 20 years of his life as a girl. He recalls being happy with his then identity as a girl and was comfortable wearing girl's clothing. At age 22 he suddenly developed facial hair and his voice deepened. He recalls that this period was traumatic as he was taunted by his brothers and faced social ostracism. However, within a short period of time he started wearing men's clothing and adopted the male name Raja. What Raja 's story tells us is that one's gender is not necessarily fixed and invariable. His story queers the idea that we all have and need *only* one gender throughout our life and that this gender is salient in defining an individual.

The necessity of having either of two genders at birth is an idea that is reflected in the law as well. In the Delhi Births and Deaths Registration Act, 1969, for example, a Birth Report is required to be submitted to the Registrar of Births within 30 days of birth of the infant. That report must contain, apart from the names and addresses of the parents, the name and the gender (either 'M' or 'F' has to be ticked on the prescribed form) of the infant. This can only be changed if the registrar finds that the entry was erroneously, improperly or fraudulently made. Thus, in the absence of any of these conditions, one's legal gender remains unchangeable. Thus, in the case of Raja, while he lives as a man, his legal personality remains that of a woman.

Returning to the treatment protocols, what is also evident is that masculinity and femininity are treated in an asymmetrical manner. It is also clear that heterosexism pervades the treatment as the diversity of sexuality and sexual behaviour is reduced to vaginal penetration by a penis. For a penis to be successful, it must easily be recognised as a real penis; that is, it must have the potential to become erect and flaccid at appropriate times and to act as a conduit through which urine can flow and semen can be expelled into a vagina. On the other hand, very little is needed for a surgically constructed vagina to count as successful save that it must be able to accept a reasonably sized penis. All that is required is a receptive orifice. Thus, the proper way to be male is to be able to have an erection and penetrate a vagina and fertilise a female and by contrast, all one needs to do to be properly female is to receive a penis.[22]

Apart from portraying all persons as inherently heterosexual who only engage in peno-vaginal sex, this anxiety over the future sexual performance, at a more fundamental level, also betrays the construction of all people as predominantly sexual; meaning that all people must engage in sexual intercourse and that all sexual intercourse involves one penis penetrating one vagina. Raja, however, says that he has never felt the desire to have sex and he is perfectly comfortable with the hijras, some of whom do make passes at him. As he puts it, 'it (sex) is something which is important to them, while it's not important to me, so I'm perfectly comfortable with it.'

Another condition for a gender assignment to be 'successful' is that the person, on whom this surgery is performed, should be told as little as possible about the surgery that was performed when the individual was an infant. Following from the logic that nurture determines sex and not biology, it is argued that the intersex individual must be consistently reared in the assigned gender, and that any mention of gender ambiguity will lead to confusion as to her/his gender identity, which is what was meant to be avoided by surgery.[23]

It is, for example, argued that women with Androgen Insensitivity Syndrome (AIS) should not be told that they are genetically male:

> The AIS patient who is told she is genetically male is likely to experience confusion or strong emotions that could diminish her sense of rationality, her ability to deliberate effectively.... The fact the patient has the XY chromosome pattern appears to be more of academic than physiologic importance to the AIS female who is diagnosed as infertile. On the one hand there is no alternative course of action she can take because this disorder cannot be corrected. On the other hand, a heterosexual AIS who is satisfied with her current sexuality may suffer from confusion or a loss of dignity when informed that she is genetically male. This may affect not only her, but also her husband or partner. I believe that it would be cruel to disclose this finding to the patient, since it would not enable her to make any decisions that

would improve her life in any possible way. In fact, it could produce unnecessary and devastating emotional and psychological effect that will impede her chances of leading a normal life.[24]

What this reasoning fails to appreciate is that hiding the facts of the condition will not necessarily prevent a patient and family from thinking about it. Failure to experience bodily changes at puberty, such as the onset of periods in girls, and/or taking disguised hormone therapy pills arouse questioning in the mind of people with intersex conditions. Often people whose intersex condition is hidden from them find other ways of discovering what is actually happening to their bodies.[25] As one intersexed person writes, 'Mine was a dark secret kept from all outside the medical profession (family included) but this is not an option because it both increases the feelings of freakishness and reinforces the sense of isolation.'[26]

Another woman who had her 'enlarged' clitoris removed when she was a child insists that, 'to be lied to as a child about your own body and to have your life as a sexual being so ignored that you are not even given the decency of an answer to your questions, is to have your heart and soul relentlessly undermined.'[27] It has also been noted that 'secrecy as a method of handling troubling information is primitive, degrading and often ineffective. Even when a secret is kept, its existence carries an aura of unease that most people can sense...secrets crippled my life'.[28]

Notions that withholding information and selective truth telling will protect the child and ensure that the child grows up properly adjusted in his or her gender is clearly based on false premises. Such practices are paternalistic and naïve in the sense that it assumes that the medical profession is the only source of information about bodies. It assumes that people will do what the medical establishment tells them to do and will go along with what their doctors tell them about their bodies.

It should be noted that practice in India when it comes to dealing with children with ambiguous genitalia is different from treatment protocols. A study was conducted on 30 individuals with male pseudohermaphroditism by the Christian Medical College, Vellore.[29] It was found that in all but one case (this one patient being a new born), all children had already been assigned a gender by their parents on the basis of external genitalia. Of these children, 16 were being raised as boys prior to medical consultation; all 16 had visible testes, whereas, according to the study, the phallic size and urogenital orifice positions were variable. The remaining 13 were being reared as girls by the parents, of whom eight had female type vulvar outlets. Five girls had visible testes, although, the study states that parents thought them to be swellings or hernia.

In treatment of these children, the study went along with the parents' choice of gender, and therapy was directed towards hypospadias repair and removal of pseudo vaginas. Four children who were being reared as girls 'who had reasonable sized phalli... were converted into boys with enthusiastic parental concurrence'. However, a sex change from a boy to a girl was not accepted by the parents in any case. This is in contrast to treatment protocols in the West where feminising surgery is the accepted solution for most children.

The study explains this deviation from western treatment protocols as indicative of the male bias in Indian society.

> Man is the traditional bread winner in India and woman, the housewife and mother. A sexually imperfect man has more economic independence and social acceptability than an infertile and imperfect female, who will remain an unmarriageable, financial and social burden, especially in rural areas.[30]

Thus, while feminising surgery is not performed in intersex infants as often as it is in the west, it is not as if intersex infants in India emerged unscathed from their encounters with the medical profession. While surgical intervention in the West appears to favour creating females, in India surgical intervention seeks to make the infants as male as possible.

Human rights concerns

When doctors perform surgeries on intersex infants, in all probability, they are not doing so to harm the child. Doctors, most probably, are doing what they think is the right thing to do for the child.[31] Their actions would approximate what is termed in the Conventions on the Rights of the Child, as the 'best interests of the child standard'.

The 'best interests of the child standard' appears in Article 3 of the Convention on the Rights of the Child, to which India is also a signatory. According to Article 3, state parties to the Convention shall take the 'best interests of the child as a primary consideration in all actions concerning the child'. This principle, which forms one of the core values of the treaty, reaffirms that in every circumstance and decision affecting the child, the Convention requires that the child's best interests be considered and given due weight.[32]

However, there has been considerable debate in recent times within the medical community, on whether performing irreversible, non-life saving surgery on intersex infants is actually in the best interests of the child.

One of the first and 'classic' cases to test Money's theory on gender identity is known as the John/Joan case. In this case two genetic male twins were undergoing circumcision procedures, when the penis of one of the twins was accidentally ablated. The child, whose penis was accidentally ablated, was then raised as a girl, Joan. Surgery was performed later that year in order to create a vagina and more followed to facilitate feminisation. The management of Joan's bodily and psychological gender was closely monitored. Early reports indicated that Joan was developing successfully and that John was doing well as Joan. John Money, the doctor who performed the surgeries on Joan and subsequently monitored her status, states, 'Now 9 years old, she has differentiated a female gender identity in marked contrast to the male gender identity of her brother. Some of the other patients are now adolescent or adult in age. They demonstrate that the twin can expect to be feminine in erotic expression and sexual life. Maintained on estrogen therapy, she will have normal feminine physique and a sexually attractive appearance.[33]

However, subsequent reports indicate that Joan's upbringing as a girl was not as successful as Money claimed it to be.[34] Joan's mother recalls in the report that Joan rejected dresses and wanted to shave like the father. Joan, the report states said that she did not like dresses and the toys that she was given and had thoughts of suicide. Despite the absence of a penis, Joan refused to enter the girls' bathroom and would attempt to use the boys' instead.

At age 12, Joan was put on an oestrogen regime but she rebelled against taking the hormones and would often dispose off her daily dose. Though she did develop breasts, she refused to wear a bra. The local medical team, noticing her preference for boys' activities and refusal to accept her female status, explored Joan's male gender with her. At the age of 14 years, Joan decided to switch to living as a male.

Joan, now John, began taking male hormone shots and was happy, the report suggests living as a man. It states, 'Subsequent to his return to male living he felt his attitudes, behaviours and body were in concert; they weren't when living as a girl.'

The report concludes by saying that after a review of literature, there is no known case where a genetic male has ever easily and fully accepted an imposed life as a heterosexual female regardless of physical and medical intervention. It also states that there is no support for Money's theory that individuals are psychosexually neutral on birth or that healthy psychosexual development is dependent upon the appearance of the genitals. While it may be easier, surgically, to create a vagina than to construct a penis, this is done at considerable and unacceptable psychological cost, which is certainly not in the best interests of the child.

Another core value of the Convention is that of participation. Article 12 recognises the child's right to participate in all aspects of life within the family, the school, and the community. This right to participate empowers the child to claim all the rights described in the Convention. Article 12 accords a child 'who is capable of forming his or her views the right to express those views freely in all matters affecting the child'. The right to participate requires the adoption of measures and mechanisms to ensure that children have opportunities not only to express their views, but also to be heard in the decision-making processes affecting his or her life.

As stated earlier, the dominant treatment protocols of intersex conditions postulate that in order for the sex assignment to be successful, the parents must raise the child in the assigned gender and must constantly affirm that this is the true gender of the child. The child must also be given age-appropriate explanations, which often means that the doctor and the parents will not disclose the intersex condition to the intersex person. Therefore, when a child is undergoing therapy and treatment after a gender assignment, the child, according to dominant treatment protocol, is constantly told what his or her gender should be, irrespective of what the child feels is his or her true gender. These two conditions directly contradict the child's right to participation.

No studies were found that analysed the widespread effects of this non-disclosure, but the impact can be seen from the Joan/John case. The report on the Joan/John case documents that Joan felt frustrated at not having his feelings and desires recognised. 'Without consideration of genitals, with the obvious absence of a penis, he nevertheless knew he was not a girl. When he tried to express such thought, the doctor would "change the subject whenever I tried to tell the doctor how I felt. He didn't want to hear what I had to say but wanted to tell me how I should feel".'

Moreover, as was stated earlier, doctors and parents are not the only source of information to intersex individuals. Most patients will eventually become aware of their diagnosis one way or another. Some people articulate feelings of anger, distrust, and betrayal directed towards their doctors and families.[35] Policies of non-disclosure preclude access to community-support groups for shared support, learning and experiences

The individual who is forced to undergo this surgery should not, in fact, have to deal with choices made by others for them, especially since these are based on false premises that govern the 'treatment' of intersex conditions. Undoubtedly, an infant is not in any position to give or deny consent to medical procedures and this is why, this essay argues that surgery, unless in the context of a life-threatening condition, should be postponed. If at all conducted, it should be done only when the child concerned can convey what he or she feels is the gender that he or she wants to live as in that moment. Children do give expression to their feelings and thoughts about their gender identity and they have the right to have their opinions taken into account before surgical intervention takes place.

In 1999, two cases of intersex infants were brought before the

Constitutional Court of Columbia.[36] The two main questions before the Court were: first, when and in what circumstances parents of intersex infants could consent to surgery to be performed on their children and, second, what constitutes valid consent. The Court declared that parents' authority to consent to medical procedures on behalf of children who are too young to consent for themselves depends upon (1) the exigency and urgency of the procedure; (2) how invasive and risky the procedure is; and (3) the age and degree of autonomy of the child. For instance, it is obvious that parents may consent to a vaccination for their child and it is equally obvious that they may not force a teenage child to undergo cosmetic surgery.

The court found that although surgical modification of intersexed infants has been standard medical practice for some 40 years, there is no evidence that it is necessary, safe, effective, or that an early decision is urgent. An alternate model, in which surgery is performed only if desired by a patient who consents for herself, is backed by Intersex Society of North America (ISNA) and a growing number of medical experts. These factors weigh against authorising parents to consent on behalf of their children.

On the other hand, the Court acknowledged that the State has an interest in protecting the privacy and autonomy of the family. The State assumes that parents will act in the best interests of their children and that parents are in the best position to determine what is best for their particular child. Therefore, the State should not be allowed to intervene unless there is a clear risk to the child.

In the case of intersexed infants however, the Court found that parents are likely to make decisions based upon their own fears and concerns rather than what is best for the child, especially if they are pressed to decide quickly. 'In some sense, parents who consent to the surgery may actually be discriminating against their own children.' The Court held that parents cannot give consent on a child's behalf to surgeries intended to determine sexual identity. The Constitutional guarantee of free development of one's own personality implies a right to define one's own sexual identity.

The Court required the legal and medical community to

establish a new category of consent, 'qualified, persistent informed consent', intended to force parental decisions to take into account only the child's interest.

The Judges held that parents may consent to surgery only if they have been given accurate information about the risks and the existence of alternate treatment paradigms which reject early surgery. Furthermore, the consent must be in written form, and must be given on more than one occasion, over an extended period of time, so that the parents have time to really understand their child's condition and the ramifications of alternate treatment paradigms.

From the early 2000s, owing to pressure from groups like the ISNA, treatment protocols for intersex conditions began to similarly change. In 2001, an editorial in the British Medical Journal argued that, 'With a serious deficiency of any evidence based, emotive debates on ethics and clinical concerns over the long term consequences of interventions, it is time to stand back and rethink every aspect of this management.'

In 2006, a Consensus Statement on Management of Intersex Disorder moved away from previous treatment protocols. Doctors, according to this consensus statement, should emphasise that the child does not have a shameful condition but one that occurs naturally. It recommends that gender should be assigned—meaning that the child should be given and raised in a particular gender. With regard to the central postulate that all infants are psycho-sexually gender neutral at birth, it states that this generalisation should be treated with caution and viewed conservatively. 'In children and adolescents with significant gender dysphoria, a comprehensive psychological evaluation and an opportunity to explore feelings about gender with a qualified clinician is required over a period of time.' If the wrong gender is assigned and if the individual desires to change gender then that wish should be supported.

It supports the process of disclosure 'concerning facts about karyotype, gonadal status and prospects for future fertility in collaborative, ongoing action that requires a flexible individual-based approach…. Disclosure is associated with enhanced psychosocial adaptation.'

With specific regard to surgery it states that, 'It is generally felt that surgery that is performed for cosmetic reasons in the first year of life relieves parental distress and improves attachment between child and parents. The systematic evidence for this belief is lacking.' It goes on to further state that vaginoplasty or vaginal dilation should not take place before puberty and only be performed in adolescence when the patient is psychologically motivated and a full partner in the procedure. With regard to hormone therapy as well, the consensus statement recommends that this be commenced at puberty and that this time should be used to discuss the condition and set a foundation for long-term adherence to the hormone therapy.

More recently in 2006, an International Panel of Experts in International Human Rights Law and on Sexual Orientation and Gender Identity adopted the Yogyakarta Principles on the Application of International Human Rights Law in Relation to Sexual Orientation and Gender Identity. Principle 18(b) states that,

> States shall take all necessary legislative, administrative and other measures to ensure that no child's body is irreversibly altered by medical procedures in an attempt to impose a gender identity without the full, free and informed consent of the child in accordance with the age and maturity of the child and guided by the principle that in all actions concerning children, the best interests of the child shall be a primary consideration.

This principle recognises the bodily sanctity even of children and seeks to protect the body of a child from medical procedures that fix a gender identity—the same type of painful, traumatic medical procedures that have been and perhaps are being performed on intersex children today. Also, this principle echoes the principle of participation that is present in the Child Rights Convention and obliges states to take into account the opinions of the child when performing any such medical procedures.

Conclusion

While the 2006 consensus statement does go some way in responding to concerns about performing unnecessary and potentially harmful surgery upon infants, it does not address the more basic rationale for understanding intersex as a medical problem.

Intersex conditions in most cases do not represent a threat to the life or health of the infant and instead are socio-cultural emergencies where the body of the intersex infant must be made to conform to culturally defined notions of a male and female body. Where there is a threat to the physical health or life of the child, only then should the medical profession intervene. Surgery intended to render genitalia cosmetically acceptable and to fix the gender of the infant causes a great deal of physical and mental trauma to the individual and such surgery prevents the full discovery of one's own sexuality and gender. If an individual wishes to undergo surgery to change the appearance of the genitals or to assign a gender then that surgery should be performed at an age where the individual involved can be an active participant in the process.

Notes

[1] Raja came to the office of Alternative Law Forum (ALF) with the objective of seeking legal redressal. The problem he faced was that he was not allowed to take an examination to be a teacher because the examiners felt that his birth certificate said female, but he acted and dressed like a male. The name has been changed to ensure confidentiality.

[2] S.E. Preves, 'Sexing the Intersexed: An Analysis of Sociocultural Responses to Intersexuality', *Signs: Journal of Women in Culture and Society*, Vol. 27, No. 2 (2001).

[3] P.K. Donahoe, 'The Diagnosis and Treatment of Infants with Intersex Abnormalities', in B. Churchill and C. Sheldon (eds), *Management Principles in Paediatric Urology* (Philadelphia: Saunders, 1987).

[4] Michel Foucault, *Abnormal: Lectures at the College de France* (New York: Picador, 2003), p. 66.

[5] *Ibid.*, p. 72.

[6] V.A. Rosario, 'Is it a Boy or a Girl? Introduction to the Special Issue on Intersex', *Journal of Gay and Lesbian Psychotherapy*, Vol. 10, No. 2 (2006).

[7] Marcus de María Arana, *A Human Rights Investigation into the Medical 'Normalisation of Intersex People: A Report of a Public Hearing by the Human Rights Commission of the City and County of San Francisco* (Published on 8 April 2005), available at www.sfgov.org/humanrights (accessed on 16 April 2007)

[8] P.A. Lee, C.P. Houk et al., 'Consensus Statement on Management of Intersex Disorders', *Pediatrics: Official Journal of the American Academy of Pediatrics* [www.pediatrics.org/cgi/content/full/118/2/e488, accessed on 9 April 2007].

[9] A.D. Dreger, 'Ambiguous Sex or Ambivalent Medicine', *The Hastings Center Report*, Vol. 28, No. 3 (May/June 1998).

[10] Most men inherit a single X chromosome from their mother and a single Y chromosome from their father. Men with Kleinfelter syndrome inherit an extra X chromosome from either parent; their karyotype (sex chromosome make-up) is 47XXY.

[11] The typical female karyotype ('sex' chromosome make-up) for females is 46,XX. This means that the typical female has 46 chromosomes including two that look like X's. People with Turner syndrome have only one X chromosome present and fully functional. This is sometimes referred to as 45,XO or 45,X karyotype. In a person with Turner Syndrome, female sex characteristics are usually present but underdeveloped compared to the typical female.

[12] 'What is Intersex?', *Intersex Society of North America* [http://www.isna.org/faq/what_is_intersex, as accessed on 7 April 2007].

[13] M. Diamond and K. Sigmundson, 'Sex Reassignment at Birth: A Long Term Review and Clinical Implications', *Archives of Pediatric and Adolescent Medicine* (March 1997).

[14] S.J. Kessler, 'The Medical Construction of Gender: Case Management of Intersexed Infants', *Signs: Journal of Women in Culture and Society*, Vol. 16, No. 1 (1990), p. 7.

[15] Section on Urology, 'Timing of Elective Surgery of the Genitalia of Male Children with Particular Reference to the Risks, Benefits and Psychological Effects of Surgery and Anesthesia', *Pediatrics*, Vol. 97, No. 4 (April 1996).

[16] Diamond and Sigmundson, 'Sex Reassignment at Birth', p. 8.

[17] *See* note 10.

[18] J. Money, 'Ablatio Penis: Normal Male Infant Sex Re-assigned as a Girl', *Archives of Sexual Behaviour*, Vol. 4, No. 1 (1975).

[19] Cytologic evaluation is the analysis of cells under a microscope. This is done to determine what the cells look like, where they came from, and how they form and function. This evaluation is done on the gonads to determine whether they are ovarian or testicular tissue.

[20] Gonadotropins are protein hormones secreted by gonadotrope cells of the pituitary gland. These hormones target the ovaries or testes to simulate the production of other hormones by these organs. Gonadatropin and steroid analysis determines if these gonadatropins are capable of being secreted, and if they are being secreted by the pituitary gland. Additionally these tests determine whether the target organs, the ovaries or the testes respond to the gonadotropins.

[21] P.K. Donahoe et al., 'Evaluation of the Newborn with Ambiguous Genitalia', *Pediatric Clinics of North America*, Vol. 23, No. 2 (May 1976), pp. 361–70.

[22] Dreger, 'Ambiguous Sex or Ambivalent Medicine'.

[23] A. Dreger, 'Shifting the Paradigm of Intersex Treatment', Intersex Society of North America [http://www.isna.org/compare, accessed 15 June 2007].

24 A. Natarajan, 'Medical Ethics and Truth Telling in the Case of Androgen Insensitivity Syndrome', *Canadian Medical Association Journal*, Vol. 154 (1996), pp. 568–70.

25 S.A. Groveman, 'Sex, Lies and Androgen Insensitivity Syndrome', *Canadian Medical Association Journal*, Vol. 154 (1996), pp. 1827–34.

26 Anon., 'Once a Dark Secret', *British Medical Journal*, Vol. 308, No. 542 (February 1994).

27 M. Coventry, 'Finding the Words', *Chrysalis: The Journal of Transgressive Gender Identities*, Vol. 2 (1997), pp. 27–30.

28 A. Dreger, 'Shifting the Paradigm of Intersex'.

29 M. Jini, S. Sen, J. Chacko, N. Zachariah, P. Raghupathy, K.E. Mammen, 'Gender Assignment in Male Pseudohermaphroditism: An Indian Perspective', *Pediatric Surgery International*, Vol. 8 (1993), pp. 500–1.

30 *Ibid.*

31 S. Creighton, 'Managing Intersex', *British Medical Journal*, Vol. 323 (2001), pp. 1264–65.

32 R. Rios-Kohn, 'The Convention on the Rights of the Child: Progress and Challenges', *Georgetown Journal on Fighting Poverty*, Vol. 139, p. 145.

33 See note 10.

34 Diamond and Sigmundson, 'Sex Reassignment at Birth'.

35 A. Green, 'My Beautiful Clitoris', *Chrysalis: The Journal of Transgressive Gender Identities*, Vol. 2, No. 5, p. 12. See also A. Moreno, 'Letter to My Physicians', *Chrysalis: The Journal of Transgressive Gender Identities*, Vol. 2, No. 5, p. 42.

   If I had not persisted in obtaining my medical records, I might never have known the specifics of my intersex status…I am shocked and angered to realize that you have lied to me, convinced my parents to lie to me and that you never intended to disclose my diagnosis to me – the patient. I wonder how you thought that deceiving me might have been therapeutic or even ethical. I wonder if you thought so little of me as to believe that I would never discover the truth on my own.

36 J.A. Greenberg and C. Chase, 'Background of Colombia Decisions', *Intersex Soceity of North America* [http://www.isna.org/node/21].

II. De-Pathologisation

A Comparative Study of Homosexuals and Heterosexuals with Respect to Quality of Life, Substance Abuse and Suicidality[1]

DR. BHARATH REDDY

History of medical research on homosexuality

Homosexuality has been defined as relating to, or characterised by a tendency to direct sexual desire toward individuals of one's own sex according to the Merriam Webster's Medical Dictionary and likewise heterosexuality has been defined as relating to, or characterised by a tendency to direct sexual desire toward individuals of the opposite sex.

Even within medicine and psychiatry homosexuality was not universally viewed as pathology. Richard von Kraft-Ebbing described it as a degenerate sickness in his *Psychopathia Sexualis*,[2] but Sigmund Freud and Havelock Ellis both adopted more accepting stances. Early in the twentieth century, Ellis (1901) argued that homosexuality was inborn and therefore not immoral, that it was not a disease,[3] and that many homosexuals made outstanding contributions to society (Robinson, 1976).[4]

Sigmund Freud's basic theory of human sexuality was different from that of Ellis. He felt that all human beings were innately bisexual and that they become heterosexual or homosexual as a result of their experiences with parents and others (Freud, 1905). Freud agreed with Ellis that a homosexual orientation should not be viewed as a form of pathology.

Later psychoanalysts did not follow this view and Sandor Rado (1940) rejected Freud's assumption of inherent bisexuality, arguing instead that heterosexuality is inborn and that homosexuality is a phobic response to members of the other sex. Other analysts later argued that homosexuality resulted from pathological family relationships during the Oedipal period (around 4–5 years of age) and claimed that they observed these patterns in their homosexual patients (Bieber et al., 1962). Charles Socarides (1968) speculated that the aetiology of homosexuality was pre-oedipal and, therefore, even more pathological than had been supposed by earlier analysts.[5]

Zoologist and taxonomist Alfred C. Kinsey[6] in his groundbreaking empirical studies of sexual behaviour among American adults revealed that a significant number of his research participants reported having engaged in homosexual behaviour to the point of orgasm after age 16.[7] Furthermore, Kinsey and his colleagues reported that 10 per cent of the males in their sample and 2–6 per cent of the females (depending on marital status) had been more or less exclusively homosexual in their behaviour for at least three years between the ages of 16 and 55. His work revealed that many more American adults than previously suspected had engaged in homosexual behaviour or had experienced same-sex fantasies. This finding cast a doubt on the widespread assumption that homosexuality was practised only by a small number of social misfits.

Other social science researchers also argued against the prevailing negative view of homosexuality. In a review of published scientific studies and archival data, Ford and Beach (1951) found that homosexual behaviour was widespread among various non-human species and in a large number of human societies. They reported that homosexual behaviour of some sort was considered normal and socially acceptable for at least some individuals in 64 per cent of the 76 societies in their sample; in the remaining societies, adult homosexual activity was reported to be totally absent, rare, or carried on only in secrecy.[8] As with Kinsey, whether this proportion applies to all human societies, cannot be known because a non-probability sample was used. However, the findings of Ford and Beach demonstrate that homosexual behaviour occurs in many societies and is not always condemned. Although dispassionate scientific research on whether homosexuality should be viewed as an illness was largely absent from the fields of psychiatry, psychology, and medicine during the first half of the twentieth century, some researchers remained unconvinced that all homosexual individuals were mentally ill or socially misfit. Berube (1990) reported the results of previously unpublished studies conducted by military physicians and researchers during World War II. These studies challenged the equation of homosexuality with psychopathology, as well as the stereotype that homosexual recruits could not be good soldiers

Today, a large body of published empirical research clearly refutes the notion that homosexuality per se is indicative of or correlated with psychopathology. One of the first and most famous published studies in this area was conducted by psychologist Evelyn Hooker.

Hooker's (1957) study was innovative in several important respects.[9] First, rather than simply accepting the predominant view of homosexuality as pathological, she posed the question of whether homosexuals and heterosexuals differed in their psychological adjustment. Second, rather than studying psychiatric patients, she recruited a sample of homosexual men who were functioning normally in society. Third, she employed a procedure that asked experts to rate the adjustment of men without prior knowledge of their sexual orientation. This method addressed an important source of bias that had vitiated so many previous studies of homosexuality

Hooker administered three projective tests (the Rorschach, Thematic Apperception Test [TAT], and Make-A-Picture-Story [MAPS] Test)[10] to 30 homosexual males and 30 heterosexual males recruited through community organisations. The two groups were matched for age, IQ, and education. None of the men were in therapy at the time of the study. Unaware of each subject's sexual orientation, two independent Rorschach experts[11] evaluated the men's overall adjustment using a five-point scale. They classified two-thirds of the heterosexuals and two-thirds of the homosexuals in the three highest categories of adjustment. When asked to identify which Rorschach protocols were obtained from homosexuals, the experts could not distinguish respondents' sexual orientation at a level better than chance. A third expert used the TAT and MAPS protocols to evaluate the psychological adjustment of the men. As with the Rorschach responses, the adjustment ratings of the homosexuals and heterosexuals did not differ significantly.

Hooker concluded from her data that homosexuality as a clinical entity does not exist and that homosexuality is not inherently associated with psychopathology. Hooker's findings have since been replicated by many other investigators using a variety of research methods. Freedman (1971), for example, used Hooker's basic design to study lesbian and heterosexual women. Instead of projective tests, he administered objectively scored personality tests to the women. His conclusions were similar to those of Hooker.

Although some investigations published since Hooker's study have claimed to support the view of homosexuality as pathological, they have been methodologically weak. Many used only clinical or incarcerated samples, for example, from which generalisations to the population at large are not possible. Others failed to safeguard the data collection procedures from possible biases by the investigators. For example, a man's psychological functioning would be evaluated by his own psychoanalyst, who was simultaneously treating him for his homosexuality.

Some studies found differences between homosexual and heterosexual respondents and then assumed that those differences indicated pathology in the homosexuals. For example, heterosexual and homosexual respondents might report different kinds of childhood experiences or family relationships. It would then be assumed that the patterns reported by the homosexuals indicated pathology even though there were no differences in psychological functioning between the two groups.

In a review of published studies comparing homosexual and heterosexual samples on psychological tests, Gonsiorek (1982) found that, although some differences have been observed in test results between homosexuals and heterosexuals, both groups consistently score within the normal range. Gonsiorek concluded, 'Homosexuality in and of itself is unrelated to psychological disturbance or maladjustment. Homosexuals as a group are not more psychologically disturbed on account of their homosexuality'.[12]

Confronted with overwhelming empirical evidence and changing cultural views of homosexuality, psychiatrists and psychologists radically altered their views, beginning in the 1970s.

Removal from the DSM

The Diagnostic and Statistical Manual of Mental Disorders (DSM) is the most widely used diagnostic reference book utilised by mental health professionals in the United States and other countries including India.[13] It is a manual by which all diagnostic codes are derived for diagnosis and treatment; every single physician (an estimated 850,000) in the United States and even India refers to this book in order to code for a diagnosis.

Prior to the 1970s, homosexuality had been treated as a mental disorder under 'section 302. Sexual Deviations' in the DSM-II. Section 302 said, in part:

> This category is for individuals whose sexual interests are directed primarily toward objects other than people of the opposite sex, toward sexual acts...performed under bizarre circumstances.... Even though many find their practices distasteful, they remain unable to substitute normal sexual behaviour for them.

Homosexuality was listed as the first sexual deviation under 302.

In 1973, the weight of empirical data, coupled by changing social norms and the development of a politically active gay community in the United States led the Board of Directors of the American Psychiatric Association to remove homosexuality from the DSM. Their decision was supported in 1974 by a vote of the membership of the APA. Once that diagnostic code for homosexuality was removed, physicians, including psychiatrists, stopped diagnosing homosexuality as a mental disorder.

Subsequently, a new diagnostic category, ego-dystonic homosexuality, was created for the DSM's third edition in 1980. Ego-dystonic homosexuality was indicated by: (1) a persistent lack of heterosexual arousal, which the patient experienced as interfering with initiation or maintenance of wanted heterosexual relationships, and (2) persistent distress from a sustained pattern of unwanted homosexual arousal.

The new diagnostic category, however, was criticised professionally on numerous grounds. Many saw this as a political compromise to appease those psychiatrists (mainly psychoanalysts) who still considered homosexuality as pathology. Others questioned the appropriateness of having a separate diagnosis that described the content of an individual's dysphoria. They argued that the psychological problems related to ego-dystonic homosexuality could be treated as well by other general diagnostic categories and that the existence of the diagnostic category perpetuated anti-gay stigma.

Moreover, widespread prejudice against homosexuality in the United States meant that 'almost all people who are homosexual first go through a phase in which their homosexuality is ego-dystonic,' according to the American Psychiatric Association.

In 1986, the diagnostic category was removed entirely from the DSM. The only vestige of ego-dystonic homosexuality in the revised DSM-III occurred under 'Sexual Disorders Not Otherwise Specified', which included persistent and marked distress about one's sexual orientation (American Psychiatric Association, 1987).[14]

The APA promptly endorsed the psychiatrists' actions and has since worked intensively to eradicate the stigma historically associated with a homosexual orientation (APA, 1975; 1987). Although some psychologists and psychiatrists may personally hold negative attitudes toward homosexuality, empirical evidence and professional norms do not support any linkage of sexual orientation with psychopathology.

The APA voted in 1987 to 'urge its members not to use the "302.0 Homosexuality" diagnosis in the current ICD-9-CM or the "302.00 Ego-dystonic homosexuality" diagnosis in the current DSM-III or future editions of either document' (APA, 1987). They took this action because the American Psychiatric Association had dropped homosexuality from the DSM-IIIR. The most recent version is the 'Text Revision' of the DSM-IV, also known as the DSM-IV-TR, published in 2000, which also does not include homosexuality.

The Indian context

In India the medical establishment—The Medical Council of India, Indian Medical Association and Indian Psychiatric Association—has adopted the WHO system of classification of mental and behavioural disorders known as ICD-10 (1992). It distinguishes between 'ego-syntonic' and 'ego-dystonic' homosexuality and categorises ego-dystonic homosexuality, bisexuality and heterosexuality as psychiatric disorders.

The existence of this category has meant that in India many psychiatrists and psychologists still regard homosexuality as a psychopathological condition. Underlying this conception is the notion that heterosexuality is the normal, natural outcome of sexual development against which other forms of sexual expression are to be compared. Furthermore, the idea of a 'cure' is implied when homosexuality is viewed as pathological. Of course, not all psychiatrists and psychologists subscribe to this perspective, but a sufficient number have greatly affected the way people conceive homosexuality as well as the direction research has taken with respect to studying homosexuality.

Although psychoanalytic studies of homosexuality have had considerable influence in psychiatry and in the larger culture, they have not been subjected to rigorous empirical testing. Instead, they have been based on analysts' clinical observations of patients already known by them to be homosexual.

Two major problems result from this procedure. First, the analyst's theoretical orientations, expectations, and personal attitudes are likely to bias her or his observations. This is why scientists take great pains in their studies to ensure that the researchers who actually collect the data do not have expectations about how a particular research participant will respond. An example is the 'double blind' procedure used in many experiments. Such procedures have not been used in clinical psychoanalytic studies of homosexuality.

A second problem with psychoanalytic studies is that they have only examined homosexuals who were already under psychiatric care; in other words, homosexuals who were seeking treatment or therapy. Patients, however, are probably not representative of well-adjusted individuals in the general population. Just as it would be inappropriate to draw conclusions about all heterosexuals based only on data from heterosexual psychiatric patients, we cannot generalise from observations of homosexual patients to the entire population of gay men and lesbians.

This study is an effort at remedying the paucity of empirical material in India on homosexuality, which does not use as its subjects those already under psychiatric care. This study thus attempts to compare the homosexual and heterosexual population with respect to quality of life, substance abuse and suicidal tendencies using standardised questionnaires and protocols. The results of this study will enable us to answer the question whether homosexuality is a pathological condition as compared to heterosexuality in the Indian context, based upon an empirical, non-biased sampling.

Methodology

Between 26 June 2006 and 13 August 2006, male homosexuals from a gay group, Good As You, were invited to participate in the study to assess their mental status and risk of drug abuse and suicidal tendencies. All the subjects were requested to be present on a single day when data was collected from them. Heterosexuals matched for age and educational statuses were later selected and administered the same questionnaires as the homosexual subject sample. The objectives of the study were explained to both the heterosexuals and homosexuals; anonymity and informed consent of all the participants was assured and ensured. All the subjects were self-identified as homosexuals and heterosexuals based on a question posed to them according to the definitions of the same mentioned earlier.

Measures

Part One of the questionnaire pertains to the Quality of life (QOL) of the participants as a part of assessing their mental health status. This was done by administering the standardised questionnaire published by the World Health Organisation—WHOQOL (BREF).

Part Two consisted of questions to assess the risk of drug abuse among the participants using the DAST scale (Drug Abuse Screening Test). The items were modelled in Part Two from a validated survey. It was a 28-item questionnaire with Yes or No type of questions. The score was equal to the number of questions that were answered YES.

A score of five or less points indicated a Normal Score. A score of six or more points indicated a Drug Problem.

Part three of the questionnaire consisted of two parts:

- Assessing the presence of a Major Depressive Episode among the participants.
- Assessing the risk of Suicidal Tendencies among the participants.

This was assessed using another validated questionnaire—OCD Clinic Structured interview, Mini Plus 5.0.0, Jan 2002, Yale Family/Genetic study—A Self Reported Questionnaire. Responses were evaluated and the points and risk stratification was done as per the validated study.

These three validated items were chosen because they were relevant to our objective and have been used previously in studies done earlier in the US and elsewhere.

Data analysis

Data were coded for each question, and basic descriptive statistics were computed using SPSS. Survey responses were summarised and described by the following groups: age, QOL, risk of drug abuse, and risk of substance abuse as obtained from the three-part questionnaire.

Results

Subjects

The study consisted of 30 participants each from the homosexual and heterosexual communities. These participants volunteered to take part in the study and gave an informed consent for the same. Table 1 shows the age distribution of the study subjects.

Part One was intended to assess the QOL of both homosexuals and heterosexuals and report if there were any significant differences between the two. The assessment of the same was done using the WHOQOL (BREF) which consisted of 26 questions through four domains pertaining to different areas of an individual's life. The scores of the subjects were assessed with respect to the range and

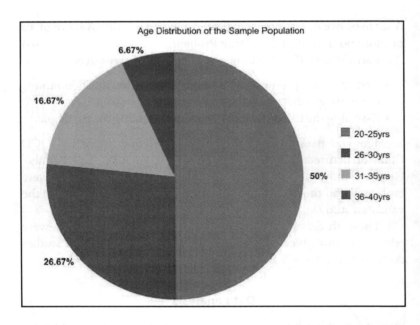

Age range	Homosexuals (%)	Heterosexuals (%)
20–25	15 (50)	15 (50)
26–30	8 (26.67)	8 (26.67)
31–35	5 (16.67)	5 (16.67)
36–40	2 (6.67)	2 (6.67)

median values. A chi square test was performed on the values to statistically quantify and evaluate any significant difference in the two study populations.

Domain 1 which assessed **physical health** showed that the scores obtained for the two groups were **not significantly different.**

Domain 2 which assessed **psychological health** showed that the results obtained for the two groups were **not significantly different.**

Domain 3 which assessed **social relationships** showed that scores obtained for the two groups were **not significantly different.**

Domain 4 which assessed **environmental relationships** showed that scores obtained for the two groups were **not significantly different.**

Part Two of the questionnaire was directed at assessing the risk of drug abuse amongst the participants. This was assessed using a validated questionnaire, Drug Abuse Screening Test (DAST) and the responses reported were analysed. The respondents were stratified according to the scale given. The same is shown in Table 3.

TABLE 3
Risk of drug abuse in the study population

	Homosexual males, n=30 (%)					Heterosexual males, n=30 (%)				
	20–25 (%)	26–30 (%)	31–35 (%)	36–40 (%)	Over all (%)	20–25 (%)	26–30 (%)	31–35 (%)	36–40 (%)	Over all (%)
Normal (<5)	12 (80)	4 (50)	5 (100)	1 (50)	22 (73.33)	11 (73.33)	7 (87.5)	5 (100)	2 (100)	25 (83.33)
Drug Problem (>=5)	3 (20)	4 (50)	0	1 (50)	8 (26.67)	4 (26.67)	1 (12.5)	0	0	5 (16.67)

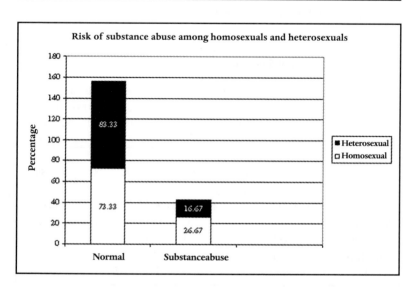

Risk of substance abuse among homosexuals and heterosexuals

The table and relevant graph show that:

- Eight (26.67%) of the respondents from the homosexual group turned out to have a drug problem and five (16.67 %) from the heterosexual population were found to have a drug problem.
- Chi-square test was done to see if the values obtained revealed any significant difference with respect to risk of drug abuse and with a value of 0.88 there was **no significant difference** in the risk of substance abuse among the two study groups.

Part Three of the questionnaire was directed at assessing the risk of suicidal tendencies and Major Depressive Episodes among homosexuals and heterosexuals. This was assessed and responses evaluated and the points and risk stratification was done as per the validated study are shown in Tables 4 and 5.

It can be seen from the Table 4 and a relevant graph that:

- Eight (26.67%) of the homosexual population were at a moderate-high risk of suicide and the same number were at a moderate-high risk of suicide in the heterosexual population.
- A total of 11(36.67%) of the homosexual population were at a low risk of suicide whereas seven (23.33%) of the heterosexual population belong to this category.

TABLE 4
Risk of Suicidality in the study population

	Homosexual males, n=30 (%)					Heterosexual males, n=30 (%)				
	20–25 (%)	26–30 (%)	31–35 (%)	36–40 (%)	Over all (%)	20–25 (%)	26–30 (%)	31–35 (%)	36–40 (%)	Over all (%)
No Risk (0)	5 (33.33)	3 (37.5)	2 (40)	1 (50)	11 (36.67)	4 (26.67)	5 (62.5)	4 (80)	2 (100)	15 (50)
Low Risk (1–5)	8 (53.33)	3 (37.5)	0	0	11 (36.67)	4 (26.67)	2 (25)	1 (20)	0	7 (23.33)
Moderate Risk (6-9)	0	1 (12.5)	1 (20)	1 (50)	3 (10)	4 (26.67)	0	0	0	4 (13.33)
High Risk (>= 10)	2 (13.33)	1 (12.5)	2 (20)	0	5 (16.67)	3 (20)	1 (12.5)	0	0	4 (13.33)

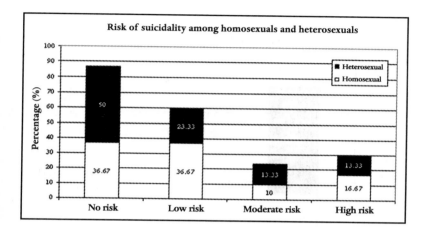

Risk of suicidality among homosexuals and heterosexuals

- About 11 (36.67%) of the homosexual population were not at a risk of suicide whereas 15 (50%) of the heterosexual population belong to this category.

  Chi-square test was done to see if the values obtained revealed any significant difference with respect to risk of suicidal tendencies and a value of 1.75 was obtained. Therefore there was **no significant difference** in the risk of suicidal tendencies among the two study groups.

Table 5 and a relevant graph show that:

TABLE 5
Risk of occurrence of a major depressive episode among the study population

	Homosexual males, n=30 (%)					Heterosexual males, n=30 (%)				
	20–25 (%)	26–30 (%)	31–35 (%)	36–40 (%)	Over all (%)	20–25 (%)	26–30 (%)	31–35 (%)	36–40 (%)	Over all (%)
Normal (<5)	14 (93.33)	7 (87.50)	4 (80.00)	2 (100.00)	27 (90.00)	14 (93.33)	7 (87.50)	5 (100.00)	2 (100.0)	28 (93.33)
Major Depressive episode (>=5)	1 (6.67)	1 (12.50)	1 (20.00)	0 (0.00)	3 (10.00)	1 (6.67)	1 (12.50)	0 (0.00)	0 (0.00)	2 (6.67)

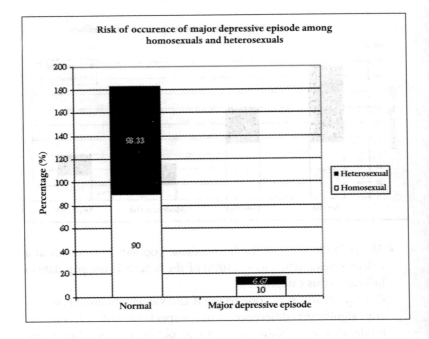

Risk of occurence of major depressive episode among homosexuals and heterosexuals

- Three (10.00%) of the respondents from the homosexual group turned out to have a Major Depressive Episode and two (6.67 %) from the heterosexual population were found to have a Major Depressive Episode
- Following application of chi square test a value of 0.21 was obtained and hence there was *no significant difference* in the occurrence of Major Depressive Episodes among the two study groups.

Conclusion

Following the study, we could conclude that there was no significant difference between homosexuals and heterosexuals with respect to quality of life, substance abuse or suicidal tendencies. Myths regarding the high incidence of the same in the homosexual population should be dispelled by wholesome education and awareness. Considering the sample size of this study was as small as 60 subjects, it should be noted that the results cannot be taken as representative of the entire population at large. As far as the risk was concerned among the subjects who weren't already under the influence of addictive substances it could be concluded that both communities were at equal risk of falling prey to substance abuse. It can be noticed from the study that substance abuse was per se higher in the age groups of 20–25 years irrespective of sexual orientation. However among the older age groups after 30 years, it can be seen that there was a higher incidence of substance abuse among homosexual men. This could probably be attributed to the social problems faced by this section of the subjects.

The same trend is noticed while studying the risk of suicidality and the risk of Major Depressive Episodes also. Here again the risk was highest among the 20–25 years age group and likewise a slightly higher prevalence of suicidality could be seen among heterosexual youngsters and homosexual men above 30 years. Whether this can also be attributed to the societal pressures faced by this group needs to be further researched.

It can however, be concluded from this study that substance abuse, suicidality, and major depressive episodes did exist in equal proportions in both the study subject groups. What existed was more of an intra group variation in the prevalence due to other confounding factors and was surely not attributable to the sexual orientation of the subjects.

Acknowledgements

Dr. Padmini Prasad, Bangalore (For her guidance); Dr. Sachin Srinivasan, Bangalore (For co-authoring the paper); Vinay Chandran, Executive Director, SWABHAVA Trust, Bangalore; Arvind Narrain, Alternative Law Forum, Bangalore; and all the subjects who participated.

Notes

[1] This paper was presented at the National Conference of Sexology and Reproductive Health in October 2006, conducted in Ambedkar Bhavan, Bangalore and received the second place among research paper presentations.

[2] R.V. Ebing and B. King, *Psychopathia Sexualis, With Especial Reference to Contrary Sexual Instinct : A Clinical-Forensic Study*(Burbank, California: Bloat, 1999)

3   H. Ellis and J.A. Symonds, *Sexual Inversion* (Washington D.C: Wilson and Macmillan,1897).

4   'Homosexuality and psychology', *Wikipedia* [http://en.wikipedia.org/wiki/Homosexuality_and_psychology].

5   For a detailed history, see Lewes, 1988; for brief summaries, see Bayer, 1987; Silverstein, 1991

6   M. Yudell, 'Kinsey's other report', *Natural History*, Vol. 108, No. 6 (July 1999).

7   A.C. Kinsey, W.B. Pomeroy and C.E. Martin, *Sexual Behavior in the Human Male*, (Philadelphia: W. B. Saunders,1948); A.C. Kinsey, W.B. Pomeroy, C.E. Martin and P.H. Gebhard, *Sexual Behavior in the Human Female*, (Philadelphia: W. B. Saunders, 1953).

8   C.S. Ford et al., 'Patterns of sexual behaviour', in Ronald Bayer (ed.), *Homosexuality and American Psychiatry* (New York: Basic Books,1981).

9   E. Hooker, 'Homosexuality: Summary of studies', in E.M. Duvall and S.M. Duvall (eds), *Sex Ways in Fact and Faith* (New York: Associated Press, 1961).

10 'Thematic apperception test', *Encyclopedia of Mental Disorders* [http://www.minddisorders.com/Py-Z/Thematic-Apperception-Test.html]

11 See 'The Rorschach test', *S.P.A.R.C* [http://www.deltabravo.net/custody/rorschach.php] and W. Mons, *Principles and Practice of the Rorschach Personality Test* (2nd edition) (London: Faber and Faber, 1950), p. 31.

12 J.C. Gonsiorek, 'Results of psychological testing on homosexual populations', in W. Paul, J.D. Weinrich, et al. (eds), *Homosexuality: Social, Psychological and Biological Issues* (Beverly Hills, California: Sage, 1982), p. 74; see also reviews by Gonsiorek, 1991; Hart, Roback, Tittler, Weitz, Walston & McKee, 1978; Riess, 1980

13 'Diagnostic and statistical manual of mental disorders', Fourth Edition (DSM-IV)', *AllPsych Online* [http://allpsych.com/disorders/dsm.html].

14 See M. Wilson, 'DSM-III and the transformation of American psychiatry: A history', in *American Journal of Psychiatry*, Vol. 150, No. 3, (Mar. 1993) pp. 399–410; and R.L. Spitzer, 'The diagnostic status of homosexuality in DSM-III: A reformulation of the issues', *American Journal of Psychiatry*, Vol. 138 (1981), pp. 210–15.

Further References

Anderson, S.C. and D.C. Henderson, 'Working with lesbian alcoholics', *Social Work*, Vol. 30, No. 6 (1985), pp. 518–25.

Bayer R. and R.L. Spitzer, 'Edited correspondence on the status of homosexuality in DSM–III', *Journal of the History of the Behavioral Sciences*, Vol. 18 (1982), pp. 32–52.

Davis, R.M., M. Genel and J.P. Howe, 'Health care needs of gay men and lesbians in the United States', *JAMA: Journal of the American Medical Association*, Vol. 275, No. 17 (1996), pp. 1354–59.

Flavin, D.K., J.E. Franklin and R.J.Frances, 'The acquired immune deficiency syndrome (AIDS) and suicidal behavior in alcohol-dependent homosexual men', *American Journal of Psychiatry*, Vol. 143, No. 11 (1986), pp. 1440–42.

Ghindia, D.J. and L.A. Kola, 'Co-factors affecting substance abuse among homosexual men: An investigation within a midwestern community', *Drug & Alcohol Dependence*, Vol. 41, No. 3 (1996), pp. 167–77.

Rubinstein, G., 'The decision to remove homosexuality from the DSM: Twenty years later', *American Journal of Psychotherapy* Vol. 49 (1995), pp. 416–27.

Stall, R. and J. Wiley, 'A comparison of alcohol and drug use patterns of homosexual and heterosexual men: The San Francisco men's health study', *Drug & Alcohol Dependence*, Vol. 22, No.s 1&2 (1988), pp. 63–73.

Stoller, R.J., J. Marmor, I. Bieber, 'A symposium: Should homosexuality be in the APA nomenclature?', *American Journal of Psychiatry*, Vol. 130 (1973), pp. 1207–16.

Winters, K.C., G. Remafedi and B.Y. Chan, 'Assessing drug abuse among aay-bisexual young men', *Psychology of Addictive Behaviors*, Vol. 10, No. 4 (1996), pp. 228–36.

World Health Organisation, 'The mental and behavioral disorders: International classification of diseases' (10th edition), *WHO* [http://www3.who.int/icd/vol1html2003/fr-icd.htm].

Validity of 'Ego-dystonicity' in Homosexuality

An Indian perspective[1]

DR. AMI SEBASTIAN MAROKY, DR. SHEKHAR SESHADRI, DR. SURESH BADA MATH, DR. C.R. CHANDRASHEKAR, DR. ASWIN RATHEESH, DR. BIJU VISWANATH

Introduction

Homosexuality is generally considered a taboo subject in Indian society and is rarely discussed in open forums. Texts such as the *Kamasutra* indicate that there was relative openness to homosexuality in ancient India. This changed with the coming of the British and the drafting of the Indian Penal Code by Lord Macaulay, which made homosexuality a criminal offence. Homosexuality remained a crime from 1860 to 2009 when the Delhi High Court decriminalised it. While there has been a change in the legal field, there are still huge strides to be made in the field of mental health. In this connection, this essay will focus on the categorisation of homosexuality as a disorder within mental health categories and the lack of scientific rationale for such categorisation.

Homosexuality as a mental disorder

Homosexuality had been officially classified as a mental disorder with the publication of the American Psychiatric Association's (APA) first edition of the Diagnostic and Statistical Manual of Mental Disorders (DSM-I) in 1952. There it was designated as a 'sociopathic personality disturbance'. In 1968, the second edition of the DSM (DSM-II) still listed homosexuality as a sexual deviation. Following the 1969 Stonewall riots in New York City, gay activists began to confront the

APA about its position on homosexuality. In 1973, the APA officially accepted a normal variant model and removed homosexuality from the DSM and replaced it by sexual orientation disturbance in DSM-II. It was further revised to ego-dystonic homosexuality in DSM III, and finally removed from DSM-III-R in 1987. However, the ICD 10 which is followed in India still retains the diagnostic category of ego-dystonic sexual orientation. The use of this diagnostic category is debated, due to the vagueness of the term 'ego-dystonic' which is defined only as 'the person wishes it were different'.

The key debate is between understanding ego-dystonicity as a phenomenon of intra-psychic stress or as a term to describe various external stressors faced by homosexual individuals. What factors play a role in the manifestation of ego-dystonicity? Are these determined purely by intra-psychic factors or by the adverse responses from society—lack of support systems, role models and companionship? Does lack of religious support and lack of legal recognition impact ego-dystonicity? There has generally been a dearth of research in this regard, especially in the Indian population. This essay hopes to get to the root of the validity of the diagnosis of ego-dystonic sexual orientation, which is still widely used in the treatment of homosexual clients in India.

Ego-dystonicity and its relation to stigma and discrimination

The study of ego-dystonicity with respect to societal stigma and minority stress has gained momentum in recent years. Much of the research done on ego-dystonicity has revealed that discomfort and stress arise as homosexual desire is viewed using heterosexuality as the frame of reference. In a heteronormative society, there is no choice for one's sexual identity other than heterosexuality (known as heterosexism).

Heterosexism devalues and stigmatises non-heterosexual behaviour, relationships, and community while *homophobia* is the 'irrational fear, hatred, and intolerance of gay, lesbian, and bisexual persons'. The internalisation of these societal attitudes is conceptualised as 'internalised homophobia'. Traditionally, internalised homophobia was equated with ego-dystonicity and there have been many studies in the West addressing this concept. But internal homophobia overlaps with other concepts (such as self esteem) and there is a lack of clear differentiation between internal homophobia and intra-psychic or behavioural issues (depression). Another trend in this area is the conceptualisation of internalised homophobia as a component of minority stress. This concept views homosexuals as a minority group subject to chronic stress related to their stigmatisation. Long before they realise their own homosexuality, homosexual people internalise societal anti-homosexual attitudes resulting in internalised homophobia.

When heterosexism is the norm, homosexuality is stigmatised. A study conducted in young (15 to 21 yrs) homosexual individuals reported that as a result of their sexual orientation 80 per cent of them had experienced verbal insults, 44 per cent had been threatened with violence, 33 per cent had objects thrown at them, 31 per cent reported being chased or followed, and 17 per cent reported being physically assaulted. D'Augelli summarised data from a number of surveys and research studies demonstrating that lesbian, gay, and bisexual youth were more likely to be victimised within their families and in the community.

Sexual minorities: Stigma and discrimination

A national survey conducted by the advocacy organisation Gay, Lesbian, and Straight Education Network reported that those surveyed experienced verbal harassment (61%), sexual harassment (47%), physical harassment (28%), and physical assault (14%). A majority of them (90%) sometimes or frequently heard homophobic remarks at their schools, with many (37%) reporting hearing these remarks from faculty or school staff.

Lesbian, Gay and Bisexual (LGB) people were twice as likely as heterosexual people to have experienced a life-event related to prejudice, such as being fired from a job. Gay and bisexual male workers were found to earn from 11 per cent to 27 per cent less than heterosexual male workers with the same experience, education, occupation, marital status, and region of residence. Approximately 1/5th of the women and 1/4th of the men experienced victimisation (including sexual assault, physical assault, robbery, and property crime) related to their sexual orientation.

The Indian situation also shows significant discrimination against sexual minorities. The South India AIDS Action Programme (SIAAP) report of 2007 studied sexual minorities in Tamil Nadu, Maharashtra, and Karnataka regions. In 2006, the percentage of MSM (men who have sex with men) who reported the following was: forced sex (46%); physical abuse (44%); verbal abuse (56%); blackmail for money (31%); and threat to life (24%). In health care settings, they have had to face verbal abuse, sub-optimal care and even denial of medical services.

The People's Union for Civil Liberties–Karnataka (PUCL-K) report was published in 2001 based on the testimonies of sexual minorities in the Bangalore area. It revealed that oppression by the police was one of the major concerns, the modes of which included extortion, illegal detention, both physical and sexual abuse, and blackmail.

Figure-1 Depicts that ego-dystonicity is dependent on various environmental variables rather than a single intra-psychic phenomenon. If societal acceptance is present then this pseudo-classification of ego-dystonicity disappears.

Figure 1

ORIENTATION	Heterosexual	Homosexual	Bisexual
SOCIETAL ACCEPTANCE		Stigma, Discrimination, Ostracisation, Violence from society and family members, Religious Sanction, Illegal status, un-conducive political milieu and poor support	
SELF ACCEPTANCE	PRESENT	DENIAL / FLUCTUATING INSIGHT / ACCEPTANCE Depending upon the environment	

Most sexual minorities dare not be open about their sexuality at their work space for the fear of ostracism or even termination of employment. Routine social interaction (talking about husbands and wives, women and men one finds attractive, etc.) becomes difficult for sexual minorities. Most of the time when people of the same sex live together and the couple are found to be lesbian or gay, discrimination ensues. Instances have been noted wherein the couples have been asked to move out of their homes after coming out in the open.

Most of the major world religions also propagate the stigma against homosexual individuals. Heterosexism and homophobia appear to be woven into the liturgical quilt of all traditional world religions. In recent times, certain progressive religious groups have proposed a non-discriminatory stance although these remain marginal opinions. A high degree of religiosity has been found to be positively correlated with increased dissonance and negative mental health effects for LGB individuals.

Most cultural institutions have constructed an environment wherein homosexuality is considered a perversion, or they refuse to talk about homosexuality. The resultant lack of space for positive and affirming constructions of homosexuality, appear to have created mindsets in which homosexual individuals feel lonely, desperate, and even suicidal.

Ways of coping with stress based on sexual orientation

In its most general form, stress is concerned with external events or conditions that are taxing to individuals and exceed their capacity to endure, therefore having the potential to induce mental or somatic illness. Many individual studies as well as meta-analyses have found that sexual minorities are at a higher risk to develop mental health problems due to the discrimination that they face. Compared to their heterosexual counterparts, gay men and lesbians suffer from more mental health problems including substance use disorders, affective disorders, and suicide.

Gay adolescents generally begin to question their sexual orientation between the ages of 12 and 14, with the awareness that their behaviour and feelings are considered non-heteronormative, and realise that society views it negatively. Many may begin to fear humiliation and physical violence on discovering their sexual orientation or feel ashamed due to their own internalised values and judge their attractions as deviant or unhealthy.

Subsequently, they employ coping strategies as varied as social withdrawal, substance abuse, striving for achievements in other areas like academics and extracurricular activities or by going out of their way to pretend to be heterosexual. Some date opposite-sex partners to avoid gossip and with the hope of 'curing' themselves of their desires. Others marry at a young age and have children early; still others remain celibate, while some turn to religion with the hope of eradicating sexual thoughts.

Despite the many hurdles, a young person may face the fears they may have about self-disclosure and go through the process of telling others about their identities; a process referred to as 'coming out'. The responses these youth receive to their self-disclosure are varied. Studies show that one of every three gay youth experiences verbal abuse from family members, one of four receives physical abuse from peers at school, and one of three has attempted suicide. Approximately 40 per cent lose at least one friend after disclosure. The challenges of 'coming out' in an atmosphere that includes verbal and physical harassment, threats, and victimisation has an impact on self-esteem, academic performance, risk-taking behaviour, and overall mental health.

The sense of community which acts as a buffer for other minorities in the development of self-identity is often unavailable to homosexual individuals; the most important of them being parents and family. Supportive and understanding, or at least tolerant parents are a great resource for children. Studies have found that family support significantly reduces the stress and symptoms of victimisation experienced by gay teenagers (99) and improved self-image and self-esteem. However, research estimates that 25 per cent of gay youth are thrown out of their homes by their parents after coming out and 42 per cent experienced deterioration in their relationship with them.

Gay male adolescents are less likely to come out to their parents if they grow up in a family with more traditional values, particularly families where religion is important and there is an emphasis on marriage and having children. A study of 111 families with gay and lesbian children found that following the disclosure of their gay or lesbian identity, 5 per cent of the children received 'Hostile Recognition' and non-acceptance, with total estrangement; 36 per cent experienced a 'Resentful, Denial' relationship, in which little contact occurred between parents and their child; 48 per cent had a 'Loving, Denial' relationship, with a positive relationship between parent and child, but the parents being unable to discuss their child's sexual orientation; and only 11 per cent experienced 'Loving Open' relationships with their parents, with the parents being accepting and also positive in sharing information about their child's sexual orientation with others. Existing research appears to reinforce the belief of these individuals of a high probability of non-acceptance by family following disclosure.

In India, even though data is limited, it is indicated that following disclosure homosexual males may face outright rejection and eviction from home, verbal abuse, physical violence, and denial of their property rights. Parents may even force their homosexual child to undergo psychiatric treatment in an attempt to convert them to heterosexuality or to push them into marriage.

Studies regarding other support systems are few. Most homosexuals initially believe that there is nobody else like them. There is a paucity of healthy role models for gay youth. Isolation corrodes self-esteem and leads individuals to accept the prevailing homophobia, which induces the belief that all gay persons are promiscuous and incapable of forming loving relationships. The prevailing culture focuses on the sexual component of sexual minorities' orientation, excluding feelings of attraction, love, and companionship, with the result that 'gay adolescents tend to view themselves as the problem, and fear the ostracism to which revealing their 'difference' might lead'.

To ward off potential stigma, discrimination, and violence, homosexuals tend to maintain constant vigilance. They may conceal their sexual orientation in an effort to either protect themselves from real harm (e.g., being attacked, getting fired from a job) or out of shame and guilt. Studies have shown that homosexuals engage in identity disclosure and concealment strategies in order to reduce discrimination on the one hand and attempt to improve self-integrity on the other. These strategies range from 'passing', which involves trying to be seen as heterosexual; 'covering', which involves censoring clues about one's self so that homosexual identity is concealed; being 'implicitly out', which involves telling the truth without using explicit language that discloses one's sexual identity; and being 'explicitly out'. Factors related to the hiding and concealment of identities requiring vigilance and expectations of rejection, are specific stressors that homosexual men and women experience. Concealment also prevents them from identifying and affiliating with others who are gay, thereby depriving them of the positive impact of affiliation.

These strategies also have an adverse impact on the quality of their sexual lives. Gay youth were also noted to engage in heterosexual dating and sexual activity; the reasons frequently cited for the same being denial of same-sex feelings, curiosity, a desire to conform to societal norms, and an attempt to reduce personal stress around coming-out issues. Their description of opposite-sex sexual experiences was that it was 'sex without feelings'—that it felt unnatural and lacked emotional intensity. Studies have also shown that this affects the development of a healthy sexual identity. Youth who were in romantic relationships had high self-esteem, while those denied opportunities for peer dating and socialisation turned to anonymous sexual encounters with adults, placing them at increased risk for sexually transmitted diseases, including HIV.

It is clear that the lives of homosexual individuals are filled with stress that results from attempts to suppress their sexuality and appear 'normal' or is the result of being open and facing the consequent difficulties. Silverstein opines that it is the social factors (e.g., rejecting families, hostile peer interactions, and disapproving society) that are to be held responsible for people seeking sexual orientation change. He and other authors indicate that what were historically viewed as 'ego-dystonic' responses to homosexuality are really internalised reactions to a hostile society.

Methodology

The conceptual basis of the research question in this study is the methodological distinction between inter-personal and intra-psychic factors. An internal factor is intrinsic to being human whereas an external factor produces change because of external reasons. By making this distinction between experiences such as stigma, discrimination or rejection as inter-personal/external factors and traits as enduring phenomenon not linked to external factors, the study aims to zone in on the cause of ego-dystonicity. Thus if something called ego-dystonicity existed intrinsically, then any measure of this intrinsic or internal factor should correlate with a degree of ego-dystonicity. Whereas, if external factors (non-acceptance by family and friends, stigma and discrimination, negative life-events related to homosexual orientation, lack of awareness regarding non-heterosexual lifestyles, etc.) correlate with ego-dystonicity then ego-dystonicity would not be an intrinsic phenomeneon but rather a result of external factors.

The study used six tools (viz., Visual Analogue Scale, Reactions to Homosexuality Scale, Perceived Acceptance Scale, Modified China MSM Stigma Scale, Trait Version of Positive and Negative Affective Scales, and Awareness Scale) to understand whether ego-dystonicity depends on external or internal factors, in addition to socio-demographic details and a written narrative of experiences. These tools were administered to a sample consists of 51 male homosexuals who were 18 years and above. They were identified through NGOs and support groups. The data was collected through online distribution of questionnaires

Out of the six tools used, two tried to assess the participant's degree of comfort with his own sexuality. Three were used to evaluate possible external influences such as acceptance by friends and family, stigma including legal and religious disadvantages and awareness regarding homosexual lives, availability of support systems and acceptance of these lives. One was used to assess intra-psychic factors of positive and negative traits. In the written narrative, they were asked to write down their feelings regarding their sexual orientation, how these changed over time and to link these feelings to their life experiences. The results were tabulated and analysed.

Findings: External and internal factors associated with ego-dystonicity

The socio-demographic details of the participants showed a mean age of 30.8 years and high income (mean of Rs 96,694 per month). The educational status was also high with an average of 17.5 years of education. Majority of the respondents (86%) were residing in India and in an urban setting (94.1%). Nearly three-fourth (74.5%) of them were single, about one-fifth (19.6%) were in a relationship and a minority (5.9%) were married. Nearly half (47.1%) were staying alone, while a quarter (27.5%) stayed with parents and the rest with partners, friends, spouses and others.

The study found that the great majority of participants were very comfortable with their sexual orientation and this negatively correlated to their own sense of internalised homophobia. This meant that the more comfortable the participants were with their own sexuality, the less they suffered from internalised homophobia. The study also found a significant positive correlation between the participant's self-perception of comfort with their sexual orientation and the perceived acceptance from friends and family. There is also a positive correlation between the participant's self-perception of comfort and awareness of legal discrimination, awareness of homosexual lives as well as support systems for homosexuals.

The results in this study support the hypothesis that external/inter-personal factors are more strongly associated with the degree of dystonicity than internal/intra-psychic factors. The study also finds that one's self-comfort is directly linked to having a supportive network of friends. This network of friends plays an important role in mitigating the discomfort related to one's homosexuality. The narratives also support this conclusion. Many of the respondents recall that when they first realised that they were homosexual, they experienced discomfort related to it. This discomfort gradually reduced as they got to know more about homosexuality, met other gay people, made friends, and availed support from NGOs, counsellors or support groups. Some have also cited the support they received from family members after coming out as a significant factor in reducing their discomfort.

Many of the negative self-perceptions of participants which emerged in the narratives also indicate the role that external factors play. Some refer to public or family disapproval:

> I've felt ashamed/scared because I would be made fun of for being effeminate and/or not 'man' enough.
>
> My family knows I am gay and they have been disapproving for the last 3.5 years.

Others state fears of criminalisation,

> I still continue to feel that I was and would probably forever be socially disadvantaged and at risk (due to Section 377).

And some others mentioned the role of religious restrictions,

> I was brought up in a religious environment and being a homosexual was the biggest challenge of my spiritual life. For many years I prayed that God should rid me of my homosexuality, as it is wrong.

The role of social pressures/obligations like marriage were also mentioned,

> I started realising that being gay would be quite a big problem. I would face issues like finding a boyfriend, maintaining the relationship, conveying my choices to my parents, marriage pressure, etc.

These narratives allow us to conclude that many respondents feel and have explicitly stated external factors as being causative of their feelings of discomfort regarding their homosexuality. This warrants further exploration and rethinking regarding the whole construct of ego-dystonicity.

Implications of current study findings

The study's findings that the external factors are more strongly associated with degree of discomfort regarding one's homosexuality, has potential implications in the social, legal and medical realms.

Social implications
The findings of this study make it clear that external factors determine the degree of dystonicity a person experiences. The persistence of overt as well as subtle discrimination in societal and family settings, maintains the discomfort levels, thereby resulting in impaired integration of the homosexual individual into the social milieu. The lack of support produces further discomfort and social withdrawal, which proceeds into a vicious cycle. To break the cycle it is important for all social sectors to take gay-affirmatives stances.

Legal implications
The current study findings indicate that homosexuality is not abnormal and therefore there is a need to establish a framework of laws that will provide homosexuals with constitutional and civil rights on par with those enjoyed by heterosexuals.

Medical implications
The implications of the current study findings in the medical field run primarily along two lines. First, with respect to the intervention strategies employed for individuals who seek help, and second, with respect to the diagnosis itself (de-medicalisation).

There is an ongoing debate as to whether help should be offered to homosexual individuals wishing to change their orientation, considering that it continues to be a significant stress factor for many, and continues to be a diagnostic entity as 'ego- dystonic sexual orientation' in the ICD-10, while on the other hand, former studies have opined that homosexuality is not a disorder and does not require interventions to change it.

In the light of the current study findings, a better alternative would be to focus and promote gay affirmative psychotherapeutic models which focus on mental health issues faced by homosexual individuals and help the individual to develop a better self-identity, and cope with the external factors mediating discomfort. Since homosexual orientation is not a disorder, interventions through support groups could reduce discomfort in the client.

With respect to diagnostic issues, from the current study findings, it appears that ego-dystonicity is not a construct in itself and is dependent on various external factors. Hence the diagnostic entity of 'ego-dystonic sexual orientation' in ICD-10 needs to be re-evaluated. It could then be considered that the distress experienced by homosexual individuals may be coded along with stress-related disorders as is done in case of distress in other minority populations, without reference to the cause of stress, thus completely removing homosexuality in all forms from the classificatory system.

Such a move would also serve to avoid ambiguity regarding how to diagnose ego-dystonicity and also help in promoting gay affirmative therapeutic interventions as discussed above. It would also de-medicalise homosexuality, and thereby assist in bringing about the social and legal reforms mentioned earlier.

Conclusions

The current study findings are supportive of the importance of external factors such as severity of adverse responses faced, availability of buffers, support systems, role models and companionship, religious affiliations and institutions and legal restrictions in the manifestation and degree of discomfort with one's homosexuality (ego-dystonicity). Ego-dystonicity not being a primary construct in itself should not act as a determining factor for medical diagnosis or intervention. Hence, there is an urgent need to de-medicalise and de-stigmatise homosexuality.

Notes

[1] This article is based upon the thesis submitted to the National Institute of Mental Health And Neurosciences-NIMHANS (Deemed University) in part fulfilment of the requirements for the degree of Doctor of Medicine in Psychiatry.

Further References

Anderson D. Family and peer relations of gay adolescents. Adolesc Psychiatry. 1987; 14: 162–78.

Badgett L. The wage effects of sexual orientation discrimination. Industrial and Labor Relations Review. 1995; 48: 726–39.

Cochran S, Mays, VM. Lifetime prevalence of suicide symptoms and affective disorders among men reporting same-sex sexual partners: Results from NHANES III. American Journal of Public Health. 2000; 90: 573–8.

Cochran SD. Emerging issues in research on lesbians' and gay men's mental health: does sexual orientation really matter? Am Psychol. 2001 Nov; 56(11): 931–47.

Coleman E. The development of male prostitution activity among gay and bisexual adolescents. J. Homosex. 1989; 17(1–2): 131–49.

Cramer DW, Roach AJ. Coming out to mom and dad: a study of gay males and their relationships with their parents. J. Homosex. 1988; 15(3–4): 79–91.

D'Augelli AR, Grossman AH, Hershberger SL, O'Connell TS. Aspects of mental health among older lesbian, gay, and bisexual adults. Aging Ment Health. 2001 May; 5(2): 149–58.

D'Augelli AR, Hershberger SL, Pilkington NW. Lesbian, gay, and bisexual youth and their families: disclosure of sexual orientation and its consequences. Am J Orthopsychiatry. 1998 Jul; 68(3): 361–71; discussion 72–5.

D'Augelli AR, Hershberger SL. Lesbian, gay, and bisexual youth in community settings: personal challenges and mental health problems. Am J Community Psychol. 1993 Aug; 21(4): 421–48.

Dohrenwend BP. The role of adversity and stress in psychopathology: some evidence and its implications for theory and research. J Health Soc Behav. 2000 Mar; 41(1): 1–19.

Fisher B, Akman J. Normal Development in Sexual Minority Youth. In: Jones B, Hill M, editors. Mental Health Issues in Lesbian, Gay, Bisexual, and Transgender Communities Washington, DC: American Psychiatric Publishing; 2002.

Fontaine JH, Hammond NL. Counseling issues with gay and lesbian adolescents. Adolescence. 1996 Winter; 31(124): 817–30.

Gilman SE, Cochran SD, Mays VM, Hughes M, Ostrow D, Kessler RC. Risk of psychiatric disorders among individuals reporting same-sex sexual partners in the National Comorbidity Survey. Am J Public Health. 2001 Jun; 91(6): 933–9.

GLSEN, National School Climate Survey, 1999. http://www.glsen.org/binary-data/GLSEN_ATTACHMENTS/file/2-1.pdf. Accessed in June 2010.

Godfried M, Godfried A. The importance of parental support in the lives of gay, lesbian, and bisexual individuals. JCLP/In Session: Psychotherapy in Practice. 2001; 57: 681–93.

Griffin P. From hiding out to coming out: empowering lesbian and gay educators. J Homosex. 1992; 22(3–4): 167–96.

Herek GM, Gillis JR, Cogan JC. Psychological sequelae of hate-crime victimization among lesbian, gay, and bisexual adults. J Consult Clin Psychol. 1999 Dec; 67(6): 945–51.

Herek GM. Heterosexism and homophobia. In: Cabaj RP, Stein TS, editors. Textbook of Homosexuality and Mental Health. Washington, DC: American Psychiatric Press; 1996. pp. 101–13.

Johnson CC, Johnson KA. High-risk behavior among gay adolescents: implications for treatment and support. Adolescence. 2000 Winter; 35(140): 619–37.

King M, Semlyen J, Tai SS, Killaspy H, Osborn D, Popelyuk D, et al. A systematic review of mental disorder, suicide, and deliberate self harm in lesbian, gay and bisexual people. BMC Psychiatry. 2008; 8.

Meyer IH. Minority stress and mental health in gay men. J Health Soc Behav. 1995 Mar; 36(1): 38–56.

Meyer IH. Prejudice, Social Stress, and Mental Health in Lesbian, Gay, and Bisexual Populations: Conceptual Issues and Research Evidence. Psychological Bulletin. 2003; 129(5): 674–97.

Muller A. Parents Matter: Parents' Relationships With Lesbian Daughters and Gay Sons. Tallahassee, FL: Naiad Press; 1987.

Newman BS, Muzzonigro PG. The effects of traditional family values on the coming out process of gay male adolescents. Adolescence. 1993 Spring; 28(109): 213–26.

Parish TS, McCluskey JJ. The relationship between parenting styles and young adults' self-concepts and evaluations of parents. Adolescence. 1992 Winter; 27(108): 915–8.

Pilkington NW, D'Augelli AR. Victimization of lesbian, gay, and bisexual youth in community settings. Journal of Community Psychology. 1995; 23: 33–55.

PUCL-K. Human Rights Violations Against Sexuality Minorities in India. A Fact-finding Report about Bangalore. A Report of PUCL-Karnataka, February.: People's Union for Civil Liberties-Karnataka; 2001

Reis B, Saewyc E. Eighty-three thousand youth: selected findings of eight population based studies. Safe Schools Coalition of Washington; 1999.

Ross MW, Rosser BR. Measurement and correlates of internalized homophobia: a factor analytic study. J Clin Psychol. 1996 Jan; 52(1): 15–21.

Sadock BJS, Virginia A. . Kaplan and Saddock's Comprehensive Textbook of Psychiatry. 8 ed.: Lippincott Williams & Wilkins 2005.

Savin-Williams R. Gay and Lesbian Youth: Expressions of Identity. Washington, DC: Hemisphere; 1990.

Savin-Williams RC. Coming out to parents and self-esteem among gay and lesbian youths. J Homosex. 1989; 18(1–2): 1–35.

Shildo. Internalized Homophobia: Conceptual and Empirical issues in Measurement. Greene,B. and Herek, G. ed.: Sage, Thousand Oaks; 1996.

SIAAP. A report on the situational assessment conducted by the consortium supported by HIVOS. European Commission 2007.

Silverstein C. Homosexuality and the ethics of behavioral intervention. J Homosex. 1977 Spring; 2(3): 205–11.

Troiden RR, Goode E. Variables related to the acquisition of a gay identity. J Homosex. 1980 Summer; 5(4): 383–92.

Weinberg MS, Williams CJ. Male homosexuals: Their problems and adaptations. New York: Oxford University Press; 1974.

Williamson IR. Internalized homophobia and health issues affecting lesbians and gay men. Health Educ Res. 2000 Feb; 15(1): 97–107.

Why Should Therapists be Sensitive to Sexual and Gender Nonconformity?

RADHIKA CHANDIRAMANI

Psychotherapy is informed by prevailing socio-cultural thinking; as are therapists. The way sexuality issues are looked at by most people does influence, to some extent, the way therapists view and respond to these issues. Conversely, the opinion and reactions of therapists and other so-called experts shape larger public opinion. One has only to look at the way the media cites a particular line of thinking to be the 'expert's opinion' to realise how strong a role this thinking plays in moulding public attitudes.

Sexuality issues themselves are not discussed easily in a professional setting by most people, even when they need to be. There is much hesitation to talk about extra-marital affairs, casual sexual relationships, or any sexual activities that are commonly regarded as being somewhat risqué. The fear is of revealing to the therapist that one has passions different from others' or that one engages in activities that might reflect a lack of 'decency'. What if the therapist is shocked, surprised, disapproving...? Talking about one's sexual life to anyone but one's closest friends, if at all that, is in any case difficult. Talking about it in a 'clinical' situation is all the more so.

In a society where heterosexuality is the dominant sexual style/ choice/preference, so much so that it is frequently unquestioned and goes unchallenged unlike homosexuality, many questions arise. If most therapists are heterosexual and/or assume heterosexuality in their clients, what does this mean for homosexual clients? And what does it mean for therapists who themselves experience and express a different sexuality? And, in a strongly patriarchal society, where rigid gender roles are defined and expected to be conformed to, what happens if one is transgender or expresses any manifestations of gender variance that is not in keeping with how 'men' and 'women' are expected to dress, walk, behave, live, work, love, etc?

Let's begin with sexual non-conformity before we go to gender non-conformity. Until a little more than three decades ago, homosexuality was seen as pathological and only after intense campaigning was it removed as an illness category from the Diagnostic and Statistical Manual (DSM). Unfortunately, there are still many mental health professionals who subscribe to the view that homosexuality is 'unhealthy'. Worse and more insidiously damaging are those who are informed enough to know that it is not a diagnostic category and will state this view but probe a little below the surface and you will find that they believe homosexuality to be a sign of psychological immaturity, a result of trauma, and hold other such unexamined beliefs that are based on the assumption of pathology. Faced with heterosexual clients, these therapists would never question their clients' heterosexuality or arrive at formulations to explain heterosexuality.

The term 'ego-dystonic homosexuality' actually does a great disservice because it allows mental health professionals to hide behind their own discomfort with non-heteronormative expression and behaviour. What is actually causing the 'dystonia' if not the larger societal views that mirror the mental health professionals' own discomfort with the fact that there exist people who love, are attracted to and want to fuck people of the same gender as themselves? And, then these very same professionals claim that it is ok and rightful to 'treat' ego-dystonic homosexuality with aversion therapy because their clients are 'not happy' being homosexual. This begs the question why their clients are 'dystonic' or 'not happy'. Could it be because of the lack of acceptance, the discrimination, the awkwardness their clients feel due to a societal non-recognisance, and even further because the therapists themselves perpetuate this non-acceptance rather than challenge it? Is the 'dystonia' in the client or in the way society reacts to them?

The scenario is not totally bleak however; there is a growing number of therapists who are becoming more open to looking at gay[1] issues with an unprejudiced eye. There are those who are perceptive enough to know that 'partner' does not always refer to one of the opposite gender. The usage of gender-neutral pronouns may deliberately camouflage the gender of the person being spoken about. Clients often resort to these techniques to put out feelers and check the sensitivity and openness of the therapist. Of course there are naive therapists who unwittingly stumble by unthinkingly using a gender-specific pronoun in response. This then makes it even more difficult for the client to come out to the therapist as it reinforces the client's apprehensions that the therapist 'will not understand'.

Just what is it that the therapist 'will not understand'? Many lesbian and gay friends have discussed with me their hesitation to enter therapy as they have heard (often sensationalised) stories of therapists trying to 'cure' homosexuality, using in their arsenal techniques such as aversion and electro-convulsive therapy. Even when potential clients see that not all therapists operate from a pre-1970s stance, there is always the desire to find a gay or lesbian therapist. 'Can you suggest a gay-friendly or at least a non-homophobic therapist?' A valid request, I think, given that in daily life there is so much denial and erosion of lesbian and gay experience.

You might turn around and say that heterosexual clients do not worry unduly about the sexuality and sensibilities of their therapists (though they may worry about how the therapist would react to knowing about certain sexual activities they have engaged in). They do not need to as yet. In a predominantly gay sub-culture they might need to, however, if they feel that their heterosexuality is being falsely held by a gay therapist to be the source or cause of whatever it is that ails them.

It is true that a sexuality and lifestyle different from that of the majority does at times place a person in situations of greater stress and also prevents them from using stress relieving mechanisms that others may use. A lesbian who is not out to her friends cannot speak of ups and downs in a current relationship with the same openness, facility and spontaneity as her heterosexual friends do. To conclude from this, that it is therefore the 'different' sexuality that is the 'cause' of the stress is not only fallacious, but also demeaning to the client. Similarly, lesbian, gay and bisexual clients at times are hesitant to discuss or even mention in therapy sexual difficulties with their partners, in case the therapist is uncomfortable or uncomprehending. There is a desire to protect the therapist from discomfort and oneself from the therapist's possibly voyeuristic curiosity.

However, there are times when clients themselves attribute far more to their (homo)sexuality than the situation warrants. When this is pointed out by the therapist, the client reacts by saying that the therapist is not gay-sensitive and does not understand. Therapists must adequately comprehend the issues if they are to avoid both insensitivity as well as a bending over backwards to appear sensitive and gay-sympathetic.

There is no way of predicting your next client's sexuality, though of course you might wish to refer a client to someone who knows more about or is better equipped to handle gay, lesbian and bisexual issues. That does not take away from the fact that therapists must be more aware of these issues because the first contact with a mental health professional influences clients' attitudes about and expectations from therapy.

Therapists who themselves are not heterosexual are often not 'out' in the larger community. This may be because they do not wish to be defined professionally by their sexual choices. It may also be difficult for them to be open about their sexuality in a society that tends to view non-heterosexual expression, be it homosexual or bisexual, as an aberration and might then, because of a lack of awareness, denigrate their professional standing on account of their sexuality. Many activists feel that gay, lesbian and bisexual therapists have a responsibility to be open about their sexuality so that they are not reacting defensively or operating from positions of shame or being apologetic about their own sexuality. Yes, therapists' own openness about their sexuality would help dispel myths about non-heterosexual expression being psychologically unhealthy. Be that as it may, I do not buy that line wholly: the fact that a psychologist does something does not make that action right or wrong or healthy or unhealthy. It is true that individuals in positions of power can and do bring about change in attitudes by the actions they take in their personal and professional capacities; however, these are personal struggles that each one undertakes and ultimately resolves for oneself.

In the Indian context, there are many misconceptions about sexuality issues and problems. However, the lesbian and gay community is becoming more visible and stronger and engaging with the mental health community to bring about substantive change. Bisexuality is still under wraps and is a contentious issue even among lesbian and gay people.

A newer and far less understood area for mental health professionals to engage with is that of the issues of transgender people, i.e., people who believe that their experienced gender identity is at variance with their anatomy. In the past few years I have been called upon to certify several individuals as being eligible for sex reassignment surgery (SRS), and I have been happy to do so. But what makes me uncomfortable as I engage with this issue in my activist circles, is that in my certification of transgender people as requiring and being eligible candidates for SRS, I have to say that they suffer from Gender Identity Disorder (GID). However, I do not think that they themselves suffer from any disorder save that which society imposes on them by rigid definitions of who is female and who is male.

I have seen such a diversity of gender expression, not just in India, but in other countries as well, that I am now loathe to use the term GID. But, on the other hand, if I do not use it, many transgender people will not get the 'certificate' or official letter that will allow them to proceed with the SRS. In the United States as in other countries that offer a national health service scheme, this category allows people to access treatment with insurance cover. But, at the same time, it also gives them a mental disorder diagnosis that is unwarranted. This is a larger political battle. It has at its base, patriarchal society's unwillingness to accept more than two rigid ways of being—as 'woman' or as 'man'. It perpetuates stereotypical, sexist ideas. Just because gender-variant people have had to hide themselves for so long, not because of an internally or individually produced 'gender dysphoria' but because of societal un-acceptance, does not mean that they do not exist or that they do not have a right to exist.

Lack of visibility does not mean lack of existence. Existence transcends mere physical existence. It implies social and psychological existence as well. The rejoinder to why therapists must be sensitive to sexual and gender variance can well be a one-line question—why must therapists be sensitive at all?[2]

Notes

[1] I am using 'gay' as an umbrella term, to cover both men and women who experience same-sex sexual attraction and am in no way intending it to privilege one set of experiences over another. It is being used for ease of reading, merely as a 'short form'.

[2] An earlier version of this essay was published in the Indian Psychologist, June 1997 issue as 'Why "Gay-Sensitive" Therapists?' Thanks to The Psychological Foundations for allowing me to expand the paper for this publication.

A Psychologist's Journey to the Understanding of Sexual Orientation

DR. LATA HEMCHAND

> The popular view of sexual instinct is beautifully reflected in the poetic fable which tells how the original human beings were cut up into two halves—man and woman—and how these are always striving to unite again in love. It comes as a great surprise therefore to learn that there are men whose sexual object is man and not a woman.[1]

Human sexuality is a complex phenomenon which is influenced in different ways by biological, social, economic, cultural and even political factors. Freud's work in the nineteenth century was a pioneering effort at understanding sexuality in the framework of psychopathology. It introduced some invaluable insights and for the first time, psychologists were made aware of the importance of 'eros' in determining human behaviour.

However, his theory of sexuality was rooted in understanding pathological behaviour. It dwelt on why and how sexual instincts contribute to neurotic behaviour. Though he did formulate a theory of normal psychosexual development from infancy to adulthood, the emphasis was mainly on how sexual desire was invested in different 'objects' of satisfaction at different stages and how if there is a lack of satisfaction due to poor object relations, the individual's psyche remains cathected at this stage and leads to neurotic behaviour. Freud and his colleagues were concerned with the nature and meaning of erotic experience as this mediated through body zones and organs and with sexual object choice. Freud's conceptions of gender identity or how we cognise the sense of masculine and feminine are tied to our genital constitution. Consequently, the creation of sexual orientation develops for the boy or the girl due to the presence or absence of the penis.

Freud viewed homosexuality as the phenomenon of 'inversion', which according to him was one of the sexual aberrations found in man. He postulates that when the sexual object of choice is from the same sex, it can be described as having 'contrary sexual feelings or as inverts'. He attributed it to certain circumstances in the individual's life such as the opposite sexed parent being less nurturing than the same sexed parent or seduction and mutual masturbation experience with an individual of same sex during adolescence.[2]

The Behaviourists, who emerged largely as a reaction against the theory of unconscious and intra-psychic conflicts proposed by Freud, had their roots in the principles of learning theory. Their postulates were mainly based on experiments done in the laboratory performed both on animals and humans. These findings were then extrapolated as techniques of behaviour therapy to treat maladaptive behaviour. Their view of sexuality was that it was a biological drive like any other such as hunger and thirst. They did not view sex beyond the scope of being a motivational force. Behaviour therapy viewed sexual behaviour in terms of sexual deviation, sexual dysfunction and its treatment.

According to them what was sexually 'maladaptive' needed to be treated so that 'sexually healthy' behaviour could be strengthened. The concept of 'sexual health' and what was 'maladaptive' were determined mainly by statistical norms. Heterosexuality was considered 'normal' because a majority of people were 'believed to be hetero'. Any deviation from this norm was considered pathological and hence required treatment.

There were two areas of sexuality where behaviour therapy techniques were widely used and research reported convincing benefits. One was the area of sexual dysfunction within the heterosexual population and the other was in the area of sexual deviation or perversion. Symptoms such as erectile dysfunction, premature or delayed ejaculation among males, and lack of sexual desire, *vaginismus* among women were all considered to fall under the category of sexual dysfunctions. Whereas homosexuality, paedophilia, transvestism, etc., were classified as sexual deviations and were treated using aversion therapy methods. The founding principles of this therapy were based on the classical conditioning paradigm of extinction postulated by Pavlov. This was later modified and used as a behaviour therapy technique by several researchers.[3] The basic rationale in aversion therapy is that if a response is followed by pain or punishment, the frequency of that response reduces. In other words, the association between a stimulus and a response gets weakened when followed by a painful consequence.

Feldman and MacCulloch[4] showed slides of partially or fully nude men and women to male homosexuals. When the male image was on the screen the subject had to signal quickly for another slide or he got a painful shock. A picture of a woman was shown. After 15 sessions of 20-minute durations, the study was terminated. The authors reported that homosexual behaviour was eliminated in about half the cases with a follow-up of 14 months.

However, later behaviour therapists[5] considered that there are psychological as well as ethical and humanistic objections to using a painful electric shock as a part of a treatment. Much of the professional and public distaste for behaviour therapy stems from the fact that it is viewed as being simplistic, mechanistic and lacking in human values.

The preceding discussion makes it clear that psychologists with their emphasis on sexual deviation and its treatment have a tunnel vision with regard to sexuality. Richmond,[6] a well-known practising psychologist states:

> As strange as it may seem, psychology really cannot say much about human sexuality. It is true that psychology can be used to treat sexual dysfunction and psychologists know that coerced sex, such as child abuse or rape leaves lasting emotional scars on the victims. But psychology cannot offer much advice to consenting adults as to what sexual activities are appropriate or inappropriate.[7]

Against the backdrop of this prevailing climate within psychology, the author would like to focus on three landmark events which changed the views on sexuality in the field of psychology namely:

- Sexuality Continuum—proposed by Kinsey report.
- The APA Declaration of 1973.
- The advent of the AIDS epidemic.

Kinsey's Report and Scale was developed by Alfred Kinsey in the early 1950s. Research done on existing sexual practices showed that there is a broad spectrum of sexual orientations and not just the binary division of heterosexual and homosexual. Instead of looking at the sexual orientation as an either-or condition Kinsey developed a seven-point continuum based on the degree of sexual responsiveness people have to the members of the same and other sex. The seven-point continuum is as follows:

0 – Exclusively heterosexual
1 – Predominantly heterosexual, incidentally homosexual
2 – Predominantly heterosexual, but more than incidentally homosexual
3 – Equally heterosexual and homosexual
4 – Predominantly homosexual, but more than incidentally heterosexual
5 – Predominantly homosexual, incidentally heterosexual
6 – Exclusively homosexual

Over a follow-up period of three years the study indicated that 6 per cent of men were rated under the seventh continuum point (category 6—exclusively homosexual). 10 per cent were in category 4 and 5. 37 per cent of all men experienced orgasm in a sexual activity with another man. 60 per cent of men had some type of homosexual relationship before they were 16 years of age. These findings were supported by Masters and Johnson's study in later years.[8]

In spite of these findings the practising psychologists of that era continued to treat homosexuality as a condition to be treated. Homosexuality was believed to be a mental illness due to the unfortunate fact that mental health professionals furnished society with incorrect information. Most studies about homosexuals only involved gay men and lesbians who were in therapy, which painted an untrue portrait of gay men and lesbians.

Mental health professionals took three decades to wake up to the facts of the Kinsey's report. In 1973 the APA passed a resolution removing homosexuality from the classification of mental illness. This was supported by the American Psychologist's Association in 1975. Both Associations urged the public to help dispel the stigma and discrimination towards homosexuals. However, to dispute a theory learned early in life is sometimes impossible.

The AIDS epidemic exacerbated anti-gay attitudes. Anti-gay hate crimes became a serious national problem in the US.[9] The current research data concludes on five important myths with regard to sexual orientation:

1. Gays and lesbians are no more likely than heterosexual men or women to suffer from mental illness.
2. The origins of homosexual orientation are not due to experiences of seduction with individuals of same sex.
3. Homosexuals are not any more likely to be involved in child molestation than heterosexuals.
4. Homosexual parents are quite capable of rearing developmentally secure children who are psychologically well adjusted.
5. Organisational efficiency and morale does not get lowered if there are more number of gays and lesbians.

Social scientists have contemplated for many years that sexual preference is a learned behaviour that is developed during early childhood. Some scientists believe that sexual orientation develops at an early age through interaction of biological, psychological and social factors. Other mental health professionals share the view that homosexuality may be genetically determined. Since sexual orientation develops in adolescence without any previous sexual experience, it is believed that it is not chosen. For the same reason contemprary psychologists do not consider sexual orientation to be a conscious choice that can be voluntarily changed.

In India the voice of the gay community was heard by the public through articles written by gay men that got published in the media during the early 1990s. It coincided with the advent of the AIDS epidemic and the efforts made for its mitigation and prevention.

Mental health professionals in India have relied more on the ICD-10 (1992) system of classification, which distinguishes between ego-syntonic and ego-dystonic homosexuality. In ego-dystonic homosexuality the sexual preference is not in doubt but the individual wishes it were different and seeks treatment. In such a case according to WHO, treatment is warranted. In ego-syntonic homosexuality, by contrast, the individual is comfortable with his/her sexual preference and treatment is not warranted. The mental health community in India latched on to this concept of ego-dystonic homosexuality and has been dealing with the same by using aversion therapy as treatment.[10]

Being a practising psychologist in India for more than two decades I have gone through similar phases in working with gays, lesbians and bisexuals. However, in the latter half of the 1990s, when I became closely associated with this community in connection with my work in the field of HIV/AIDS, my attitude went through a sea change. I could clearly see that I would be rendering a great injustice to the LGBT people if I continued to believe in the ICD-10 classification and suggest treatment to change their very identity! Since then my approach has been to help them accept their identity despite the homophobia that exists around them. My efforts have been to educate them on the world-wide understanding of these issues and to affirm their identity as legitimate and to mitigate their guilt and shame.

In this connection, the following are two such cases which were referred to me by psychiatrists for aversion therapy.

19-year-old M, an engineering student felt attracted to his lecturer who encouraged M to confide in him. Once he knew the truth, the lecturer's attitude became totally negative. A bright student in the past, M became totally disinterested in studies; he began to have disturbed sleep and suicidal thoughts. His family consisted of parents and an elder brother who was studying abroad. M was emotionally close to his parents and told them the truth. M's father brought him for therapy, to be converted into a *normal heterosexual* individual. Efforts were made over several sessions to educate the client about the current understanding about homosexuality and to affirm his identity as well as to reduce his sense of guilt and shame which was making him suicidal. The therapist also made an attempt to liaison with a gay organisation involved in helping such individuals. Several sessions of family counselling were held to help the family accept the situation. By the end of these sessions M was less depressed but his family continued to feel that he could never have a happy life with a gay identity. M was forced to look at himself as a 'freak' and had to accept what the family wanted.

A bright Computer Science student from Hassan, 22-year-old A came from an upper middle-class, conservative Marwari family. Since his adolescence he felt that his bone structure and distribution of hair on the body was more feminine than masculine. He felt that other males got attracted to him due to this. He came out about it to his parents. They tried physical punishment to change his ideas and finally when they were unsuccessful referred him to a psychiatrist. The psychiatrist diagnosed him as psychotic and put him on treatment. His sexual orientation was never addressed and he continued to be awkward and hesitant in social interaction.

It is clearly evident from the above cases that people in general continue to be homophobic, which prevents gay people from 'coming out' in the open, free from shame and guilt. It's time that we woke up to these realities and realised that the only way we can psychologically support these clients is by respecting their identity and creating a space for them in our society.

The crusade against stigma and discrimination towards sexual minorities has to be supported by mental health professionals more aggressively than before. We need to make sure that LGBT people lead a happy and productive life just as much as straight men and women.

In the Indian scenario, we are at least a decade behind the west. The sporadic efforts made by a handful of professionals are inadequate even to change the attitudes within the community.

As a therapist I urge my fellow professionals to stop 'converting' and 'normalising' and become more humane and sensitive.

Views of the Karnataka Association of Clinical Psychologists (KACP) on LGBT issues

Members of the KACP are of the opinion that when they come across clients with LGBT issues, the main focus should be on alleviating psychological distress, both at the individual and family level, if there is a felt need for the same. With regard to 'treatment' of homosexual behaviour or 'converting' homosexuals to heterosexual individuals, no coercion is used and the members opined that it was no longer ethical or relevant to use aversion therapy to treat them (in keeping with the current classification of diseases—DSM IV and ICD 10). On the other hand networking with gay groups who are dealing with these issues in a professional manner would be an option that they would like to give clients.

Notes

1. S. Freud, *Three Contributions to the Theory of Sex: Nervous and Mental Disease* (Washington DC: Publication Co., 1920).
2. S. Freud, *An Outline of Psychoanalysis: The Standard Edition of the Complete Psychological Works of Sigmund Freud*, Vol. XXIII (London: The Hogarth Press and the Institute of Psychoanalysis, 1964).
3. M. Kushner and J. Sandler, 'Aversion therapy and the concept of punishment', *Behaviour Research and Therapy*, Vol. IV (1966), pp. 179–86; D.L. Whaley and R.W. Malott, *Elementary Principles of Behaviour* (New York: Appleton Century Crofts, 1971).
4. M.P. Feldman and M.J. MacCulloch, 'The Application of Anticipatory Avoidance Learning to the Treatment of Homosexuality: I. Theory, technique and preliminary results', *Behaviour Research and Therapy*, Vol. III, p. 165–183.
5. A.A. Lazarus, *Behaviour Therapy and Beyond* (New York: McGraw Hill, 1971).
6. R.L. Richmond, 'The fourth pleasing idea', *American Psychologist*, Vol. 52 (1997), p. 1244.
7. *Ibid.*
8. A. Kinsey, W. Pomeroy, C. Martin and P. Gebhard, *Sexual Behavior in the Human Female* (Philadephia: W. B. Saunders Co., 1948).
9. G. M. Herek, 'Hate crimes against lesbians and gay men. Issues for research and policy.', 1989.
10. A. Narrain and V. Chandran, '"It's not my job to tell you it's okay to be gay"— Medicalisation of Homosexuality: A Queer Critique', A. Narrain and G. Bhan (eds), *Because I Have a Voice* (New Delhi: Yoda Press, 2005).

Transgender and Transsexual Issues

Clinical Dilemmas and Best-practice Guidelines in Mental Health Care

VIDYA SATHYANARAYANAN and POORNIMA BHOLA

> I was three or four when I realised that I had been born into the wrong body, and should really be a girl. I remember the moment well, and it is the earliest memory of my life.
>
> Jan Morris, *The Conundrum*

Born James Humphrey Morris, the celebrated travel writer chronicled a personal journey of transformation to Jan Morris after living as a man for 36 years. *The Conundrum* exemplifies the struggles and strengths of the transgender experience.

In recent years, public awareness of transgender issues has increased and many transgendered people have identified themselves openly. Rose Venkatesan became India's first transgender television show host. The 2011 Indian Census has taken a progressive step to include a third gender category—'others'—apart from male and female, so that the transgendered have a voice. Many support groups and non-governmental advocacy organisations are gaining visibility and momentum in India. However, public acceptance has not kept pace with growing awareness. Indian transgenders—hijras or aravanis— have long been part of the social fabric but are still vulnerable to discrimination and marginalisation.

Many transgendered people continue to remain invisible and vulnerable to mental health difficulties. Some of them access the available mental health services in our country, while many slip through the net. Mental health professionals need to be prepared to provide informed, comprehensive and inclusive care attuned to the needs of this clientele. In this chapter, we discuss what we have learnt (and unlearnt) through our training as clinical psychologists and through our interactions with transgender clients in our practice.

Labels and little boxes:
Reforms in psychiatric nosology and intervention

The major mental health diagnostic systems; the International Classification of Diseases (ICD–10) and the Diagnostic and Statistical Manual (DSM–IV) include categories related to transgender experiences. There is an ongoing debate about the terminology of Gender Identity Disorder in the DSM-IV and the potentially stigmatising definition as a medical condition. It has been argued that this categorisation promotes a dualistic and bipolar concept of gender. On a pragmatic level however, the diagnosis can help individuals to access insurance and other health-care benefits in some countries. In response to advocacy and calls for understanding that *'our identities are not disordered'*, revisions in the forthcoming fifth version of the DSM are being discussed.

Historically, mental health professionals attempted to 'change' the gender identity of transgendered individuals through reparative or conversion therapies. In India, Khanna, Desai & Channabasavanna[6] described a six-month behaviour therapy package with motor training, social skills training, fantasy training, aversion therapy, supportive psychotherapy, and occupational therapy with 'marked improvement in gender role and identity' with the person remaining 'symptom-free two years after termination'.

With the changes in awareness and understanding, these 'treatments' are no longer supported by the major mental health associations and informed ethical professionals. There is a shift to creating safe spaces where the transgendered individual's perspectives and experiences can be shared. The mental health professional needs to be aware of the inherent power imbalance in the interaction and attempt to forge a respectful collaborative relationship. Therapist openness and sensitivity is the key to understanding the clients' needs and reasons for seeking help. Inevitably for all therapists, their own gender identity, expression, and concepts about gender influence the therapeutic relationship and process. Biases about gender conformity and uncomfortable emotional reactions can emerge even for sensitive and competent therapists. Therapists must create spaces for self-introspection and awareness and increase knowledge and skills through professional training avenues as well as interactions with relevant community agencies.

Mental health professionals need a contemporary gender primer to be in tune with the multiple and sometimes overlapping terms like gender identity, gender dysphoria, transgender, transsexual and transvestite. For example, while *transgender* is an umbrella term referring to people whose gender identity or expression differs from their birth sex, *transsexual* denotes transgendered people who live or wish to live full-time as members of the gender opposite to their birth sex and *transvestite* refers to persons who regularly or occasionally cross-dress. More recently, terms like gender-variant or even gender-defiant have emerged. To add to this, the nomenclature varies in different countries, and across regions in our multi-cultural nation. The mental health professional must differentiate the accepted terminology from the derogatory monikers that are often used. An area of potential confusion for clinicians relates to sexual orientation. It is important for clinicians to acknowledge that transgender people could identify as heterosexual, homosexual, bisexual or even asexual.

An affirmative stance includes the use of transpositive language. Blanchard[7] suggested that phrases like 'comorbid psychopathology', 'gender identity disorders' and 'clinical management' be replaced with client-validating ones like 'multiple mental health issues', 'gender distress/discomfort', 'gender variance/diversity' and 'transgender care'. When an individual discloses transgender issues, the therapist should ask, 'What would you like me to call you?' It is important not to assume the use of a name or particular pronouns (he/she) and to ask the client about appropriate language at the beginning of the interaction. Terms used in the transgender community are varied and changing and some locally relevant terms might be unfamiliar to Indian mental health professionals who train with textbooks written in the West. The maxim that we have found most useful in our clinical practice is: 'Ask...then ask what it means'.

Trans-specific elements in mental health practice

Individuals with transgender concerns are increasingly becoming visible in mental health settings. Clinical psychologists are an integral part of the multi-disciplinary team of professionals involved in their care. Our experiences with transgender clients, as clinical psychologists working in a general hospital setting, have underscored the need for a sensitive and informed approach with individuals on this difficult journey.

Individuals with transgender concerns reach mental health clinics through various routes and with different needs and agendas. Referrals from other professionals, like endocrinologists or plastic surgeons, often arise in the context of hormonal or sex reassignment options. We must be aware that, although the client is transgender and may have gender-related concerns, the primary concern and reason for seeking mental health services may *not* be related to gender identity and/or gender dysphoria.

The primary challenge for the therapist is to understand the complex multiple layers of the client's difficulties. The initial contact provides a window of opportunity for the therapist to engage with the client, who might be ambivalent, anxious or even mistrustful. Each client is unique and the presentation of the transgender experience is heterogeneous.

Therapists need to have their antennae up for hidden gender issues and clients should be made to feel comfortable to disclose their uncertainties and concerns. Unrecognised gender problems are occasionally diagnosed when patients are seen with anxiety, depression, bipolar disorder, conduct disorder, substance abuse, dissociative identity disorders, borderline personality disorder, other sexual disorders, and intersexed conditions.

Presentations might sometimes masquerade as transgender issues and the clinician needs to use skill and time to distinguish these from other psychopathology. Conflict and confusion about sexual orientation, body dysmorphic disorder, malingering, and gender dysphoria occurring exclusively during psychotic episodes or dissociative states are some difficulties that might initially present like transgender issues. Bockting and Coleman also pointed out that gender dysphoria may be part of another presenting problem, such as psychological pain stemming from a history of abuse, depression, anxiety, or loneliness. Further discussion of hormonal or surgical options would not be appropriate for this group.

There is a growing trend of transgendered individuals directly accessing mental health professionals for assessments and certification in their journey towards hormonal treatments and sex reassignment surgery. The clinician needs to guard against tunnel vision and specifically look for additional psychological and medical problems that might occur either as sequelae of their difficulties or as independent disorders. These most commonly include anxiety disorders and depression. Additional areas to be assessed are substance abuse, personality disorders, eating disorders and a history of suicide attempts. Possible medical conditions that might require attention include the fallout of unsupervised hormone use, hepatitis and HIV.

While the focus is often on the transgendered individual, clinicians often need to expand the ambit to assess the involvement and needs of significant others. Cultural issues such as the salience of family relationships, the concept of family 'honour' and 'name' in the community and the role of marriage in India, are all important contextual factors. Individuals might be brought by family members who place clinicians in the role of advising 'counselling' or medication to change gender identity. Families might be in turmoil following disclosure and couples are often concerned about family and societal censure and the impact on children. In our experience, marital discord might be the presenting problem and sensitive interviewing might unearth the transgender issues. Both the complex individual and dyadic issues would require attention. In addition, transgender people might experience conflict, rejection, and separation from family members and view other significant others as family. The clinician should integrate this 'family of choice' into the assessment and intervention process if the client wishes.

Gender issues and mental health issues can often get intertwined in terms of aetiology, treatment and self-understanding. As clinicians navigate these complexities, what must be remembered is that mental health issues will not get resolved only by addressing gender issues, or by ignoring them.

Some of the varied client presentations and challenges will be illustrated though clinical vignettes. Client narratives are always the most powerful learning ground for clinicians at any stage of professional development.

> Prakash, 48 years old, married with two children, was referred to the clinical psychology consultant by the endocrinology department for psychological evaluation for sex-reassignment surgery. Prakash described the difficult process of coming to terms with this decision and said, 'The make-up artiste in Vegas helped me live as a woman for a weekend and that's when I decided to take the final step. See my photographs.... Please give me a letter'.

The client's agenda was very specific and the expectation from the clinician was clearly articulated. The therapeutic interaction was viewed as a time-limited pathway to the letter of recommendation for reassignment surgery. This circumscribed involvement can lead to a feeling of incompleteness for the therapist. Therapists should be cautioned that some clients might fabricate or exaggerate experiences or conversely conceal vulnerabilities, as they fear refusal of the recommendation letter for surgery.

> 27 year old Ashok was diagnosed with recurrent depressive disorder and two suicidal attempts by his psychiatrist. He was then referred to a clinical psychologist for 'social skills training' for his 'effeminate' gestures. Gentle probing revealed a history of cross-dressing from early childhood, almost exclusive play with girls and a few sexual encounters with male classmates in late adolescence. He described the internal turmoil while growing up and said, 'Every P.T. (physical training) class, I ran around on the football field, hiding behind the other boys, just waiting for it to end'. Ashok appeared hesitant and uncomfortable during these disclosures. He had got hormonal investigations done on his own to 'confirm that I was a man'. His diary was full of statements about the need to be more manly and labelling of his sexual thoughts about men as sinful and against religious teachings. 'Please teach me to fit in,' asked Ashok.

This vignette illustrates how individuals might struggle to accept their transgender identity. Internalised transphobia has been described as discomfort with one's own transgenderism stemming from internalised normative gender expectations. For a clinician who is accepting of gender non-conformity and works towards empowering transgendered clients, this can pose a therapeutic dilemma. Clinicians need to be accepting of prolonged stages of uncertainty and ambivalence and should not push the client.

> Vanitha, a 25 year old working professional came in with multiple cuts on her forearm after being compelled to wear a saree and bangles for a family wedding. 'Please explain to my sister and mother that I cannot change. I have always been like this. They want me to be a normal girl.' A meeting with the one supportive sibling was followed by a multigenerational session involving six family members. The session included discussions about their misconceptions, professional opinions about transgender experiences, future issues like marriage and their varied emotional reactions.

The therapist must be prepared to play the role of 'translator' and advocate on behalf of the transgendered individual. Sessions with the family might sometimes take precedence and therapeutic flexibility helps in judging the priorities for intervention.

> 40 year old Bhaskar, single, being treated for schizophrenia for 19 years presented with extreme distress associated with repeated thoughts that his genitalia were 'changing and becoming female'.

> 18 year old Somen, with a history of academic difficulties was noticed to be muttering to himself in the last year. The family also revealed cross-dressing behaviour of uncertain duration and recent demands for surgical removal of his penis.

These vignettes illustrate the potential difficulties in assessing transgender experiences in the presence of psychosis. When gender identity concerns arise only after the onset of psychosis or appear episodically during exacerbations, the distinction is clearer. However, this might not always apply and there have been rare case reports describing the co-existence of schizophrenia and transsexualism.

These personal stories speak to the importance of empathy and engagement in the therapeutic space, the different roles demanded from the clinician and the power of learning from clients and from other therapists' experiences.

Best practice guidelines in transgender care

Working with transgender and transsexual clients calls for specialised knowledge and expertise on the part of mental health professionals. It is essential for therapists to have specific knowledge and training with regard to diagnosis, differential diagnoses and common co-morbid disorders often associated with transgender issues, as has been discussed earlier. In any clinical practice, it is paramount that protocols be tailored to the specific needs of each client/patient, and mental health practice is particularly dynamic in this regard. Research in transgender health is still in its infancy, and there are widely diverging clinical (and consumer) opinions about 'best' practice. In this document, we offer suggestions based on published literature specific to transgender mental health, the authors' clinical experience and interactions with other professionals and NGOs working with this client population. Ongoing interdisciplinary research and dialogue are important in further developing practice protocols.

A key role that clinicians play is as gatekeepers determining which clients are appropriate for sex reassignment surgery (SRS) or hormone treatment and which are not. Guidelines and recommendations for this decision, called the Standards of Care, were drafted in 1979 by the Harry Benjamin International Gender Dysphoria Association (now the World Professional Association of Transgender Health, WPATH). The current version describes the general goal of psychotherapeutic, endocrine, or surgical therapy for persons with gender identity disorders as lasting personal comfort with the gendered self in order to maximise overall psychological well-being and self-fulfilment. After the diagnosis of Gender Identity Disorder is made, the therapeutic approach usually includes three elements or phases (sometimes labelled triadic therapy): a real-life experience in the desired role, hormones of the desired gender, and surgery to change the genitalia and other sex characteristics.

According to the WPATH guidelines, mental health professionals who work with individuals with gender identity disorders may be regularly called upon to carry out many of the following responsibilities:

1. To accurately diagnose the individual's gender disorder;
2. To accurately diagnose any co-morbid psychiatric conditions and see to their appropriate treatment;
3. To counsel the individual about the range of treatment options and their implications;
4. To engage in psychotherapy;
5. To ascertain eligibility and readiness for hormone and surgical therapy;
6. To make formal recommendations to medical and surgical colleagues;
7. To document their patient's relevant history in a letter of recommendation;
8. To be a colleague on a team of professionals with an interest in gender identity disorders;
9. To educate family members, employers, and institutions about gender identity disorders;
10. To be available for follow-up of previously seen gender patients.

Clinical Assessment and Evaluation

The tasks of the mental-health professional include assessment, individualised treatment, advocacy, and aftercare. Assessment includes an evaluation of gender and sexual history, current self-identification and goals, body image, relationship and sexual functioning, coexisting mental-health concerns (including substance abuse), and social support.

The process of evaluation, in addition to diagnostic clarification and evaluation of mental health concerns as discussed earlier, includes detailed psychological testing and assessment of cognitive and intellectual capacity to ensure that the client has the ability to comprehend and appreciate the options and choices in store. Personality structure and organisation is assessed to understand the strengths and vulnerabilities in the individual including self concept, conflicts, emotional regulation, coping, and ego strength. Interpersonal relationships such as the ability to relate to others, peers, superiors, subordinates, sexual relationships, family dynamics are understood. Diagnostic Assessment helps in evaluation of diagnostic possibilities of psychotic/affective/neurotic/organic features and/or the presence of maladaptive personality traits. In addition, the nature of reality contact and testing or impending break with reality are evaluated. Prognostic factors as seen on the psychological tests such as ego strength, quality of reality contact, interpersonal connectedness, availability of social support help plan psychotherapy and other management.

Treatment of mental health concerns is often necessary to assist the client in engaging in the psychotherapy that is required prior to hormone therapy or surgery. Gender-related stigma increases a transgender person's vulnerability to such mental health concerns as substance abuse, anxiety, depression, and personality disorders. Coexisting mental-health concerns need to be managed adequately so that the client is sufficiently stable to focus on the therapeutic tasks related to gender identity and expression.

A treatment plan is developed and negotiated with the client based on his or her goals and timeline, taking into account the needs of family and, if applicable, the WPATH standards of care for gender-identity disorders. Mental health treatment includes educating the client and family about current understandings of sexual and gender identity, such as distinguishing among sex assigned at birth, gender identity, social-sex role, and sexual orientation. Clarifying roles and responsibilities repeatedly during therapy is essential to managing the therapist's gatekeeping role. Whether or not to change gender roles, take hormones, or have surgery is first and foremost the client's decision. The therapist's role is to assist the client in making a fully-informed decision, help the client develop and implement a transition plan, and ascertain the client's eligibility and readiness for hormone therapy and/or surgery in accordance with the standards of care for gender-identity disorders. Ideally, the therapist is proactive in holding the client accountable to the timeline and treatment plan the client negotiated in consultation with the therapist.

Phase I of work with transgender clients usually focuses on rapport building and detailed evaluation for suitability for hormone therapy and SRS. This is especially the case if the client seeks an opinion and letter of recommendation for SRS. The process of evaluation and assessment has been described earlier. Given below is the outline of sessions:

- Session 1–3
  - Intake
  - Detailed Workup
- Session 4–5
  - Consultation Liaison Referrals: Endocrinology; Surgery; Dermatology; Speech Therapy
  - Medical Examination and tests as indicated/required
- Session 6–8
  - Psychological Assessment
- Session 9–10
  - Feedback and Letter

The letter of recommendation integrates findings on assessment with mental status examination, interview, observation and clinical findings. It is a comprehensive, meaningful report and provides a summary of the client's gender identity, personal history & development and sexual history. Family details including the degree of social support along with personality traits and the quality of interpersonal relationships are documented. Medical history along with any relevant mental health concerns and substance use are recorded with treatment details. Information obtained from psychological testing detailing strengths and areas of difficulty is included in the letter. Findings are used to recommend management including the need for psychotherapy, medication for psychiatric disorders if any. Treatment options with specific suggestions about Hormone Therapy, Real Life Experience and SRS are recommended.

Legalities/informed consent

In view of the fact that many of the treatment options sought by clients are irreversible, it is recommended that both clients and clinicians providing treatment have safeguards that ensure their interests are taken care of. Detailed informed consent documents for the hormone regime and the SRS surgery would take care of this. A similar procedure is recommended for the spouse / partner of the index client. This should ideally encompass knowledge of issues concerning the client and treatment choices available.

The focus on addressing mental health concerns and working on setting and attaining gender identity related goals specifically is often reached after the issue of the letter of recommendation is addressed as described above. At this point, negotiation of a collaborative therapeutic relationship sets the stage for psychotherapy to progress.

Psychotherapy

Psychotherapy has a multifaceted role in the gender exploration and transition process. It can provide support for coping with external stressors, treat co-morbid conditions, provide increased insight into personal history and motivations, facilitate exploration of the options of living with one's gender identity and enhance decision making regarding gender transition options. Psychotherapy often provides education about a range of options not previously seriously considered by the patient. It emphasises the need to set realistic life goals for work and relationships, and it seeks to define and alleviate the patient's conflicts that may have undermined a stable lifestyle. In every case, the therapist is challenged to provide treatment that is sensitive to the client's unique gender identity and individual circumstances.

The first phase of transgender-specific psychotherapy is reflective. The client writes and shares a detailed history of transgender feelings and expression, including how being transgender affected, first, the development of his or her overall identity and autonomy, second, relationships with family and friends, and, third, dating, intimate relationships, and sexuality. As a result of growing up with transgender feelings in a world that largely sees gender as dichotomous and frowns upon gender nonconformity, many transgender people have internalised this negative appraisal, referred to here as internalised transphobia. It is often the source of intense shame, self-hatred, and extended periods of suppression of transgender feelings. Through facilitating a 'coming-out' process, psychotherapy can aid in grieving the loss of the ideal to make room for a deeper level of acceptance of one's transgender (as opposed to male or female) identity.

The second phase of transgender-specific psychotherapy is more behavioural in nature. The client is encouraged to connect with peers and find community on the internet and in real life and to experiment with various options of transgender expression. The goal is to explore to eventually find a gender role and expression that is most comfortable. After a period of exploration and experimentation, most clients are ready to make a decision about a possible gender-role transition and the available options of hormone therapy and/or surgery. Making a full-time gender-role transition is in essence the start of the Real Life Experience (RLE). Taking this step is terrifying for most clients. The goal of the RLE remains to test the client's resolve and to prepare him or her for the implications of irreversible body modification through surgery.

Transgender individuals may find ways of living with non-traditional or cross-gendered identities that do not involve changing their bodies. Blending in as a member of the other sex is no longer an overriding concern for some individuals. For many, being transgender now means having a distinct identity, and the focus of treatment has shifted toward facilitating a transgender coming-out process. This process may or may not include hormone therapy and/or sex reassignment surgery. This seems akin to Virginia Prince's term 'transgenderist'—males who live full time as women without undergoing genital reconstructive surgery.

The tasks of the mental health professional include preparing the client for living life as a transgender or transsexual person. Sex reassignment transitioning is only one of several options to alleviate gender dysphoria. Other options range from containing or integrating transgender feelings into a gender role that is consistent with sex assigned at birth, to episodic cross-dressing, to living part or full time in the new gender role without hormone therapy or sex reassignment surgery. In our setting, other factors such as limited access to care, the costs involved, and lack of medical benefits and insurance facilities influence treatment choices.

Transgender clients often struggle with paralysing fear when it comes to disclosure to family and friends. The therapeutic strategy is to acknowledge this fear, yet counsel the client to 'do it anyway' by taking calculated risks, starting with disclosure to those most likely to be supportive. It is crucial for the client to recognise that immediate acceptance is not realistic; families go through their own coming-out process and need time to adjust.

Consultation liaison role of clinical psychologists

The role of clinical psychologists is important from the perspective of consultation-liaison between different mental health, medical and surgical specialities. The primary liaison occurs within the interdisciplinary Mental Health Team between the psychiatrist, clinical psychologist and psychiatric social worker. This is required when other mental health concerns or disorders are identified for holistic evaluation and planning regarding treatment. The psychiatric social worker works with the family and the extended social network to facilitate understanding of the concerns and issues. Many times the family is in need of support and resources that therapy can provide; also a loved one's disclosure and the subsequent crisis often is an opportunity for growth and strengthening of family relationships and friendships that can be facilitated through therapy.

Many individuals may be using hormonal preparations without supervision or may be unaware of the need for appropriate consultation and treatment. Input with regard to supervised medication management, making changes in physical appearance, voice training, etc., is often required. Referrals to the medical team for appropriate treatment from professionals such as the endocrinologist, dermatologist and speech therapist, etc., are planned and executed as and when the client is ready. Liaison with the surgical team (general surgery and plastic surgery) is undertaken where required.

Apart from the need to establish links with medical and surgical specialities, mental health professionals often work with the larger community, NGOs and Support groups in their role of advocating for their client. This includes providing assistance for legal changes in name and sex (usually in the form of supporting documentation), and consultation and training in school or workplace to facilitate changes in gender role.

Challenges in transgender mental health care

Mental health professionals working with transgender clients are faced with many challenges that need to be negotiated. Rapport and the therapeutic alliance are often fluctuating and conditional with the client's agenda occasionally being hidden. These evolve over a period of time after the professional passes 'tests' set by the client. These include sensitivity to transgender specific concerns, the use of transpositive language and addressing the client by the name he/she would prefer. There is a need for familiarity with terminology used by these clients. Bess and Stabb found expertise, empathy, and trustworthiness and avoiding pathologising diagnoses and heterosexist bias in therapists to be critical factors in engagement in psychotherapy as reported by transgender clients. The universal principles of acceptance, warmth, unconditional positive regard, flexibility, and non-judgemental attitude would stand any therapist in good stead towards achieving this goal.

Barriers mainly stem from the gatekeeping role that mental health professionals are called to play. Some transgender and transsexual clients may consider their therapists to be adversaries due to the power differentials inherent in the therapist's gatekeeping role. Such assumptions may be barriers to an effective therapeutic relationship. The gatekeeping role is a privilege with which the therapist or evaluator is entrusted that must be taken seriously and managed responsibly. Clarifying roles and responsibilities repeatedly during therapy is essential to managing the therapist's gatekeeping role.

Another challenge in working with this population of clients is the issue of ongoing follow up. Frequently, transgender clients do not remain in continuous contact with mental health professionals. Issues discussed above may be a large factor influencing drop out from treatment. Transgender coming out is a lifelong process. Hence, for those who opt for hormonal and or surgical treatment, there is a need for ongoing support. The therapist can serve as an ongoing resource for assistance with coming out, intimate relationships, sexual functioning, resurfacing of grief over lost time, aging, and other life transitions or mental-health concerns.

The lack of legal requirements for hormonal and SRS options in India currently is a concern that needs urgent attention. Gupta and Murarka highlighted a number of issues like consent for the procedure, safeguarding the surgeon or gender team from future litigation and post-operative sexual and legal status of the individual. Present Indian laws regarding marriage, adultery, sexual and unnatural offences, adoptions, maintenance, succession, labour and industrial laws will require modifications when dealing with these individuals and protecting their rights.

At present, there is self-regulation by many medical and mental health professionals who attempt to educate themselves regarding the special concerns of this population rather than there being a legal mandate for care provided to the transgender population. This also reflects in the emphasis in training provided to professionals regarding the needs of the transgender population. There is a need for sensitising and setting up liaison with other medical and surgical specialties so that myths, misconceptions and stereotypes do not cause barriers in accessing optimal treatment and care of these individuals.

An important issue is the profile of clients accessing help and presenting for treatment in a general hospital setting. Presentations vary from clear request for certifying fitness to undergo SRS to uncertainty and conflict regarding gender identity. Clients have different degrees of awareness and plans regarding their treatment goals. A large majority of the transgender population do not access the medical setting due to stereotypes, stigma and discrimination, social class and financial barriers. The kothi/hijra community

S

depends on their own strong bonds and social support networks and connections with non-governmental organisations and advocacy groups. Mental health concerns may often take a backseat vis-à-vis issues of day-to-day survival, coping with harassment, abuse and sexual violence. This is an area where mental health professionals in India still need to bridge the gap to understand the unique requirements of this group.

In conclusion, currently, mental health issues for transgender care does not find place in the training curriculum of mental health professionals. There is an urgent need for training of mental health professionals with regard to these issues through curriculum reform. As discussed earlier, there are challenges for developing professional competency in this sphere. Increased dialogue between professionals through peer consultations and culturally relevant, multidisciplinary workshops would help address the lacunae and build competencies from a strengths-based perspective.

It is imperative that we evolve legally mandated and regulated multidisciplinary guidelines that keep in mind cultural relevance and the ground realities that exist in our country. Awareness of legal rights and government-supported schemes are crucial to providing optimal care. Mental health professionals need to step out of their ivory tower and build bridges and referral pathways with community agencies and support groups. Together, we can work to provide comprehensive, ethical and inclusive mental health care for the transgender community.

References

American Psychiatric Association. (2000). Diagnostic and statistical manual of mental disorders (4th ed., Text revision). Washington, DC: American Psychiatric Association.

Bhargava, S.C. & Sharma, B.D. (2002). Transsexualism and schizophrenia: a case report. Indian Journal of Psychiatry, 44(2): 177–8.

Blanchard, R. (1989) The concept of autogynephilia and the typology of male gender dysphoria. Journal of Nervous and Mental Disease, 177: 616–623.

Bockting, W. O. (2008) Psychotherapy and the real-life experience: From gender dichotomy to gender diversity. Sexologies, 17, 211–224.

Bockting, W., & Coleman, E. (1992). Gender Dysphoria: Interdisciplinary Approaches in Clinical Management. Haworth Press.

Bockting, W., Knudsen, G., & Goldberg, J. M. (2006). Counselling Transgender adults and their loved ones. www.vch.ca/transhealth/resources/library/.../guidelines-mentalhealth.pdf

Bockting W. and Coleman, E. (2007), Developmental stages of the transgender coming out process: toward an integrated identity. In: Ettner R, Monstrey S, Eyler E, Editors. Principles of transgender medicine and surgery. p. 185–208. New York: The Haworth Press.

Bockting, W.O. & Goldberg, J.M. (2006) Editors. Guidelines for transgender care. Binghamton, NY: The Haworth Medical Press.

Blanchard, R. (1989). The concept of autogynephilia and the typology of male gender dysphoria. Journal of Nervous and Mental Disease, 177: 616–623.

Brown, M. L., & Rounsley, C.A. (1996), True selves: Understanding transsexualism for families, friends, coworkers and helping professionals. San Francisco: Jossey-Bass Publishers.

Chakrapani, V. (2010), Realizing right to health for MSM and transgender people. http://ilga.org/ilga/en/article/mwD0JkZ1Pi

Fontaine, J.H. (2002), Transgender issues in counseling. In L. Burlew & D. Capuzzi (eds), Sexuality counseling (pp. 177–194). New York: Nova Science Publishers, Inc.

Feinberg., L. (1996), Transgender Warriors: Making History from Joan of Arc to Dennis Rodman. Boston, MA: Beacon Press

Gainor, K. A. (2000). Including transgender issues in lesbian, gay, and bisexual psychology: Implications for clinical practice and training. In B. Greene & G. L. Croom (eds), Education, research and practice in lesbian, gay, bisexual, and transgendered psychology: A resource manual (pp. 131–160). Thousand Oaks, CA: Sage Publications.

Gupta, R. & Murarka, A. (2009), Treating transsexuals in India: History, prerequisites for surgery and legal issues. Indian Journal of Plastic Surgery. 42(2), 226–233.

Israel, G. E., & Tarver, D. E. (1997), Transgender care. Philadelphia: Temple University Press.

Lev, A.I. (2004), Transgender emergence: Therapeutic guidelines for working with gender-variant people and their families. New York: Haworth Clinical Practice Press.

Meyer, W., Bockting, W. O., Cohen-Kettensis, P., Coleman, E., DiCeglie, D., Devor, H., Gooren, L., et al. (2001), The Harry Benjamin International Dysphoria Association's standards of care, 6th version. Retrieved on September 16, 2002, from http://www.hbigda.org.socv6sm.pdf

Morris, J. (1974), Conundrum. London: Faber and Faber.

Ramsey, G. (1996), Transsexuals: Candid answers to private questions. Freedom, CA: Crossing Press.

Report of the APA Task Force on Gender Identity and Gender Variance (2008), http://www.apa.org/pi/lgbt/resources/policy/gender-identity-report.pdf

Revathi, A. (2010), The Truth About Me: A Hijra Life Story. New Delhi: Penguin India.

Stabb, S. D. (2009), The experiences of transgendered persons in psychotherapy: voices and recommendations. ["http://findarticles.com/p/search/?qa=Sally%20D.%20Stabb"]; Bess, J. ["http://findarticles.com/p/search/?qa=J.%20Alison%20Bess"]; Journal of Mental Health Counseling, 31 (3), 264–282. ["http://findarticles.com/p/articles/mi_hb1416/"]

Winters, K. (2008), Gender madness in American psychiatry: Essays from the struggle for dignity. Dillon, CO: GID Reform Advocates.

World Health Organisation (1992), The ICD-10 classification of mental and behavioural disorders. Clinical descriptions and diagnostic guidelines. Geneva: WHO.

Contexts of Distress for LGBT People

A Counsellor's Guide

VINAY CHANDRAN

Introduction

People identified as lesbian, gay, bisexual or transgender (LGBT) have always been defined within the framework of abnormality in healthcare. Considering sexual orientation and gender identity as pathology, mental health professionals have promoted various 'treatments' like conversion therapy. There is a dearth of documentation of distress situations regarding LGBT persons for counsellors. In fact, much of the literature available on counselling for LGBT people has largely been based on international (particularly North American) sources. The Indian material in journal articles focus only on the efficacy of conversion therapy for homosexuals.

LGBT people visit counsellors for a large number of reasons. There are often complaints that many counsellors have no awareness on how to deal with LGBT clients. Instead of focusing on curing homosexuality, counsellors need to be aware of the kinds of distress that LGBT individuals may go through and ways of helping them deal with this distress. This essay lists the different contexts of distress that LGBT people face and provides some indications as to what directions counselling can take.

The material in this essay is drawn from two sources. The first is a training manual for volunteers on a telephone helpline, Sahaya (estd. 2000), a project of the Swabhava trust in Bangalore. The helpline focused on providing counselling and access to information about other support services for people identified as LGBT or those who were confused about their sexual orientation and gender identities. The manual was prepared in order to train new volunteers who were already trained counsellors. Additional material is sourced from a paper on self-esteem and psychosocial stress amongst Men who have Sex with Men (MSM) and transgender populations, which was presented at a consultation in New Delhi, and from author experiences as a counsellor on the Sahaya helpline since the year 2000.

Counselling concerns

There are three issues that need to be addressed before engaging with counselling for LGBT populations. These are (a) counselling skills especially useful in LGBT counselling; (b) counsellor empathy towards LGBT issues in general; and (c) therapist's sexual orientation and gender identity.

Certain counsellor response skills used in general counselling sessions can be especially powerful in LGBT counselling. These include warmth, listening skills, transparency and being supportive. Experience of people who have been involved in LGBT counselling indicates that techniques like paraphrasing, making the process obvious to the client, and reference to earlier sessions can help ease conversation. Counsellors need to be aware that for many LGBT clients, talking about their sexuality to a total stranger (in a country where conversation on sex in public is still frowned upon) can be stressful. Any response that can assist the client in disclosing these issues will be extremely useful. Sometimes responses like 'I know it is difficult for you to talk to absolute strangers about your sexual life. I do not know what worries you, but please understand that you can speak about any issue...including those related to lesbian, gay, bisexual or transgender identities, or confusion and information about these identities....' can provide an avenue for the client to initiate conversations about these topics. The technique of using trigger questions to get the client to speak, especially using informal language, as opposed to a clinical one, needs to be emphasised. When dealing with clients who may not have access to information about LGBT identities, for whatever reason, it may be necessary to adopt a more descriptive approach (e.g., talking of men who are attracted to and have sex with other men, women who are attracted to and have sex with other women, rather than talking of LGBT identities) to encourage communication and to help the counselling process along.

The second issue that needs to be addressed is about counsellor empathy. While counsellors are expected to be empathetic to all clients, the value-laden socialisation that all individuals go through in society does not spare counsellors. Considering the links that are made between 'immorality' and sexual orientation, can counsellors be empathetic on these sensitive issues? Many in the LGBT movement believe that counsellors who perceive homosexual desires or different gender identities as being abnormal or unnatural, cannot be expected to give an objective hearing or support to LGBT clients.

The third issue is about the circumstances under which the therapist should disclose his or her sexual orientation. It has been argued that only a member of a minority group can understand what another member of the same group has experienced. In the same way, many LGBT people feel that only an LGBT counsellor can understand what they are going through and this becomes a particularly important source of anxiety for these clients. Since this anxiety can often harm a session or prove an obstacle to accessing support services, it is necessary for counsellors to address this early on in the sessions.

While the advantage of having an LGBT counsellor addressing the counselling needs of an LGBT client cannot be underestimated, there are a few concerns to keep in mind. The first is that of disclosure. LGBT counsellors have to gauge for themselves, depending on the nature of the client's distress, about the value of disclosing their sexuality identity to the client. Obviously this poses a greater challenge to counselling in general because counsellors perceive themselves as objective listeners. However, when clients repeatedly focus on how there are no positive role models for LGBT people and that they perceive LGBT identities as being abnormal through statements like 'Gay relationships don't work...' or 'LGBT people will never be happy', counsellors may have to explore the potential for revealing their own identities. The second concern is about transference. In instances where clients are looking for partners or there is potential for transference due to the fact that the client sees the counsellor as being the only other LGBT individual and therefore a possible ideal partner, disclosure might not be beneficial. Additionally, if clients request counsellor disclosure of sexuality identity, it may be useful to explore why this would benefit the client through responses like, 'Does it matter if I am LGBT?' or 'May I know how the knowledge about my identity will help you in this matter?' or 'Would it make a difference to you, if I am or am not LGBT?'

Not many counsellors agree that only LGBT counsellors can understand LGBT client's issues. The argument here is that by promoting this, there is a negative reinforcement that LGBT people have 'special' problems that need 'special' treatment. These counsellors suggest that the effort should be in mainstreaming LGBT distress counselling and motivating general counsellors at any institute or private practice to provide sensitive and non-judgemental support to LGBT clients. In such a scenario, counsellors may want to disclose their non-LGBT identities in the context of supportive responses so that the client can perceive that the support or referral is being given without judgement. Whatever the situation, it is imperative that the counsellor does not avoid the question of self-disclosure as this may be seen in a negative light and may reinforce wrong perceptions about LGBT individuals as a whole.

Contexts of distress for LGBT people

For the sake of simplifying the numerous concerns that need to be addressed, the following list is used to indicate the broad categories of stressors that LGBT people encounter. Obviously, the list can only be a preliminary framework for thinking about LGBT distress counselling. Some of the contexts of distress which have been identified are related to:

a. Identity;
b. Sexual behaviour;
c. Legal status;

d. Violence;

e. Relationships;

f. Support systems;

g. Health; and

h. Others.

We will examine each of these areas of distress in a little depth and indicate what directions counselling sessions can take.

Identity

Confusion about being attracted to the same-sex, or of wanting to express a different gender identity, internalised beliefs about abnormality of same-sex desire identification, and other concerns are all important in this context of distress. There is often depression, anxiety and fear of revealing these feelings, which acts as a major source of stress for these clients. These often get expressed in phrases like 'I had sex with another woman...I think I am lesbian...I don't know what to do...' or 'I'm a man and I like wearing women's clothes, is that normal?' or 'I'm 50 years old, I've always been homosexual, but I've never come across anyone else like me...Is there something wrong with me?' or 'I'm really depressed and can't get any work done because I'm attracted to other men' or simply 'I think I am gay.'

In situations related to adolescent or youth counselling, the confusion may come from school or college students who may be having crushes on same-sex peers or may feel that they have fallen in love with their same-sex classmates or friends. In one counselling experience, the author has provided counselling and referral support for a 16-year-old male student who said, 'I'm a boy but I've always felt like a girl, I would like to become a girl, what do I need to do?'

Counsellors have to pay close attention to the need for addressing violence related to disclosure of identities. Transgender individuals by virtue of their gender identities often experience violence (both within the family and in public spaces).

Sexual abuse is another factor that some LGBT clients may speak about and there is often a rationalisation, both from the client as well as the counsellor, that their current LGBT identity is linked to this experience. It is necessary for the counsellor to deal with this sensitively and delink their experience of abuse from their sexual orientation.

Religious belief causes a great number of conflicts for many LGBT clients. This conflict often gets expressed as 'I'm lesbian but my religion is against these feelings…I feel very guilty and don't know what to do.'

Clients also bring in their confusions about sexuality identity when they are being forced to consider arranged marriages as intended by their families. Here many of them feel conflicted because of their desire to be responsible to their family. This gets expressed as, 'My family is forcing me to get married, but I don't want to because I'm transgender…How can I deal with this? How can I tell them?'

Counsellor response

To address these issues the counsellor needs to be empathetic about the client's experience of sexual orientation or gender identity and also enable clients to explore their own identities without imposing categories like LGBT. For instance, saying, 'There is nothing wrong with being gay, so don't worry if you are. However, tell me why you feel that *you* may be gay?' may provide a clear motivation for the client to express his feelings more clearly without fear of disclosure.

In the scenario where the client is depressed, the counsellor may have to explore the feelings associated with the depression saying, 'Tell me why you feel depressed about being attracted to your own sex?', again reinforcing that being LGBT is not the problem. Often, counsellors use this expression of distress (or depression) related to identity as ego-dystonicity and do not engage with what the cause of distress may be. The argument that 'if a client feels distressed about being gay, then there is something wrong with being gay' is not empathetic. Encouraging the client to explore the causes of distress, which may get expressed as 'My parents may reject me… My friends will reject me…I may lose my job…I won't be able to have a relationship' and so on, will enable the counsellor to find responses that are appropriate to each possible cause of distress. Ultimately, the effort is to make the clients comfortable enough to deal with their sexuality and reframe their expectations of their lives by evaluating how handling each distress situation might actually make them stronger individuals.

When dealing with clients who express different gender identities and pose questions about surgical options, counsellors need to keep in mind the elaborate but essential protocol for sex-reassignment surgeries (SRS). While information on this is still not widely available today (though they are accessible on the internet) and there are not many surgeons in India who conduct these surgeries or are aware of the needs of these clients, counsellors can access some information on these through other transgender individuals who may have already gone through such surgeries. This obviously involves being in contact with LGBT organisations possessing such information and being able to make appropriate referrals where necessary. Additionally, if counsellors are not trained in dealing with transgender issues or SRS, it is imperative that they have a referral list of other counsellors to whom the client can be referred.

The important thing that counsellors need to remember when dealing with sexual abuse and other violence faced by LGBT individuals is that recovery and reclamation of selfhood needs to be emphasised. If counselling links abuse or violence experienced by the individual *negatively* with the sexuality of the individual, there are chances that future sexual experiences might be *negatively* affected. In such a scenario, counsellors also need to explore why the client feels that his or her identity is linked to the experience of childhood sexual abuse or violence and help bring about a positive sense of self related to identity.

Clients dealing with their conflict with religion can be exposed to narratives of other LGBT individuals who assert both their personal religious beliefs and their sexuality identities without negating either. The narratives of individuals who assert, 'I am a Christian and I am a lesbian' or 'I am a gay man and I am a practising Muslim', are invaluable in motivating LGBT clients to view religion as not in opposition to their identities but as rather an aspect of identity, which can coexist with their sexual identity.

LGBT clients undergo the same socialisation about marriage

and relationships in society. Counsellors helping LGBT clients being forced into marriages could encourage them to examine the possibilities of coming out to parents. This is in order to ensure that forced marriages do not lead to further distress and depression. With male clients, counsellors need to discuss the negative effect of forced marriages on the female partner especially where there is no disclosure. Additionally, LGBT clients can be encouraged to re-examine the importance of marriage as well as think about other forms of meaningful relationships. Counsellors may also want to encourage LGBT clients to bring their families to the counselling sessions so that any trauma about coming out can be dealt with professionally.

Sexual behaviour

Due to the high levels of stigma attached to LGBT sexualities, LGBT individuals, especially lesbian and bisexual women, have very few private spaces to engage in pleasurable sexual relationships. In addition, there is the popular notion that gay, bisexual and transgender people are immoral because they engage in sex in public places like toilets and buses or parks. Even the clients themselves, particularly men, often express this sense of disgust with a public sexual act and such disgust is internalised to the extent of bruising self-esteem levels deeply. Many such men speak of their feelings in phrases like, 'I was travelling in a crowded bus. I saw an attractive man and we rubbed against each other. It felt good at the time, but I feel depressed that I have to do this.'

Another concern expressed by many gay or bisexual men is that of not being able to have a regular sexual partner. There are several reasons given for these. The first reason is the fear of discovery or the fear of being labelled homosexual. Second, the lack of a private place for having a sexual relationship is sometimes cited as another reason. Third, men may also possess a negative image about their body and self-worth, due to which they believe that they are not desirable enough for any sexual partner. This negative association may be related to their sexuality identity. Similar issues of body image and lack of self worth also affect transgender individuals.

Counsellor response

Since the Delhi High Court Judgement, 2009 decriminalised sexual acts in private, counsellors can assert that homosexual relationships are not illegal. But sexual contact in public might put the client at risk for arrest, or for blackmail and harassment from extortionists or law enforcement. So counsellors need to inform the client about such risks. The guilt and shame associated with sexual acts can be dealt with gently without reinforcing negative feelings. 'I understand that you feel bad about having had sex with another man in public, you may not have had a choice about these things, but feeling guilty may not help you understand how to deal with such a situation if it arises again...' and so on.

Fear of being discovered having sex in public could drive many LGBT individuals to severe depression. Counsellors have to address this fear in order for the client to realise what the worst-case scenario could be if such a discovery did occur. Additionally, many clients may express that they are probably aroused by the prospect of being discovered. In either case, counsellors can encourage the client to explore other avenues of sexual contact that can be considered safe, so as to reduce stress related to discovery.

The stress emerging from the lack of self-worth and negative body image has to be explored and analysed. Does low self-confidence and esteem arise from the LGBT identity or is it due to some other factor?

One concern among transgender people is that when pre-operative transgender individuals engage in sex with their partners they may not be willing to undress during the sexual act. Partners may feel unsatisfied with this, but counsellors have to help these clients and their partners to recognise the need for communicating with each other about what is desirable during the sexual act and what is not.

Legal status

The first question that most counsellors will pose is about the legal threat and punishment to homosexual activity in India. Many clients also come with the same question, 'Isn't homosexuality a crime? How can I be a homosexual in India?' Counsellors need to be aware that many times clients express that the only way they can be homosexual is by leaving the country and living in countries where being LGBT is not criminal.

In many cases, this fear of the law pushes many LGBT individuals to succumb to extortion threats from strangers or law enforcement officials. Clients may express these anxieties about being blackmailed, 'This man who is our neighbour came to us and said that he knew we were lesbians and if we didn't give him money or have sex with him, he would inform the police about us...'

Some clients may experience being disowned by family members after coming out. They may require legal assistance to gain their rights to inheritance or property and may have anxieties about this. 'My brother found out that I was homosexual and he plotted with my family to throw me out of the house and get me written out of the family property. I have nowhere to go now, what do I do?'

Clients may also bring in concerns about being dismissed from their jobs due to coming out or being outed at the workplace and the harassment related to this. 'My colleague found out that I was gay and told the management. I was asked to leave and wasn't even given notice...I feel depressed and don't know what to do....'

In many cases of lesbian couples who are 21 years or above and have planned to live together, parents who are against their relationship bring in complaints of kidnapping and forcibly restrain either or both the women in their respective houses. Clients who have gone through these experiences may be deeply disturbed by the complete breach of trust from within their own families.

Many clients bring in concerns about whether their relationships are legally recognisable or if they could get married publicly to their same-sex partner.

Transgender clients often question whether going through SRS is a legal procedure and if they could be arrested for this. Counsellors may also be concerned whether helping transgender clients access SRS is illegal.

Counsellor response
Counsellors should know that a judgement decriminalising homosexual acts in private has been in place since 2009 in the Delhi

High Court. If clients have concerns about whether the judgement has an impact on their lives they should be referred to a lawyer with a working knowledge on these issues.

Counsellors can also inform clients that extortion whether from the public or from the police is a crime and clients should be encouraged to file charges against these individuals. In such cases counsellors should also discuss personal safety measures at length once such charges are filed. Clients have to understand that it is fear that blackmailers prey on. If clients are not afraid of being outed as LGBT, there can be no fear of blackmail.

Counsellors will have to refer clients to sensitive and informed lawyers to deal with crises like being disowned by the family or being terminated from their jobs. They can then concentrate on dealing with the trauma and depression related to these incidents. Also, while dealing with the violence that a family inflicts on an LGBT person, it may be necessary to identify supportive individuals to negotiate with the remaining family members and bring the LGBT person out of harm. The loss of trust that such an experience can bring has to be addressed in the sessions. Besides this, if the threat of being disowned or being thrown out of the home is high, then counsellors have to help their client list alternative sources of support and shelter while dealing with the crisis. Many LGBT organisations in large cities can provide information about such shelters and counsellors need to be aware of these. Sometimes, counsellors can discuss with clients about delaying coming out to family until there is economic security. Suggesting basic preparations for such long-term economic security, particularly in the case of lesbians and transgender individuals, may include setting up a separate bank account that only the individual has access to and is not a joint account with family members. Such preparations may help clients in the long run.

Unfortunately, LGBT relationships are not recognised under the law. Counsellors might want to refer clients who wish to formalise their relationships to sensitive lawyers who can arrange for appropriate legal solutions for insurance, property purchase, personal wills and so on, ensuring that these are managed in such a way that they are not challenged by family members or others who disapprove of these relationships.

There is some ambiguity about SRS and their legality. However, many transgender individuals in India have had surgeries done and their basic documents like passports and so on altered. Transgender clients need to be in touch with therapists who, together with endocrinologists, plastic surgeons and psychiatrists, can help the client go through the SRS protocol.

Violence

Individuals who come out as lesbian, gay, bisexual or transgender face violence in different forms almost on a daily basis. This violence is often against those who do not fit conventional norms of gender ('effeminate' men or 'masculine' women) or conventional notions about appropriate behaviour (public displays of affection with your partner, etc.). The first source of violence for many LGBT individuals is still the family.

Clients may also talk about the constant teasing from workplace colleagues or may have experienced police harassment owing to their different gender identities or perceived sexual behaviour. A few clients may narrate experiences of violence faced from a casual sexual partner or from a partner who paid for sex or even from their long-term partners. 'My boyfriend and I have been in a relationship for three years now, and I really love him, but he is very short-tempered and gets jealous if I speak to anyone. He sometimes slaps me when we're alone, but then says he's sorry. I don't know how to stop him.'

Counsellor response

When clients report violence, counsellors have to pay attention to a couple of issues. First, the session has to address the impact of violence on personal self-worth. Many clients may dismiss the violence and may be able to get over it, but several others might not be able to cope with it and may internalise it leading to self-hate. Second, violence against LGBT has to be placed in the larger context of discrimination against LGBT people. Clients have to realise that they need not allow such experiences to demean them and should challenge such violence when it occurs.

Studies have shown that violence within relationships,

whether heterosexual or homosexual, goes through similar stages. Counsellors should empower clients to deal with violent relationships by negotiating that no further violence takes place, by analysing the relationship itself and inviting the violent partner to counselling sessions, and if feasible, by working with the violent partner separately. Counsellors should also pay attention to the difference between (a) violence that directly and deeply impacts a partner's self-value and self-worth and (b) violence used in the context of a relationship that employs sado-masochistic fantasies for sexual pleasure, for which the clients may not require counselling input. Finally, counsellors have to address the violence by 'gendering' it and seeing how much of it is actually based on internalisation of sexist ('If I'm the husband in this relationship, then I can beat my wife...' or 'I'm the wife in this relationship, so obviously he will beat me...') or heterosexist frameworks.

Relationships

'Will I ever get into a relationship?', 'How can a gay relationship work?', 'There are no role models of LGBT relationships in the media, so I don't know whether my relationship will work...' 'Everyone on the internet dating sites is looking for sex, no one is looking for relationships.' These are all phrases used by LGBT clients to speak about their stresses related to entering or sustaining a relationship. Social perceptions of LGBT relationships as not being as ideal as heterosexual relationships often prevent LGBT clients from developing deep and meaningful partnerships. Many LGBT clients internalise this belief that such relationships don't work. Therefore, they are not surprised when their partners break up with them, and they don't put any effort into sustaining a relationship.

LGBT clients may bring three kinds of issues related to marriage to counsellors: (a) Forced heterosexual marriages to fulfil familial obligations (b) Clients who are already married but continue to lead homosexual lives in private which can be a source of high-stress and (c) LGBT individuals who wish to enter into marriages of convenience.

Some clients may experience a sense of conflict and frustration about 'open' relationships in LGBT communities. Many counsellors may not have enough information or experience on dealing with these kinds of relationships.

LGBT individuals might want to adopt or become surrogates to fulfil their desire to be parents. Other stressors include the fear of loneliness and growing old alone.

Counsellor response

If clients feel that there are no role models for gay relationships, counsellors can help clients to break down this need for role models and help arrive at their own versions of how gay relationships can be. Clients need to understand that starting and sustaining a relationship in an LGBT context may probably be just as easy as a heterosexual relationship. However, while heterosexual relationships exist within certain structures and institutions that support them publicly, LGBT relationships do not have any such backing and depend entirely on the partners involved. This means partners have to strive to make a relationship work but it also means that LGBT individuals can redefine their ideas and expectations of relationships.

We have already dealt with the issue of forced marriages and the need for coming out in these situations. With married LGBT individuals, the conflict between family life and life with their same-sex partners is tremendous. Maintaining two lives separately is extremely stressful and many LGBT people have communicated their failure to successfully lead a double life. There has to be an exploration of whether this double life needs to continue and if coming out can be considered. LGBT clients have to acknowledge that while coming out might not benefit the family, the partner they are married to, the children they have parented, or their friends, it is a tremendous step towards greater self-respect (and respect for the people involved) that can prevent a lot of harm later on. Additionally, the client needs to be able to bring in his or her partner, their children and other important members of the family to counselling.

Some clients may express their need for open relationships, where they wish to have more than one sexual partner while they continue to have a primary emotional bond with one partner. The 'open'-ness being referred to here is that individuals have sexual contact outside their relationship with the open knowledge of their partners. There are two hurdles here: the first is that of the partners themselves. Does such a relationship affect the emotional stability of each partner in any way that threatens the overall relationship? Are both partners equally convinced about this arrangement? The second hurdle is that of the counsellor: Counsellors need to understand that this is not unique to homosexual relationships. So such issues need to get addressed openly without judgement.

Clients who wish to explore adopting or surrogating children can be referred to agencies that deal with these issues. But the counsellor's job here is to examine readiness, responsibilities and realities of child rearing like in any family.

Ultimately, when clients (especially homosexual or bisexual men) are unsatisfied with their relationships, or are unable to find partners, they might express the need to get into a heterosexual marriage to avoid loneliness. These clients need to understand that (a) a heterosexual arranged marriage need not necessarily help them avoid loneliness and (b) they have to be open and pro-active about meeting other LGBT people through support groups, parties, dating sites, public events, etc. Also, they should not underestimate the value of having a close set of friends who they can rely on for companionship that need not have anything to do with sex. Counsellors have to help clients understand that loneliness is not particularly a homosexual issue. Clients may get married and lose their partners to illness or bad marriages and end up being lonely anyway. What is more important is to ensure that they have friends and close family that acts as a support group for them through their lives.

Support system

Support systems are invaluable to LGBT individuals especially when they are coming to terms with their identities or when they are in crises. Many express their concerns about the lack of a support system through phrases like, 'There is no one else like me, I feel I'm the only gay man in this place....' For others, the concern is about not meeting with others like them or not having a relationship, 'No one likes me I'm always going to be alone....'

Counsellor response

Counsellors have to be pro-active about enabling clients to find systems of support. All clients need to understand that three areas of support need to be built up over their lifetime. The first is within the family where LGBT individuals can identify some supportive family members. Many LGBT individuals also identify people who may not be related to them (teachers, friends, mentors, etc.), who could become a source of support. The second involves supportive friends and peers. Many LGBT feel left out of non-LGBT peer groups because their issues are not addressed in these groups. With LGBT peer groups, like in any other homogenous peer group, there is more likelihood of making friends with people who understand and respect you. The third support system can be a support group within the LGBT community. Support groups draw from the larger community a wide range of individuals with a wide range of experiences and belonging to such groups can benefit individuals. In such groups, they may be able to benefit from listening to the experiences of other individuals who may have gone through similar situations. Counsellors need to be informed about local LGBT support groups in order to assist their clients to access these.

Health

Many health-related stressors exert their influence on LGBT people. Depression related to their identities, relationships and facing discrimination have already been discussed.

Health stress related to substance use may also come up as a counselling issue.

Transsexual individuals and hijras may have health stressors due to the sex-change operations that they have gone through. Side effects of hormones and incomplete operations, or abuse at the hands of the medical professionals may impair physical health as well as result in anxiety and depression.

Testing for various sexually transmitted infections (STI), including HIV, is also a stress factor. For LGBT individuals, the added anxiety of discovery of their identity when visiting a doctor exacerbates their stress levels. LGBT individuals who also identify as HIV-positive may experience distress due to the double discrimination they face in society.

Counsellor response

Any complaint of severe anxiety, clinical depression, self-harm or attempt to commit suicide should be addressed immediately and clients should be admitted for immediate medical attention.

Studies have shown that LGBT persons are not always at a higher risk of self-harm and substance use. Counsellors should explore what the substance use or self-harm is linked to. Conversation can include the various health risks from substance use. Counsellors can also address the risks of having unprotected sex while under the influence of substances. For some individuals substance use may be linked to addictive personality issues and therapy can focus on this.

Counsellors need to be informed enough to make referrals for transsexuals or hijras to deal with medical concerns and also to deal with their anxieties about these. Knowledge about sensitive hospitals or doctors for testing and treatment of STIs is also crucial.

HIV-positive LGBT persons need counsellor input on self-acceptance and leading a healthy life. Fears about discrimination and ostracisation have to be addressed in therapy and legal or other referrals need to be made.

Many HIV-positive LGBT people might wish to enter into relationships with other HIV-positive LGBT people or with non-HIV-positive individuals and counsellors can help explore the possibilities of these with the client. Counsellors can discuss safer sex practices through which clients can conduct their relationships.

Other stressors

Apart from all these stressors, concerns that LGBT people might bring to counsellors may include economic status related anxieties; discrimination faced due to nature of work (e.g., LGBT individuals who are sex workers); disenfranchised status (e.g., hijras who have no documents that can ensure that they can buy land or get married) and so on.

Counsellor response

Counselling about career or economic opportunities would be routine for clients who bring economic status-related anxieties. Dealing with discrimination in workplaces (both personally and politically) and dealing with police violence or violence from the public have to be addressed in cases of LGBT clients who are sex workers by referral to legal groups handling these. Counsellors can help support a larger movement to enfranchise the hijra community (e.g., as in Tamil Nadu).

Conclusion

This essay by no means represents all the stressors that LGBT people may face and is only an attempt to indicate the direction in which further work needs to be taken. Instead of focusing on 'fixing' what is not 'broken' or 'curing' something that isn't a 'disease', counsellors have to adopt a more progressive view that reflects changing social values and expectations. Knowledge about the different contexts, which LGBT people live through, and the kinds of distress they face will provide a better foundation for counselling. The need is not for special skills in counsellors but more sensitivity and greater understanding of LGBT lives. The quest is not trying to find the 'normal' or emphasise personal standards of 'morality' on the world, but to ensure that LGBT people, like others, are treated with equal standards of respect and value for human rights.

References

CDC (2006) HIV/AIDS among men who have sex with men. CDC HIV/AIDS resources. http://www.cdc.gov/hiv

Chandran, Vinay (2003), The veil behind the face: Rituals, language and sexuality among hijras in India. Paper presented for the 4th IASSCS conference "Sex and Secrecy", Johannesburg

Chandran, Vinay and Dr. Chandrashekhar Balachandran (2002), LGBT Journeys: Challenges and self-empowerment of Bangalore's LGBT community. Swabhava Trust and The Dharani Trust, Bangalore.

Crosby, Michael G. and Michael Grofe (2001), Study of HIV Sexual Risk among Disenfranchised African American MSM. Prevention #8. AIDS Research Institute, Center for AIDS Prevention Studies, University of California, San Francisco.

Dandona L., Dandona R. et al. (2005), 'Sex behaviour of men who have sex with men and risk of HIV in Andhra Pradesh, India', AIDS 2005: 19:611–19.

Germann, Stefan (2004), Psychosocial impact of HIV/AIDS on children. AIDS Bulletin, June 2004, Vol. 13, No. 2. South African Medical Research Council. http://www.mrc.ac.za/aids/june2004/impact.htm

HIV/AIDS Bureau, Health Resources and Services Administration, US Department of Health and Human Services (2005) Men who have sex with Men and HIV/AIDS. www.hab.hrsa.gov

Jaffrey, Z. (1996), The Invisibles, A Tale of the Eunuchs of India, New York: Pantheon Books.

Jagruthi (2001), Report of the study on commercially and sexually exploited male children in Bangalore, City, Jagruthi: Bangalore.

NACO (2003), National Aids Prevention and Control policy. http://www.naco.nic.in/nacp/ctrlpol.htm. (National AIDS Control Organisation, New Delhi).

Nanda, S. (1999), Neither man nor woman: The hijras of India, 2nd Edition (Belmont, CA: Wadsworth).

Narrain, Arvind and Vinay Chandran (2005), '"It's not my job to tell you it's okay to be gay"—Medicalisation of Homosexuality: A Queer Critique', *Because I have a Voice: Queer Politics in India*. New Delhi: Yoda Press.

Pembrey, Graham (2006), Overview of HIV and AIDS in India. http://www.avert.org/aidsindia.htm

PUCL (2003), Human Rights violations against the transgender community: A study of kothi and hijra sex workers in Bangalore. PUCL-K, Bangalore.

Seabrook, J. (1999), Love in a different climate. (London and New York: Verso).

Tomaszeski, Lauriann (2001) An Overview of the Psychosocial Issues That Impact Family's Affected by HIV/AIDS. June/July, 2001/Jacksonville Medicine http://www.dcmsonline.org/jax-medicine/2001journals/junejuly2001/psychosocial.htm

Vanita, R, and Saleem Kidwai (eds) (2001), Same-sex Love in India: Readings from Literature and History. New Delhi: MacMillan India.

Williams, John K., et al. (2004), Psychosocial issues among Gay and non-Gay identifying HIV-seropositive African American and Latino MSM. Cultural Diversity and Ethnic Minority Psychology, Vol. 10, No. 3, 268–286.

Use of arts-based tools and techniques to improve self esteem, self care and self expression of gay, bisexual and transgendered people in Chennai

Magdalene Jeyarathnam

Introduction

Continued discrimination lead LGBT people to experience low self esteem, various levels of clinical depression and an over-riding feeling of anxiety and stress. Having to lead a double life for the sake of their families and the mainstream—while being a different person in an LGBT-friendly environment—takes a toll on them emotionally and affects the quality of their lives. Studies show that the LGBT population are more likely to be treated for anxiety, panic disorder, depression, poor self-esteem, eating disorders or to develop alcohol/drug dependency when compared to the general population.

Violence and discrimination is also a part of everyday life for most of the LGBT community. Gay and lesbian adolescents report attempted suicide at least twice the rate of their heterosexual adolescents. The average high school student may hear anti-gay remarks at school as many as 25 times a day.

This essay comprises details of a project that used an art-based therapy to help improve self-esteem, self-care and self-expression among LGBT people in Chennai.

Why art-based (ABT) therapy?

The use of art-based therapy is not a new initiative. Fischer described a 'cumulative effect' on overall health when self expression is stifled. Since that time, others also have made a connection between self-expression and physical and emotional well being. All the above research has direct implications for art therapists working with LGBT individuals where the most important aspect of their client's self-expression often is the ability to come out and be out.

In planning counselling-based art therapy interventions with

LGBT population, several factors must be considered including the fact that the LGBT population continues to face unique challenges such as stress from stigmatisation and discrimination leading to emotional distress, substance use and suicide, among other issues. Any of these may be addressed in art therapy with LGBT clients. However, many art therapy techniques are ideally suited for exploring identity issues and a number of case studies relate the value of art therapy to LGBT individuals. Collage work has been used in individual and group therapy with gay men and lesbians to explore experiences with bigotry, hatred, internalised homophobia, and sexual identity.

Activities for the group included self-portraits, collage, group murals, and sculpture, and the participants approached concepts of family, guilt, shame, fear, anger and homophobia through individual and group art making. Fraser and Waldman described individual art therapy used with gay and lesbian clients struggling with their sexuality, gender identity, depression, homophobia, coming out, fear, fantasy, and shame. The therapy aimed at 'making visible the invisible, hidden and secret, to bear witness to pain and to celebrate courage'.

Methodology and Findings

In this project, almost two-dozen art-based methods were used to elicit individual experiences and narratives of pain. The therapeutic objectives of the art-based therapy were:

A. Improving perception of self
B. Improving caring for the self
C. Improving self expression

Various scales were used both before and after the project to see if these objectives were being met. The scales used to understand well being and sense of self included: WHO's Well being Index; Rosenberg Self Esteem Scale; Holmes and Rahe Stress Scale; Beck Anxiety Inventory; WHO's alcohol use disorders identification test (AUDIT); and Eating attitude test (Eat 26).

In addition to this, observation formats were used to assess various changes in self-expression in clients. These included observations from therapist; family and friends; self-assessment; peer assessments and through maintaining journals.

The project also used standard ABT assessment tools like the feelings chart and video recording to assess moods and feedback before, during and after sessions.

Using different methods like collage, symbolising emotions, journal making, making a *mandala*, body map, storytelling, feelings charts and so on participants engaged with their own sense of self and their relations with others. The project showed that there was a measurable increase in self-perception, self-care and in self-expression.

References

Addison, D. (2003). 'Art therapy with gay, lesbian, bisexual and transgendered clients', in S. Hogan (Ed.), Gender Issues in Art therapy, pp. 53–58. London: Jessica Kingsley publishers.

Barbee, M. (2002), 'A visual-narrative approach to understanding transsexual identity', Art therapy: Journal of the American art therapy association, volume 19, number 2, pp. 53–62.

Fraser, J. and Waldman, J. (2003), 'Singing with pleasure and shouting with anger: Working with gay and lesbian clients in art therapy. In S. Hogan (Ed), Gender Issues in Art therapy, pp. 69–91. London: Jessica Kingsley publishers.

Lynne Ellis, M., 'Images of sexualities: Language and embodiment in art therapy, International Journal of Art Therapy, Volume 12, Issue 2 December 2007, pp. 60–68.

Pelton-Sweet, L. and Sherry, A. (2008), 'Coming out through art: A review of art therapy with LGBT clients', Art therapy: Journal of the American Art therapy association, Volume 25, Number 4, pp. 170–176.

Wadeson, H. (2000), 'Art therapy practice: innovative approaches with diverse populations' John Wiley and son Inc, pp. 339–366.

Coming Out to Parents and Friends
Perspectives from Parents of LGBT

VINAY CHANDRAN

Introduction

Sexual orientation and gender identity are two under-addressed areas in clinical counselling in India. There is little information about how to deal with various contexts of distress that people who identify as lesbian, gay and bisexual (LGBT) have to face. There is even less information on how counsellors can help LGBT persons 'come out' to their family about their identities. Coming out is an extremely important process for LGBT persons as it has a positive effect on self-esteem. For many LGBT people who come out, the process of coming out is a step towards both self-acceptance as well as growing comfort with identifying as part of a community.

However if the process of coming out leads to rejection from families or friends, it may be very stressful. Studies conducted on adolescent and youth suicides internationally have linked high rates of suicide in LGBT-identified youth directly to rejection and stigmatisation from parents and friends.[1]

In such a context, understanding both the need for coming out and parent's perspectives about homosexuality is extremely important when working with LGBT youth and their parents. This compilation seeks to put together some of the documented responses by parents of LGBT persons to their children's sexuality in meetings conducted by LGBT support groups in Chennai, Bangalore and Mumbai.[2] Narratives about parents' responses to children with different gender identities are not available in this essay, which is an obvious lacuna.

The need for coming out and responses to coming out

In this section, we examine the reasons for coming out and the different responses to coming out.

Reasons to come out to family

The first question that most LGBT individuals face prior to coming out is, 'Why do you feel the need to come out at all?' There are two kinds of responses that emerged on this question during the Gay Bombay group meeting. One response linked coming out to notions of upbringing and values imparted by parents relating to trust, honesty and so on. A member of the Mumbai group states:

> Our parents are most important, we love them and share our lives with them and they are very important for us. Tomorrow if my mom finds out that I am gay from strangers, she will reflect that 'I am so far from my son that he does not trust me enough to tell me. All my years of upbringing have gone down the drain....'

Another response is that coming out is nothing but really asserting that one is not ashamed of who one is. A Mumbai group member said:

> I spend a major part of my time with my family. If I believe what I am doing is right, why should I hide? I am not saying accept or reject me since there is no choice. Another thing is that she asked me why I hadn't told her for the previous 25 years of my life? I was out of Bombay for a long time to escape this and in retrospect if I told her I would have been a lot happier.

A Bangalore member said:

> You will only feel that it is difficult to talk about being gay if you think that being gay is a problem. If you realise that there is nothing wrong with being gay, then you wouldn't have a problem talking about it to other people, whoever they may be.

Sometimes, the desire to hide the identity and the personal journey comes from fear of family responses. It's important to understand that some of the fear may be a realistic appraisal of the situation and some of it may be based on imagined negative reactions. A Gay Bombay member said:

> Very often, the child comes out to the parents in front the doctor. A very common response is that 'Why didn't you tell me earlier? Did you think I would not have had faith in what you said? We think the mother will die and get a heart attack. But see what the real responses are, they are not at all like that.'

This was also illustrated by the experience of a mother in the Bangalore meeting who said:

> The one thing I was really hurt by was that he kept going with us to these different families to see the girls there and then would reject them. In our family the boys' side goes to the girls' homes, so we must have visited more than 10 families. He would keep saying no for some reason or another. Now when everyone sees that we've visited so many girls, it becomes very difficult to reply to their questions about why he's not married. I wish he had not done that. It's not fair to us or the girls we visited.

Response of parents: 'What will people say?'

One of the first responses to coming out that parents express is their fear of the entire family knowing about their child's sexuality. This is because in India opinions of the extended family, neighbours, friends, etc., matter and the prestige of the family is tied in to the fear of 'what people will say'. One mother from Chennai observed[3]:

> In these many years of marriage and family life, it has been a struggle for me to create a sense of autonomy for this small family unit, keeping extended family and relatives as important people, but not important enough to influence and sway opinion. It has not been easy. May be as an urban, upper-middle-class woman, it has been possible for me to do so, but it has taken decades. So for me what has come to matter most is the happiness of my husband and children and now, after several years of self-negation, my own happiness. So I refuse to give much importance to opinions of people. I have had enough of those. I am paring down to things I can worry about to just a few. My children's happiness comes foremost among them.

In the Bangalore meeting, one mother articulated this fear of the larger family getting to know:

> It's okay for us, but it's very difficult to talk to our other family members. We are a huge family. It's not possible to make everyone understand. It's very hurtful when people keep asking you why your son's not getting married.

Some parents in the meeting assuaged this fear by stating:

> There's no need to listen to all these relatives. You should ignore what other people say. You'll never be happy if you keep trying to meet other people's expectations. Ultimately your child should be happy.

However, relatives and friends of the family can help play a very important role in supporting parents through the process of their children coming out to them. This was illustrated by a couple of parents in the Bangalore meeting.

Fear of the law

In sessions with parents held before the judgement in the *Naz Foundation* case decriminalising homosexuality, they expressed many fears about the law. In the Bombay meeting one parent asked:

> With article 377 of the IPC criminalising sodomy in place, how wise is it to come out?

However the positive judgement has brought about a sea change in the atmosphere of fear which parents felt about the risks their children were living with by merely being LGBT. In the discussion in Bangalore for example:

> Now that the law has changed people will also change their attitudes. But you have to give them time. Eventually, they'll change.

There was also skepticism about how much a change in the law would result in a change in societal attitudes:

> Even if the law changes, people and society are not going to change easily. Ours is a large traditional family of more than 75 members. My son is very successful and has made us very proud over the years with what he has achieved. But when he told us about this I was very

hurt. For a whole month I would just sit around and cry. I couldn't eat properly or talk to anyone.

What can be asserted is that a change in the law has the potential for lessening irrational prejudices and some of the measured and thoughtful responses to the judgement by both political parties, media as well as many ordinary people shows the changes in Indian society post the Naz judgement in 2009. One remarkable measure of how a change in the law has brought about a change in societal attitudes is dramatically signposted by the responses to those who have filed an appeal seeking to overturn the Naz judgement. In support of the Naz judgement, 19 parents of LGBT persons, 14 mental health professionals and 16 teachers have filed interventions. The intervention by the parents of LGBT persons in particular indicates how parents have become a significant source of support for their children. The parents argue that the real harm to family values is caused by divisive and discriminatory laws like Section 377 of the Indian Penal Code.

It is Section 377, which is a threat to family values, as it directly affects the rights of the Applicants to safeguard their families from illegal and arbitrary intrusion from the state authorities. Section 377 invades the sanctity of the family, home or correspondence and allows for unlawful attacks on the honour and reputation both of parents of LGBT persons as well as LGBT persons themselves.[4]

Supportive responses

Many parents provide supportive responses to their children who come out as LGBT. A few parents in the Gay Bombay meeting saw coming out not only as a positive step but were also able to empathise with the risks and stress that their child may have gone through.

These kids think of the repercussions of coming out even more than us. They have to work harder in confronting their sexualities than us. We as parents are on the sidelines, while they are actually going through all the turmoil in their minds and hearts. They are terrified of the pain their parents may be going through due to their coming out. They don't want the family name to be sullied either. It crushes them to think that their mother may be laughed at behind her back. So instead of living in terror and shame and exacerbating their pain, why not fight back against society?

> In retrospect, my suffering is lesser than that of my son. The number of mothers who stumble upon this insight on dealing with their sons' coming out is unbelievable. 'I wonder what my son must have gone through all these years keeping it within his chest', they say. The second thing that parents realise is that they have lived their lives, but their children are coming into the prime of their lives and should be able to blaze trails without all these roadblocks.

One Bangalore parent said about her gay son:

> No, I didn't know at all. It was a complete shock. I had no idea. Which mother would want their child to be gay? I could see something was bothering him, but I couldn't understand what it was about. When he told us, I kept wondering if it was somehow my fault. I didn't know how to deal with this. But I can see why it was so important for him. He is more comfortable now and much more relaxed, so I know now that it was a good idea for him to tell us.

Though some parents accept their children, they realise that their child may now have to live outside of social norms. As one parent in the Gay Bombay meeting said:

> Earlier widow remarriage was a taboo. Even customs like sati did exist, but courageous people made many sacrifices to fight against them. Hence swimming against the tide is going to be difficult. If you realise that your son is not doing anything wrong, why not support him?

A few parents did not think that they had to go out of their way to accept their children.

> I'm neither obliging him nor doing my duty by accepting my son. Because I have given birth to him, I would have accepted him if he would have been physically handicapped or mentally retarded. I don't want him to feel that I am doing him a favour.

Parents who go through the same socialisation processes realise that they were not aware of homosexuality because they did not have any frame of reference (or 'role models') for homosexuals. And now they are suddenly faced with LGBT children in their own families. As one parent in the Gay Bombay meeting said:

> Earlier I didn't have an idea that homosexuals exist to this extent, now I don't feel so surprised. Thought I'd try to explain to him but I felt that maybe I made some mistake while raising him. But he said, no, this is something intrinsic. Not interested in marriage, does not want to cheat a girl. Don't expect that I will change. After all it is our child, so I would like to accept it. He should find a friend who is loyal.

Parenting parents

Obviously not all parents hold sensitive views with respect to homosexuality. The fear of social repercussions, disease, multiple-partner relationships, lack of safety and security are all perceived as being associated only with homosexuals. If the potential for conversion to a heterosexual life exists, these parents would support such conversion therapies. Many LGBT people are taken to counsellors and psychiatrists because of these beliefs. As one parent at the meeting said:

> Your life does not have a legal protection. Your lives have nothing; don't you have any fear of HIV and AIDS, etc.? Changing partners will lead to problems. I am not saying that all the men and women are Ram and Sita. But along with no legal aspect being present to support you, you will not have any security. If you put your mind to becoming straight, it is possible.

But LGBT people have to give their parents time to deal with these issues. As a group member put it, this was a process of parenting your parents:

> Most mothers go through this phase of anger and denial and it is easy to pass judgement on them. Most mothers go through the stages that she has: considering homosexuality to be an illness or an addiction like alcohol, where the affected person has to abstain; unnatural; irreligious, etc. So the solutions for these? Repent, go to straight therapy and so on. These are obviously phases that mothers go through. Some even see being gay as mental retardation. Or pity—

one of the saddest things to do to your child. In order to achieve real understanding, she needs to get this insight on her own. We need to give her the space. Children need to understand that we need to parent our parents after we come out to them. Give her time.

The question of marriage

Marriage in India is constructed both as a religious ritual as well as a social identity. Its association with reproduction is considered fundamental. Most parents subscribe to the dominant social opinion that views marriage as an inevitable social obligation.

So, when LGBT individuals say that they do not want to fulfil this obligation by getting married particularly because they would not be able to satisfy their partner's sexual needs, parents respond by saying:

> It is not necessary that a married couple should have a physical relationship. So many people live together for care giving. The sexual part should not come first.

This viewpoint obscures the fact that sexual intimacy is a sensitive and important relationship which many human beings develop and which is actually central to family life, well being of the community as well as integral to the development of the human personality.

Many parents and counsellors also see marriage as a 'solution to the problem of homosexuality'. The understanding here is that if the child is married, then the 'other' feelings will stop. Not many may empathise with the future partner of their children and how this forced marriage affects both the individuals and their families. A couple of parents in the Bombay meeting showed their concerns about this:

> If it is a natural instinct, if there is no natural attraction to girls at all, what is the use? It is not that he is going against nature. If we are forcing him to get married, we are spoiling someone else's life.
>
> Homosexuality was always there, it is also natural. Only thing was it was not open earlier during our time. Lots of problems arise

if a forceful straight marriage is undertaken. It's not necessary that marrying a girl will make him happy it can even make things worse. I will support my son. I haven't told my husband, but I have told my daughters. Earlier, people were ashamed. Marrying and producing two children is not all the aim in life.

Some parents have sought to understand social obligation differently. A parent at the meeting said:

The solution of heterosexual marriage for your gay son that you are suggesting is like trying to blanket one problem with a bigger problem. As far as social obligations are concerned, you can even meet them by taking care of the education of an underprivileged child. It is not necessary to self-destruct in order to meet social obligations.

Loneliness and marriage

When parents get past the initial stages of accepting the sexuality of their children, the concern very often voiced is about who will take care of the child when the child grows old. Parents worry that their children will end up being lonely. A parent at the meeting said:

Husband and wife remain loyal and stay with each other for kids. If you think someone will remain with you all your life it is very difficult. If you want a partner it is okay, but where will you find one? Tomorrow when you grow old, nobody will even offer you a glass of water.

This concern was voiced very touchingly in the Chennai meeting where a parent said:

Initially I was reluctant to accept my son's sexuality, but now I understand him to the fullest. I also pray to God that he should not suffer loneliness and to provide him a partner as per his wish for his lifetime.

Another approach to the question of loneliness is to show that relationships are not the sole basis of building a more caring environment. What is deeply devalued is the role that networks of friends can play in alleviating loneliness. A parent said:

If you are alone, you have to handle your loneliness by having people around you. You are not alone simply by not having a boyfriend. You should have people around you."

A gay man in the Bangalore meeting said:

> The question of loneliness is something that parents of LGBT children worry about. But I have a large set of friends that I'm very close to and who I meet on a regular basis. So really the way gay people handle being alone is by surrounding themselves with friends who become a kind of support group.

The consequence of marriage

Many LGBT individuals get married with the view of fulfilling the social obligation of marriage. The experience has generally been painful for the individual, the partner, as well as both the families. For the family member who has experienced or witnessed the consequence of a gay man getting married to a woman, the tragedy is felt deeply. The situation of a woman, in such a marriage, who may feel lied to and used, is one that both parents and the gay man have to acknowledge. In the meeting, one member said:

> I am a sister of a gay man. You have no right to make your son marry a girl and ruin her life. As a woman and human being you have no right to do it. I have seen how the girl a gay man gets married to gets disgraced....

The crucial lesson to learn about forced heterosexual marriages for LGBT individuals comes from those individuals who have gone through these experiences and have borne the brunt of a collapsed marriage, an ignorant, indifferent family and offended in-laws. In one narrative, a Gay Bombay group member who faced all these despite having a supportive wife, relates his experience.

> I am a gay man recently gone through a divorce from a straight marriage. As marriage pressure was building and an arranged marriage was being finalised I came out to my mom and sister, and even dad. But I got married to the girl anyway. We didn't have a physical relationship for 15 months, though we were in the same bed. We didn't have any fights, but I knew what I was going through and so did she. I was

282 Nothing to Fix

uncomfortable with everything. I couldn't adjust with her and didn't feel like sharing my feelings, happiness or life with her, though she did a lot for me. The parents got me married but then washed their hands off me. They said it was my responsibility to keep my wife happy. My in-laws said it was my responsibility to keep their daughter happy. So I was under the burden of the expectations of two sets of parents. My wife was getting all the material comforts, money, etc. But the thing she wanted the most, my love, I couldn't give her. Finally, one day, I told her and came out that I am gay. She was shocked. But incredibly, she took it on to find out as much as she could. She did a detailed study later, went on the internet, etc. She even went to the Humsafar centre and met the counsellor, made me meet them. She understood exactly what being gay is. Then she told her own parents. The parents did not understand. There was a big *hungama*, both the extended families came to know. My wife's family created a major scene and immediately took her back to her hometown. It was a big hurt for our family, but I accepted that it was my mistake. We paid a huge amount of alimony. We have taken divorce one year ago.

Heterosexual marriage as a solution for a person's homosexuality runs into two major problems. First, it would be unethical as it is often based upon not disclosing the sexual orientation to the proposed bride or groom. Second, the marriage runs into problems sooner or later, with the two parties then having to go through the often painful process of divorce.

Conclusion: Changing belief about homosexuality

The best narratives of coming out and support from parents are those where parents make their own journeys from denial and anger into tolerance and finally acceptance of their LGBT children. Some even envy the remarkable deep meaningful relationships that many LGBT share with each other and their partners. Says one Bombay meeting member:

Sometimes my boyfriend and I live at my place, and sometimes at his place. About a year and a half back he came out to his mother. About a week after that he told her about me. All he said was that 'I want you to meet him'. She comes from a traditional Maharashtrian family.... She thought here was someone who had spoilt my son. A month later, on her own, she said let's go meet him. I insisted that they come home. She did and we had a nice two hours together. After that, she left. Her words to him as she left in the lift were: 'He's a good human being, nice guy, mature, good for you.' What a contrast from 'I don't want to meet him at all'. Then the second time was at a movie. The sweetest words she ever said was 'He now seems like a son-in-law to me.' She said 'I wish the straight relationships in our family could have a love like yours.'

Notes

[1] For instance, see R. Brown, 'Self harm and suicide risk for same-sex attracted young people: A family perspective', *Australian e-Journal for the Advancement of Mental Health*, Vol. I, No. 1, (2002) http://auseinet.flinders.edu.au/journal/vol1iss1/brown.pdf

[2] The narratives that are being analysed in this essay were drawn from the minutes of a support group meeting conducted by Gay Bombay in September 2007. The narratives have also been drawn from a support group meeting for parents held in Bangalore hosted by Swabhava in 2010 as part of the Bangalore Pride as well as in Chennai as part of the Chennai Pride in 2011.

3 Quoted from http://orinam.net/resources-for/friends-and-family/

4 Petition filed by 19 parents supporting the Naz Judgement, 2009 in the case of *Suresh K Kaushal Vs. Naz Foundation*, in the Supreme Court of India.

Annexure 1: For Family and Friends of LGBT individuals (from Parents, Families, Friends and Allies of Lesbians and Gays)	
Do	*Don't*
Do listen to what your loved one's life is like, and what kind of experiences he or she has had in the world.	Don't put the blame for your own feelings on your loved one.
Do take the time to seek information about the lives of LGBT people from parents of LGBT people, friends of your loved one, literature, and, most of all, directly from your loved one.	Don't rush the process of trying to understand your loved one's sexuality or gender identity.
Do get professional help for anyone in the family, including yourself, who becomes severely depressed over your loved one's sexuality or gender identity.	Don't assume that your loved one should see a professional counsellor or encourage them to participate in 'reparative therapy' (conversion therapy).
Do accept that you are responsible for your negative reactions.	Don't criticise your loved one for being different.
Do respect your loved one's right to engage in loving relationships.	Don't try to break up loving relationships.
Do try to develop trust and openness by allowing your loved one to be who she or he is without pressure.	Don't try to force your loved one to conform to your ideas of proper sexual behaviour.
Do be proud of your loved one's capacity for having loving relationships.	Don't blame yourself because your loved one is lesbian, gay, bisexual or transgender.
Do look for the injured feelings underneath the anger and respond to them.	Don't demand that your loved one live up to what your idea of what a man or woman should be.
Do defend him or her against discrimination.	Don't discriminate against your loved one.
Do support your loved one's individual goals, even though they may differ drastically from your own.	Don't force your own life goals on your loved one.
Do say 'I love you.'	Don't insist that your morality is the only right one.

Religion and Sexual Orientation
Reconciling Faith with Same-sex Love

VINAY CHANDRAN and ARVIND NARRAIN

I realise that Christianity will never accept me being gay.

(28-year-old Christian gay man)

During my mid-twenties, I read about my religion and homosexuality. I prayed to ask God to tell me what to do. I wondered about people who mean a lot to me; would they accept me?

(40-year-old Muslim gay man)

It would have been extremely difficult if I lived with my parents. The concept of guilt hangs heavy in the house. I think I am an honest person. I would not want to live a life of lies with my parents.

(32-year-old Christian gay man)

Introduction

The conflict between one's religious faith and one's experience of sexuality is a key source of distress for some LGBT individuals. Religion answers a deeply felt need within the psyche of numerous individuals and religious faith is integral to the well-being of many LGBT persons. At the same time, when there is no correspondence between religious norms pertaining to appropriate sexual orientation and gender identity and one's deeply felt experience of gender or sexuality, the result is feelings of conflict and distress for the individual concerned. Particularly in cases where individuals so deeply empathise with their religion and are therefore conflicted about their sexual orientation, there is no easy path of privileging one identity over the other. It is not always possible to say, as some gay people have said, that they would refuse to '... wander around searching for meaning in a religious tradition which says that they don't have a right to exist.'[1]

For those who feel that religion and sexuality are both an integral aspect of their identities, it's important to be able to reconcile these seemingly conflicting aspects of their existence. There is greatest intra-psychic conflict in the case of those who are followers of Christianity and Islam because of perceived explicit textual prohibition of homosexuality. Those who are Hindu and identify as lesbian, gay, bisexual or transgender (LGBT) by contrast, appear to face little by way of conflict between their religion and their sexuality.

The dominant homophobic interpretations of both Islam and Christianity have provoked a counter interpretation of both Islam and Christianity by those who identify as both religious and LGBT. In fact, it should be noted that what is emerging is a theology which attempts to reconcile homosexual feelings and expression with religion faith.

In this essay, we examine some experiences of same-sex desire among individuals who are religious. We attempt to understand some of the concerns related to the perceived lack of congruence between the practice of religion (particularly Islam and Christianity) and the experience of desire that leads to the feeling of distress, conflicted emotions and exclusion. We also argue that it is possible to continue to have a religious faith as well as have an LGBT identity as experienced by many individuals. We will share some of the narratives of these experiences.[2] This position of embracing both identities is also supported by textual interpretations of key religious texts.

Homosexuality, Hinduism and Buddhism

The non-judgemental attitude towards homosexuality is documented extensively by the important work of Saleem Kidwai and Ruth Vanita who refer to an array of sources from ancient and medieval India to conclusively show how homosexual expression was intertwined with

Hinduism right from its very origins.[3] The first and perhaps most celebrated instance is in the writings of Vatsyayana (compiled circa 3rd century B.C.E). The *Kamasutra*, which Vatsyayana put together in his lifetime and provides important insights into different aspects of sexual pleasure, and devoted an entire chapter on pleasurable sex between males.[4] While it is currently being marketed more as a sex manual, the text was originally meant as an exploration of one of the three objectives of Hindu spiritual life, i.e., *Kama* (aesthetic and erotic pleasure). The other two objectives were *Dharma* (virtuous living) and *Artha* (material prosperity).[5]

However, the history of tolerance and even celebration of same sex love in ancient India has transmuted into a disavowal of homosexuality as something 'foreign' and not a 'part of our culture'. This opinion came to a flashpoint in the year 1998 on the occasion of the release of the movie *Fire* (1996, Dir: Deepa Mehta). The film explored same-sex desire and a relationship between two women in middle-class India.[6] The protests against the screening and the subsequent banning of the film in different states brought into the Indian living room the clash between Hinduism and female sexuality in general and female homosexual desire in particular.[6] Hindu male homosexual desire had until then, relatively, escaped the public gaze.

But barring the anti-homosexual stances taken by various political parties including, but not limited to the Hindu right wing, the stance in Hindu religion on homosexuality is seen as being more tolerant and accepting of same-sex desire. Innumerable temple structures across India (Khajuraho in Madhya Pradesh, the Shiva temple in Bagali, Karnataka, and the Sun temple and Rajarani temple in Orissa) have sculptures that display every form of sexual desire and act. While the purpose of these sculptures is often debated, that they exist at all is indicative of the acknowledgement of different desires in ancient Hindu society. Additionally, there are numerous folk tales and stories within the large framework of the Hindu religion where individuals, kings, queens, gods and goddesses assume different genders or have relationships with someone of their own gender.[7]

Some Hindus argue that homosexual love is fundamentally the same as heterosexual love.

288 Nothing to Fix

Nowhere in the Hindu sacred texts is romantic love excluded to all but a man and woman, so there are no religious grounds to make a statement to the contrary. Since homosexuals can experience romantic love, homosexual sexual relationships are not all the product of lust … homosexuals should be allowed to marry…. Sexual expression within a loving relationship is encouraged by Hinduism because it is not an expression of lust, but an expression of love and devotion to each others' happiness. Therefore, homosexuals in loving relationships (i.e., marriage) should be allowed to express their love sexually.[8]

In the context of **Buddhism**, while overcoming desire is itself seen as the spiritual goal, there are non-judgemental interpretations of same-sex desire.

As homosexuality is not explicitly mentioned in any of the Buddha's discourses (more than 20 volumes in the Pali Text Society's English translation), we can only assume that it is meant to be evaluated in the same way that heterosexuality is. And indeed it seems that this is why it is not specifically mentioned. In the case of the lay man and woman where there is mutual consent, where adultery is not involved and where the sexual act is an expression of love, respect, loyalty and warmth, it would not be breaking the third Precept. And it is the same when the two people are of the same gender. Likewise promiscuity, license and the disregard for the feelings of others would make a sexual act unskilful whether it be heterosexual or homosexual. All the principles we would use to evaluate a heterosexual relationship we would also use to evaluate a homosexual one. In Buddhism we could say that it is not the object of one's sexual desire that determines whether a sexual act is unskilful or not, but rather the quality of the emotions and intentions involved.[9]

The problem of exclusion in Islam and Christianity

While Hindu and Buddhist texts appear to have some degree of tolerance for same-sex desire and different gender identities, the same is not apparent in several mainstream interpretations of Islam and Christianity. It is necessary, in this context to examine three issues: first, the problem of exclusion from religious communities; second, the need for LGBT affirmative interpretations of religious texts; and finally, the experiences of LGBT individuals with their religion.

There are two kinds of experiences of rejection felt by many LGBT individuals who are deeply connected to their faith but cannot find pathways to acceptance within their religion. The first experience of rejection comes from religious communities, where Muslim and Christian LGBT persons are excluded and have faced ostracisation, excommunication and violence.

The second experience of rejection is deeply personal where same-sex desire is seen as being incompatible with any form of religion. This is what Boellstroff calls incommensurability.[10] In effect, the experience of incommensurability forces Muslim and Christian LGBT individuals to look at their lives as spread across two distinct 'worlds'—the gay world and the heterosexual, religious world—that will never meet. Many of these LGBT individuals, for instance, expect to get married in heterosexual arranged marriages and live their homosexual lives separately, never expecting to be able to articulate a gay and Muslim or Christian identity simultaneously.

However, within Christianity, the objections to LGBT persons are increasingly discussed in the contemporary era. Ranging from debates about the position of the church on gay marriage, the potential for 'curing' homosexuality with belief and prayer, the definition of marriage as being between a man and a woman, and so on, the debate on the interface between homosexuality and Christianity has become very public. In fact, the opposition to gay marriage was one of the key electoral planks of the Republican Party in the 2004 and 2008 Presidential elections in the United States. And despite over a dozen states legalising gay marriage, opposition to gay marriage on religious grounds continues to dominate US politics.

But these debates about same-sex love in the contexts of Islam and Christianity become even more salient in the twenty-first century as the LGBT movement grows stronger and there are more and more articulations of an independent identity such as *gay* or *lesbian* that defies traditional religious modes of expressing desire.

Viewpoints of religious leaders

While the mainstream positions of these world religions continue to marginalise LGBT populations, there are many religious leaders who have spoken in public in favour of supporting the LGBT movement:

> Zaki Badawi, a scholar and head of the Muslim College in London, in 2000, said in an interview to Gay Times that 'In Britain, we Muslims are in a minority, and it should not be our task to encourage intolerance towards other minorities.... Homosexuality has always existed and continues to exist in all Islamic countries....'[11]

> Archbishop Desmond Tutu, one of the leading opponents of racial discrimination during South Africa's apartheid era, has drawn a link between apartheid and discrimination against lesbians and homosexual men. His comments—which imply that discriminating against people on the basis of their sexual preference is as immoral as discriminating against them on the basis of their race or colour—have deep implications not only for the churches in South Africa and Norway but also for churches across Africa, where homosexuality is often taboo, and for other Lutheran and Anglican churches around the world.[12]

> ... [Archbishop Desmond] Tutu said ... that he was ashamed of the Church ... believing that the Church had become homophobic. He has instead pleaded the case for an inclusive church which sees homosexuality as an orientation rather than a lifestyle choice.[13]

In the recent context of the decriminalisation of homosexuality by the Delhi High Court, It is important to note that the Roman Catholic Church as well as the National Catholic Council of India (NCCI) and some Islamic scholars have welcomed the decriminalisation of homosexuality.

Asghar Ali Engineer, a well known Islamic scholar argues that:

> The Quran condemns homosexuality, but doesn't prescribe any punishment for it. It's a sin, not a crime. Sin is between Allah and the sinner, but crime concerns the entire society. So, sexual minorities

should be left to their conscience. They are answerable to Allah for their act and should not be treated as criminals.[14]

A statement by the National Council of Churches in India (NCCI) noted that:

We recognise that there are people with different sexual orientations. The very faith affirmation that the whole human community is created in the image of God irrespective of our sexual orientations makes it imperative on us to reject systemic and personal attitudes of homophobia and discrimination against sexual minorities. We consider the Delhi High Court verdict to 'decriminalise consensual sexual acts of adults in private' upholding the fundamental constitutional and human rights to privacy and the life of dignity and non-discrimination of all citizens as a positive step. (India—Theological Roundtable on Churches' response to Human Sexuality)[15]

Dr. George Zachariah, a theologian, welcomed the Naz judgement as being based on the language of inclusiveness:

This is the vision of a rainbow community of the beloved and equals. It is a historic moment for us, the Indian Church, to make a decision. We can either continue to remain as an inhospitable religious club—a hostile community as the rapists of Sodom in Genesis 19, committing violence against the sexual minorities, or we can become a just and inclusive rainbow community celebrating our God given diversities by welcoming those who are different from us into our midst to experience Christian fellowship in a deeper way. God of love has called us as a community of friends and equals to be filled with God's love; to share God's unconditional love; to demonstrate God's love to others— whoever they are, whatever their background be; to declare and show by our actions that God loves all, and has no pre-existing conditions for loving all of God's creations. May the God of love help us to become a Church to those who are demonised, criminalised, and excluded.[16]

Similarly the Delhi Roman Catholic Archdiocese has been reported as saying:

Spokesperson of Delhi Catholic Archdiocese, Father Dominic

Emmanuel, told TOI, 'Homosexuality is a sin as opposed to a crime. But we believe that those who indulge in it should be treated with respect and compassion.' In a newspaper article, Father Dominic was even more forthright. 'It needs to be made clear that the Christian community does not (repeat it does not) treat people with homosexual tendencies as criminals. Nor does it believe that they can be regarded on par with criminals. Therefore, the church has no serious objection to the repealing of Section 377.'[17]

However it is to be noted that the Roman Catholic Church is still not fully supportive as it still considers homosexuality to be a sin. Nonetheless, the statement that it welcomes the decriminalisation of homosexuality indicates some flux in the position of the church. While these are some positive interpretations of Christianity and Islam, there are a number of religious groups which have also taken a highly negative view of the judgement.

Theology from the standpoint of LGBT persons

There is also an emerging theological scholarship from the standpoint of LGBT persons which has attempted an alternative interpretation. This scholarship asserts that it is wrong to state that homosexuality is condemned in religious texts like the Bible and the Qur'an.

For example, the recent work by scholars such as Scott Kugle has examined in detail the textual basis for the prohibition of homosexuality in Islam. After traversing through the verses of the Qur'an, the Hadith (scholarly commentaries) and Fiqh (Islamic legal reasoning), Kugle comes to the conclusion that the textual basis for the prohibition is weak.

Kugle begins by quoting a verse from the Quran:

O people, we created you all from a male and a female
And made you into different communities and different tribes
So that you should come to know one another
Acknowledging that the most noble among you
Is the one most aware of God.

Qur'an 49:13

Kugle says, in his analysis of these words,

Most Muslims cherish reciting this verse to oppose the evils of racial
superiority, ethnic chauvinism, and class arrogance. Yet some see
this verse as a call to justice that rings far beyond its terse words.
Progressive Muslims extend its implied meaning beyond its explicit
wording, to condemn also male sexism, gender injustice and social
stigmatizing of homosexuals. This verse is often cited in the internet
discussions of members of a support group for Muslims who are
lesbian, gay or transgender in the U.S., called Al-Fatiha Foundation.
Its members see themselves as a community of people—like the tribes
and communities of the Qur'anic verse—who are a natural result of
human diversity as it is created by God's divine will. Many of them
refuse to accept the allegation that they are sinful or perverse or sick,
as many Muslim authorities regularly assert. They accept that they are
merely human, as are all other Muslim believers, and that God judges
them according to their awareness of God. They strive to surrender to
God's will and not to the criticism of others informed more by social
prejudice than by awareness of God.[18]

Kugle's scholarly analysis has to be read along with the more
general point made by Whitaker that the religious texts are open
to different kinds of interpretations. 'Just like the Bible, the Qur'an
has a number of verses that are popularly regarded as condemning
homosexuality. As in the Bible, they are comparatively few and open
to a variety of interpretations ...'[19]

Similarly there is a good amount of scholarly literature
which casts doubt upon whether at all there is a textual basis for
prohibiting homosexuality in the Bible. The path breaking work of
John Boswell bears special mention in this regard. John Boswell has
asked some fundamental questions as to what exactly the verse in
the Old Testament in which the cities of Sodom and Gomorrah are
destroyed meant. In Boswell's understanding the destruction of the
cities had to do with the lack of hospitality of the inhabitants and
not to do with the sexual practices of its inhabitants.[20]

Other scholars have argued that:

... the Bible really does not fully address the topic of homosexuality...

Nowhere, however, does the Bible come close to condemning a loving and committed homosexual relationship. To use the Bible to condemn such a relationship, as we see, involves a projection of one's own bias into the Biblical texts and a stretching of these texts beyond their original intent.[21]

The work of these scholars goes to show that the general attitudes against homosexuality are more a result of politics based on religion than a specific textual interpretation. To take the case of the persecution of homosexuality in Islamic countries it has been argued that:

> … while attitudes towards homosexuality in the west over the last few decades have generally been liberalising. Muslim countries have been moving in the opposite direction. This is largely a result of international politics. Perceptions of a domineering west, coupled with fears of globalisation and modernity have brought a revival of imagined 'customs and traditions', along with the spread of rigid and puritanical versions of religion. Historically, though, Muslim societies have been relatively tolerant of sexual diversity—perhaps more so than others.[22]

Reconciling faith and sexuality

There are marked similarities in the way LGBT individuals who are religious experience their desires. The initial confusion, the conflict between belief and desire, the urge to change, probable rejection of belief or rejection of desire itself, and finally, sometimes, a reconciliation of belief and desire. Participants interviewed spoke about these concerns.

> I thought it was abnormal to be gay because of my religion. I initially ignored that I was religious, but questioned religion only after I discovered that I was gay. I asked for God to 'correct me' or show me the 'right path'. Over a period of time I realised that I could not change my sexuality. The attraction towards other men became more dominant. I took this as a positive sign. I thought if this was indeed true then as texts and others say God would have punished me and would not have given me so much of happiness in my life. May be God

wanted me to be this way. The Bible says, 'God made us in his own image', may be God created me this way. I have a personal relationship with God. If there was anything wrong in my lifestyle it would be between me and him and not the priest or others who say it otherwise.

(23-year-old Christian gay man)

There was a point when I thought I was the only one and I felt extremely guilty. But reading about sexuality I realised that it was biological. I believe that there are some things beyond our understanding. I have had many religious experiences. I studied in a Catholic school and grew up around Hindu traditions. I believe God is my only judge and on judgement day he will judge me on my good and bad decisions.

(40-year-old Muslim gay man)

Until about my 10th grade my upbringing was strictly Catholic. I knew it was condemned, but I did not feel guilty. Maybe initially I was, but eventually I grew out of feeling guilty. Probably by the time I was in my teens I started to be impartial towards religion. I started to raise questions. I was sure that God does not condemn homosexuality. I had spent enough time on confessions, prayers. Due to my Catholic upbringing, it did bring me a fear of hell, fire, etc. I wasn't comfortable about my sexuality in the initial period. While growing up I had very limited exposure towards homosexuality and references were mostly negative. I did wish that I was not gay, not because of the religion but more because I was scared what my friends and others would think.

(32-year-old Christian gay man)

When I had my first 'proper kiss' with a woman whom I met at the mosque I decided to do more reading on this issue. I came across a few paragraphs that talked about male homosexuality but of course very vague. There wasn't any writing on homosexuality between women. So I assumed that my feeling towards women was not something of an abomination. I realised that this was something deeper than religion. I thought may be God made me this way and decided that sleeping with too many people whether men or women would be a sin but that being with one person whom you love whether it's a man or a woman would not be a sin.

(37-year-old Muslim lesbian woman)

However, not too many LGBT individuals end up reconciling their beliefs and desires. Many may go through the experience of incommensurability that we spoke of earlier, believing that no reconciliation is possible in a scenario of a society where heightened religious prejudice condemns all difference. Some others give up religion and practice entirely.

> I realise Christianity may never accept me for being gay. I do not care about religious leaders and their preaching. They interpret what they think is 'right'. Maybe I won't fulfil the requirements of 'traditional catholic society', but that is fine with me. I believe that as long as one is happy and does not force another to do anything against their will, it is fine. There are a lot of conflicting studies about Christianity, lot of internal politics, politics beyond the teachings of Jesus Christ.
>
> *(30-year-old Christian gay man)*

> I have unconsciously ignored the conflict between my religion and my sexual identity.
>
> *(30-year-old Christian gay man)*

> I think God has created each one of us differently: left-handed people, people with different eye shades, skin colour, etc. God has created each one of them, then why not me? Sexuality might not be a choice, I think it is genetics. Christianity has helped in my upbringing: it is the core part of what I am, my beliefs, principles, etc. Although I did go out to see other places of worship to see how they worship. But after all this, I do not believe in God any more. I am not an atheist, I am a rationalist.
>
> *(35-year-old Christian lesbian woman)*

In these contexts, support systems like the family should have played an immense role in building self-esteem of gay or lesbian children. However, data shows that the higher number of rejection experiences come from families with strong religious beliefs.

> Mom does not seem to come to terms with my sexuality. Two months after I came out to my parents, I took up a job outside of India. Thought this would give them enough time to resolve the issues, but I don't see much of a difference now. The discussions are as tensed as they were, but she consciously tries telling me that

I am 'on a wrong path' and 'faking my religious identity'.

(23-year-old Christian gay man)

The pressure was to accept my 'responsibility'. Marriage, having kids, taking care of them, having a 'good family', etc., were supposed to be my responsibilities. People questioned why I am not adhering to these 'social norms'? At times I questioned myself, 'Am I doing something wrong'?

(36-year-old Hindu gay man)

My family was not particularly religious but questions about sexuality create more debate due to cultural than religious grounds. Anything unusual, anything out of the 'normal' would be looked down on.

(40-year-old Muslim gay man)

I realised that I had feelings towards women around the age of 12. But I did not act on it.... I shared my thoughts with my mother. She said I felt that way because I had not met the right guy. And that I am too young to have thoughts like that and I need to be with a man. I now think she knew that I was different, so she insisted that I need to be with a man. Although being religious she was quite liberal in so many aspects. She was almost a hippie at some level. But she was uncomfortable with homosexuality I think.

(37-year-old Muslim lesbian woman)

If I were to be reborn, I would ask God to make me straight. Especially when I look at my brother's perfect life as a married man: he is going to have kids soon, he has a good job, and my parents are so proud of him. My parents would like me to be like him. But I do know that I would not be able to make them happy as my brother has done.

(30-year-old Christian gay man)

Despite these experiences, a few individuals have traversed the journey from confusion about their identity to a determinedly clear articulation of being religious and gay or lesbian without seeing it as an either-or situation. All these individuals have taken it upon themselves to re-interpret their religious traditions in such a way as to preserve the essence of the religion.

I feel God has always helped me out. I have witnessed so many miracles in my life, so I know he is there to guide me if ever I need him. If there was a way to change my sexual preference now why would I change it, that too, after all these years? God would have showed me a long time back.

(23-year-old Christian gay man)

I believe in being good according to my morals. My personal religion is a combination of principles from different religions. It is a set of guidelines to make people happy. Religion is meant to guide my path, to live a better life. That should not depend on who I love. Love is pure, shouldn't matter if it is a boy or a girl. I don't think there is anything that is 'good Christian'. If I had an option of giving up my religion or sexuality, I would choose religion.

(32-year-old Christian gay man)

Probably one could say my understanding of religion changed over the years. I started to believe that if I were doing anything wrong and if I felt guilty of doing something, I would stop that activity. Strangely enough I never felt guilty of my sexual preference. I always thought that was something ingrained in me. I do pray to god, but while praying I do not think about my sexuality. My devotion to god has nothing to do with my sexual preference.

(29-year-old Muslim gay man)

The re-interpretation of religion is done from a personal standpoint wherein the individuals identify the core of the religion as being a practice of love towards all and thereby deduce that it is impossible for their religion to sanction hatred towards any group of people.

I disagree with many aspects of the Bible. I do not believe that it is the word of Jesus. Jesus would not condemn homosexuality. He always talked about loving everyone.

(32-year-old Christian man)

These personal journeys of individuals who have struggled with two aspects of their identity, indicates that it is indeed possible to reconcile religion and sexuality. The key seems to be an attitude which views religion as a personal relationship with God.

Resources (The sites were accessed in December 2007)

There are numerous websites dedicated to the complexities associated with being gay and religious. To list a few of the main ones that caters to Christian and Muslim LGBT:

- http://www.lgcm.org.uk/
- http://www.gaychristianonline.org
- http://christiangays.com
- http://www.gaychurch.org/
- www.InclusiveOrthodoxy.org
- Truth Sets Free: http://www.truthsetsfree.net/index.htm
- Beyond Ex Gay: http://www.beyondexgay.com/
- Centre for Lesbian and Gay Studies in Religion and Ministry: http://www.clgs.org/index.cfm
- Lesbian and Gay Christian Movement: http://www.lgcm.org.uk/
- http://groups.yahoo.com/group/al-fatiha-news/links or www.al-fatiha.org
- Gay-Muslims: http://www.queernet.org/lists/gay-muslims.html
- Iman: (Lesbian/Bi/TG Muslim Women & Biofemales): http://www.queernet.org/lists/iman.html
- Muslim Gay Men: http://groups.yahoo.com/group/muslimgaymen
- Trans Muslims: http://groups.yahoo.com/group/TransMuslims
- Bi Muslims: http://groups.yahoo.com/group/BiMuslims
- Partners Of LGBTQ Muslims: http://groups.yahoo.com/group/PartnersOfLGBTMuslims
- LGBTQ Muslim Youth: http://groups.yahoo.com/group/LGBTQMuslimYouth
- Parents Of LGBTQ Muslims: http://groups.yahoo.com/group/ParentsOfLGBTQMuslims
- http://huriyahmag.com
- http://www.salaamcanada.com/

Notes

[1] See Ali Potia, 'Islam and me', in Arvind Narrain and Gautam Bhan (eds), *Because I Have a Voice* (New Delhi: Yoda Press, 2005), pp. 252–58.

[2] All personal experiences shared in this essay are based on interviews conducted

by Mr. Nanju Reddy on behalf of Swabhava Trust as part of a larger study on religion and sexual orientation, Bangalore, 2009.

[3] Saleem Kidwai and Ruth Vanita, *Same Sex love in India* (New York: Palgrave, 2001).

[4] Danielou, Alain (1994) *The Complete Kama Sutra* (Maine: Park Street Press).

[5] Sinha, Indrani (1980). *The Love Teachings of Kama Sutra: With extracts from Koka Shastra, Ananga Ranga and other famous Indian works on love.* Translations from Sanskrit and commentary. London: Hamlyn. Also see: http://www.indrasinha.com/books-2/kama-sutra/ (accessed June 2015)

[6] Caleri (Campaign for Lesbian Rights), Khamosh! Emergency Jari Hai! Lesbian Emergence: A Citizens' Report (1999), p. 17.

[7] Pattanaik, Devdutt (2002) *The Man Who Was a Woman and Other Queer Tales from Hindu Lore* (New York: Harrington Park Press).

[8] 'Hinduism and Homosexuality', Religion Facts, http://www.religionfacts.com/hinduism/ethics/homosexuality (accessed in July 2015).

[9] A.L. De Silva, 'Homosexuality and Theravada Buddhism', http://www.buddhanet.net /homosexu.htm (accessed in December 2007).

[10] Boellstorff, Tom (2005) *The Gay Archipelago: Sexuality and Nation in Indonesia.* Princeton, NJ: Princeton University Press.

[11] Whitaker, Brian (2006). 'What's wrong with being gay and Muslim?' in *The Guardian*, dated 5 May 2006. http://www.theguardian.com/commentisfree/2006/may/05/whatswrongwithbeinggayand (accessed December 2007)

[12] 'Archbishop Tutu Defends Gay Christians', *The Christian Century* (20 March 1996), Vol. 63, No. 10, https://www.questia.com/magazine/1G1-18159945/archbishop-tutu-defends-gay-christians (accessed in July 2015).

[13] Daniel Blake 'Conservative Christians to Challenge Tutu on Homosexuality', *Christian Today* (24 November 2007), http://www.christiantoday.com/article/conservative.christians.to.challenge.tutu.on.homosexuality/14845.htm (accessed December 2007).

[14] *The Times of India* (4 July 2009). 'Homosexuality Immoral, But Not Criminal: Religious Leaders', http://articles.timesofindia.indiatimes.com/2009-07-04/india/28203100_1_clerics-criminal-act-sign-of-unjust-discrimination

[15] National Council of Churches in India (2009). Message to the Indian Christian Communities: India—Theological Roundtable on Churches' response to Human Sexuality, http://changingattitude.org.uk/archives/ 1629 (accessed December 2007).

[16] Dr. Zachariah, George (2009) 'Church: A Rainbow Community of the Beloved and Equals'. Sermon delivered by Dr. Zachariah at the Chapel in Gurukul Lutheran Theological College and Research Institute, Chennai on 2-8-2009. Taken from http://orinam.net/content/wp-content/uploads/2011/12/Zachariah_Church_A_Rainbow_Community.pdf (accessed June 2015).

[17] *The Times of India* (4 July 2009). http://timesofindia.indiatimes.com/

india/Homosexuality-immoral-but-not-criminal-Religious-leaders/articleshow/4736152.cms (accessed June 2015).

[18] Kugle, Scott Siraj al-Haqq (2010) *Homosexuality in Islam* (London: One World).

[19] ibid., 11. Whitaker, Brian (2006). 'What's wrong with being gay and Muslim?' in *The Guardian*, dated 5 May 2006. http://www.theguardian.com/commentisfree/2006/may/05/whatswrongwithbeinggayand (accessed December 2007).

[20] Boswell, John (1980) *Christianity, Social Tolerance and Homosexuality* (Chicago: University of Chicago Press).

[21] Cannon, Justin R. (2009) 'The Bible, Christianity, & Homosexuality'. Taken from http://inclusiveorthodoxy.yolasite.com/resources/biblestudy.pdf (accessed June 2015).

[22] ibid., 11 and 19. Whitaker, Brian (2006). 'What's wrong with being gay and Muslim?' in *The Guardian*, dated 5 May 2006. http://www.theguardian.com/commentisfree/2006/may/05/whatswrongwithbeinggayand (accessed December 2007).

III. Human Rights

Section 377 and the Medical Establishment

Changing the Terms of the Debate

ARVIND NARRAIN

Introduction

The introduction of Section 377 as part of the Indian Penal Code in 1860 for the first time in Indian history defined homosexual expression as an unnatural offence thereby embedding the perception of homosexuality as perverse and contrary to 'natural sexual expression' in law. The perception of the 'unnaturalness' of homosexuality was supplemented by the medical discourse which also began to characterise homosexuality as a mental disorder. The power of the legal discourse has been immense in terms of its ability to shape attitudes within the medical field. The criminalisation of homosexuality influences the mindsets of mental health professionals who begin to see homosexuals as part of a criminal species. This power that law has to influence mindsets and attitudes also means that if homosexuality was decriminalised it could transform the attitudes of the mental health professionals as well.

The relationship between perceptions within the mental health profession and the existing legal framework around homosexuality can be mapped through three stages. In the first stage, the existence of Section 377 influences the perceptions of homosexuality as 'unnatural' not only in wider society, but also in the mental health profession which shares many of the beliefs and prejudices of society. The second stage revolves around the contribution of scientific and medical knowledge to the decriminalisation of consenting sex between adults of the same sex in *Naz Foundation v. NCR Delhi*.[1] The final stage revolves around the historic intervention filed by fourteen mental health professionals who seek to support the judgement on scientific grounds and thereby question the scientific validity of the arguments of those who seek to overturn the judgement in the Supreme Court.

Understanding Section 377

Section 377 was introduced by Lord Macaulay in 1860 as a part of the Indian Penal Code. A plain reading of the section makes it clear that it punishes 'carnal intercourse against the order of nature' with either imprisonment of 10 years or life and fine. The provision reads,

> Unnatural Offences:
>
> Whoever voluntarily has carnal intercourse against the order of nature with any man, woman or animal shall be punished with imprisonment for life, or with imprisonment of either description for a term which may extend to ten years, and shall also be liable to fine.

The question which the judiciary has struggled with since 1860 is to determine what exactly 'carnal intercourse against the order of nature' meant. The meaning of Section 377 in 1884 was restricted to anal sex but over a period of time, by 1935, it was broadened to include oral sex and judgements in contemporary India have broadened it to also include thigh sex.

If we are to search for a principle which holds together these various sex acts prohibited by Section 377, it was laid down as early as 1935. The Court in *Khanu v. Emperor*[2] laid down that,

> ... the natural object of sexual intercourse is that there should be the possibility of conception of human beings, which in the case of coitus per os [oral intercourse] is impossible.... [Sexual Intercourse is] the temporary visitation of one organism by a member of the other organisation, for certain clearly defined and limited objects. The primary objective of the visiting organisation is to obtain euphoria by means of a detent of the nerves consequent on the sexual crisis. But there is no intercourse unless the visiting member is enveloped at least partially by the visited organism, for intercourse connotes reciprocity.

Looking at the question in this way it would seem that [the] sin of Gomorrah is no less carnal intercourse than the sin of Sodom.

In defining what constituted 'carnal intercourse against the order of nature' in *Lohana Vasanthlal Devchand* v. *State of Gujarat*[3] the Court noted that '... the act of oral sex involves enveloping of penis by the mouth, thus creating an alternative socially unacceptable activity, which is against the order of nature.'

This idea of sex without the possibility of conception was used by the judiciary over the last 140 years to characterise homosexuality as a 'perversion', 'despicable specimen of humanity', 'abhorrent crime', 'result of a perverse mind' and 'abhorred by civilised society'. What judicial interpretation did was to include both acts of consensual sex as well as acts of sexual assault under its catch-all category of 'carnal intercourse against the order of nature'. It is also important to note that, technically speaking, Section 377 does not prohibit homosexuality or criminalise homosexuals as a class but targets instead sexual acts. However, the fact that these sexual acts are commonly (mistakenly) associated with only homosexuals, has made homosexuals far more vulnerable to prosecution under the law than heterosexuals.

Since 1860, through 50 years of the Indian Constitution, the judiciary continued to follow the colonial justices of the *Khanu* era in continuing to characterise homosexuals as 'despicable specimens of humanity'. The right to equality, the right to dignity, or the right to expression were never seen fit to apply to lesbians, gay, bisexuals, hijras or others whose sexuality does not conform to the heterosexual mainstream, till the historic judgement in *Naz Foundation v. NCR Delhi*.

Prosecution under Section 377:
A case of uncontrolled state power

The way the judiciary understood Section 377, till the Naz judgement, only legitimised and reinforced state power to persecute and harass those of an alternative sexual orientation or gender identity. This

308 Nothing to Fix

enormous power in the hands of the state to enforce its vision of morality found frightening expression in the form of arbitrary and brutal state action.

The police have not hesitated to use the illegal status conferred by Section 377 to wrongfully arrest, harass and extort money from gay men. This phenomenon has been documented by some fact-finding reports in India which have sought to communicate the magnitude of the problem of harassment. One example of this form of harassment by the police was the well-documented case of the four men in Lucknow, who in 2005 were wrongfully charged of an offence under Section 377 and subsequently harassed and tortured. Their offence was merely putting up a profile on a gay website.[4]

While the issue of the state unpredictably descending upon oneself in all its fury combined with the judicial abnegation of any constitutional responsibilities is frightening by itself, it is by no means the whole story of what Section 377 means. Someone who grasped this truth very acutely is one of India's best known thinkers, Amartya Sen, who in an open letter demanding the repeal of Section 377 noted,

> It is sometimes argued that this indicates that Section 377 does not do as much harm as we, the protesters, tend to think. What has to be borne in mind is that whenever any behaviour is identified as a penalizable crime, it gives the police and other law enforcement officers huge powers to harass and victimize some people. The harm done by an unjust law like this can, therefore, be far larger than would be indicated by cases of actual prosecution.

The social impact of Section 377

The harm caused by Section 377 is not just limited to the issue of violence by the state but rather radiates out and permeates different social settings including the medical establishment, media, family and the state. Thus the perception fostered by Section 377 that homosexuality is unnatural becomes a part of the social fabric through the dominant viewpoints and opinions expressed in workplaces, families, hospitals and the popular press. This helps to create an environment where violence against queer people gains a semblance of legal acceptability. Section 377 expresses the deep societal repugnance towards queer people and provides the fig leaf of legitimacy for the harassment of queer people by families, friends, the medical establishment and other official institutions.[5]

The following examples demonstrate this. In the medicalisation study (earlier in this book), a clinical psychologist and a neuro-psychiatrist were separately quoted as saying: 'Sodomy is illegal in India'.[6] This statement by mental health professionals shows how a law such as Section 377 has to be evaluated not merely in terms of the actual prosecutions but in terms of its impact in constructing mindsets. The effect on actions by authorities right from the medical profession to the National Human Rights Commission (NHRC) should be seriously studied to grasp how Section 377 has functioned as a cultural signifier for the 'unacceptability' of homosexuality. [7]

Similarly the social intolerance fostered by the legal regime of Section 377, results in the unacceptable situation wherein one lesbian couple after another feels they have no option but to commit suicide when faced with the dire reality of the Indian norm of compulsory heterosexual marriage. Deepa from Sahayatrika has documented cases of 24 women in the state of Kerala who have committed suicide rather than be forced into marriage.[8] While this form of extreme intolerance is being combated by the emergence of queer activism, for many women from small towns without any access to the queer community it remains a lonely struggle to keep alive the revolt against compulsory heterosexuality.

The struggle against Section 377 speaks of really diverse experiences like the story of the gay man being arrested under Section 377, the hijra being tortured and abused by the police, and the lesbian who is forced by social intolerance and legal indifference to commit suicide among many. Section 377 is a visible symbol of all that is wrong with compulsory heterosexuality.

The successful challenge to Section 377:
Naz Foundation v. NCR Delhi

Section 377 thus has a serious impact upon the rights of LGBT persons in India. Cognizant of this reality, Section 377 was challenged by Naz Foundation in the Delhi High Court in 2000. The Court in *Naz Foundation v. NCR Delhi*,[9] after many legal twists and turns, finally ruled that the law violated the rights of LGBT persons to equality, dignity, non-discrimination and privacy. The Court in a moving conclusion noted that:

> In our view, Indian Constitutional law does not permit the statutory criminal law to be held captive by the popular misconceptions of who the LGBTs are. It cannot be forgotten that discrimination is antithesis of equality and that it is the recognition of equality which will foster the dignity of every individual.

The Delhi High Court after reviewing the current medical and scientific literature on the status of homosexuality observed:

> There is almost unanimous medical and psychiatric opinion that homosexuality is not a disease or a disorder and is just another expression of human sexuality. Homosexuality was removed from the Diagnostic and Statistical Manual of Mental Disorders (DSM) in 1973 after reviewing evidence that homosexuality is not a mental disorder. In 1987, ego-dystonic homosexuality was not included in the revised third edition of the DSM after a similar review. In 1992, the World Health Organisation removed homosexuality from its list of mental illnesses in the International Classification of Diseases (ICD 10).The International Classification of Guidelines of the ICD 10 reads: "disorders of sexual preference are clearly differentiated from disorders of gender identity and homosexuality in itself is no longer included as a category."

The Naz judgement was a significant watermark in the relationship between the mental health professions and the law in the context of Section 377. While prior to the judgement, Section 377 gave the judicial imprimatur to prejudices against homosexuality, what the Naz judgement did was to overturn centuries of prejudice against homosexuality through a well-reasoned judgement drawing on current scientific and medical opinion. It is significant that medical and scientific consensus on homosexuality was effectively used by the Delhi High Court to combat prejudice, stereotypical perceptions as well as bigotry against LGBT persons.

If the judges had arrived at their conclusion based on the arbitrariness of criminalising a natural variant of human nature it would have been a useful judgement. The judges however choose to tread a more ambitious path. They argued that sexual intimacy was a core aspect of human existence and made a link between sexuality and identity.

In a key passage the judges noted:

> Only the most willful blindness could obscure the fact that sexual intimacy is a sensitive, key relationship of human existence, central to family life, community welfare, and the development of human personality. The way in which we give expression to our sexuality is at the core of this area of private intimacy. If, in expressing our sexuality, we act consensually and without harming one another, invasion of that precinct will be a breach of our privacy.

The judges then went on to note that there is a strong link between sexuality and identity and stressed the importance of privacy, equality and dignity for LGBT persons.

No place for a colonial relic

We ask the Home Minister to decriminalise homosexuality in India. As an emerging global power, India cannot continue to rely on archaic colonial laws that are nearly 150 years old and which oppress a group of citizens whose sexuality is a normal variation of human behaviour. Speaking as representatives of the mental health profession, we assert that there is no evidence that homosexuality is a mental illness, now supported by a large body of research. But as a result of Section 377 of the Indian Penal Code still being law, there is government sanction of such discrimination. A group of citizens are being unjustifiably denied essential freedoms, and are often physically abused and blackmailed by the police and other malicious individuals.

Dr. E. Mohandas, President-Elect, Indian Psychiatric Society, Dr. Nada Stotland, President, American Psychiatric Association, Prof Dinesh Bhugra, President, Royal College of Psychiatrists

Hindustan Times, March, 04, 2009

As the judges noted:

> For every individual, whether homosexual or not, the sense of gender
> and sexual orientation of the person are so embedded in the individual
> that the individual carries this aspect of his or her identity wherever
> he or she goes. A person cannot leave behind his sense of gender or
> sexual orientation at home.

Therefore in the Naz judgement the sexual act is not dismissed
as simply being an act of lust but is instead viewed as being linked
to the realm of feelings, emotions and the profound human need
for establishing attachments and relationships. As such the Naz
judgement could possibly herald a new public discourse on the
perception of sex and sexuality and take the debate beyond the
terms of natural and unnatural.

The final stage? The appeal before the Supreme Court

While the judgement in Naz Foundation was remarkably progressive
in terms of its positive recognition of the link between sexuality and
identity and the importance of intimacy to human well being, the
judgment is currently being appealed in the Supreme Court. In an
unusual display of unity, 15 petitions representing Hindu, Muslim
and Christian religious groups have been filed challenging the
judgment.

The basis of challenge is that were Section 377 to go, there
would be a collapse of family values, increase of divorce rates and a
rampant spread of HIV. As is obvious, the challenges are not ground
in any rational discourse and rely for their effect upon irrational
fears and social anxieties.

The battle in the Supreme Court has also been joined by groups
which aim to support the Naz judgment. Among those arguing
that the judgment be upheld are the petitioners before the High
Court, Naz Foundation and the intervenors before the High Court,
Voices Against 377 (a coalition of child rights, women's rights and
LBGT groups). Adding support to Naz and Voices are interventions
by 19 parents of LGBT persons, 16 teachers, Mr. Shyam Benegal
(acclaimed Film Director) as well as 14 mental health professionals.

The 19 parents seek to argue that criminalising an intimate aspect of their children's sexuality offends the right to dignity, privacy and equality. The 16 teachers seek to demonstrate that the criminalisation of homosexuality offends the democratic values on which the Indian Constitution is based and the 14 mental health professionals seek to introduce a scientific and rational basis to the arguments before the Supreme Court.

What the mental health professionals seek to convey is the current scientific understanding of the basis of homosexuality and thereby lessen irrational prejudice against homosexuality. One hopes that this intervention will lessen irrational hatred and provide a basis for the Supreme Court to come to a well reasoned conclusion which takes forward the debate initiated by the Delhi High Court.

Notes

[1] (2009) 160 DLT 277.

[2] AIR 1925 Sind 286.

[3] AIR 1968 Guj 252.

[4] http://www.yawningbread.org/apdx_2006/imp-249.htm (accessed on 4 April 2011).

[5] Arvind Narrain and Gautam Bhan, *Because I have a Voice*, (New Delhi: Yoda Press, 2005), p. 8.

[6] See Chapter '"It's not my job to tell you it's okay to be gay..." Medicalisation of Homosexuality: A Queer Critique', in this anthology.

[7] *Ibid.*

[8] V.N. Deepa, 'Queering Kerala Reflections on Sahayatrika', in Narrain and Bhan, *Because I have a Voice*, pp. 175–96.

[9] (2009) 160 DLT 277.

Human Rights Violations Against the Transgender Community

A Study of Kothi and Hijra Sex Workers in Bangalore, India

PEOPLE'S UNION FOR CIVIL LIBERTIES, KARNATAKA (PUCL-K)

The medical establishment

The medical establishment has played a key role in creating a culture of intolerance towards hijras and kothis. The medical establishment is particularly significant in the lives of hijras and kothis both with respect to their ability to access treatment without being subject to discrimination and with respect to their constructing a self and identity for themselves. When hijras want to transit to another sex or gender, the role of the medical profession in facilitating this process is crucial. The medical discourse has in fact classified this need to 'transit' as a Gender Identity Disorder(GID).

According to the two main diagnostic systems, ICD 10 and DSM IV, transsexualism is a Gender Identity Disorder in which there is strong and ongoing cross-gender identification, and desire to live and be accepted as a member of the opposite sex. The transgender individual experiences persistent discomfort with his or her anatomical sex and a sense of inappropriateness in the gender role of that sex. According to the *Oxford Companion To Medicine*, 'transexualism is characterized by a passionate life-long conviction that one's psychological gender, that indefinable feeling of maleness or femaleness, is opposite to one's anatomical sex...'. There is a wish to have hormonal treatment and surgery to make one's body as congruent as possible with one's psychological sex. The objective of treatment is to harmonise the psychological sex with the physical sex.

Once GID is confirmed, one of the treatment options is sexual reassignment surgery (SRS). In SRS there is no single model of treatment; rather, variety in approach is both supported and sought as part of the continuing professional discussion of the syndrome. The currently accepted and effective model of treatment utilises hormone therapy and surgical reconstruction and may include electrolysis, speech therapy, counselling, and other psychotherapeutic treatments. The surgical reconstruction itself could include construction of a vagina, removal of the penis, testes, construction of clitoris, etc. According to a report in *Hindustan Times* (20 December 2002), the plastic surgery department in Lok Nayak J.P. Narayan Hospital in New Delhi successfully performed SRS for a 27-year-old transsexual Ranjan, one of several that this hospital has performed in the last couple of years. The surgery, which was a complicated one lasting seven hours, was done free, which in a private hospital would have cost up to Rs 15 lakhs. According to Dr. Rajeev Ahuja, who performed the surgery, every year about a dozen transsexuals approach him for this operation. Such surgeries have similarly been performed in Kerala.

However the accessibility of SRS among the hijra population in general is limited. As Dr. C. Venkatesan, a physician from Chennai notes,

> While educated and wealthy 'male-to-female transsexuals' may have access to surgeons and plastic surgeons, many hijras are from a low socio-economic status and hence might not be able to afford SRS. Further SRS is not done in government hospitals; private qualified practitioners (general/plastic surgeons) also don't do SRS. Some do SRS but charge heavily. Consequently, many hijras go to unqualified medical practitioners (quacks) who do castration.

But the so-called simple castration that many hijras undergo at the hands of 'quack doctors' or senior hijras (called 'Thai Amma') has significant health risks. As the first PUCL Report observes,

> Often such operations are undertaken by poorly qualified doctors in hazardous and unsanitary conditions. When Manorama and her two friends decided to have the operation, they found that they did not

have enough money for it and had to do sex work for a while to earn the amount. A fellow hijra took them on payment of a commission to a doctor in Dindigul who was known to do such operations for a fee of Rs 5,000, which did not include nursing care. The doctor's clinic was a tiny airless room with a toilet consisting of three benches, which served as an operation table. The operation was so painful that Manorama wondered whether it was worth going through the pain in order to become a hijra. The operation turned out to be defective leading to a severe infection, loss of urine control and other painful complications. The operation was not followed by a urine and blood check up. Since the operation was defective they have had to keep visiting other doctors to deal with the infections resulting from the operation.

This kind of risk is not just limited to a few cases but is a pervasive part of the hijra's interface with the medical establishment. As Dr. C. Venkatesan notes, 'The risks involved in traditional castration practice include death due to neurogenic shock or hypovolemic shock or due to the wound becoming septic.' Even if death is not the eventuality, many hijras complained of 'urine problem following the operation' (urinary stenosis / stricture following emasculation by Thai Amma or quacks) as the main health problem faced by their community.

The problem of access to hygienic, professional and affordable medical treatment is exacerbated by the legal position on SRS and castration. The law in India does not contemplate the phenomenon of transsexuality at all. In fact under Section 320 of the Indian Penal Code (IPC), 'emasculating' (castrating) someone is causing him 'grievous hurt' for which one can be punished under Sec 325 of the IPC. Thus technically speaking even if one voluntarily (with consent) chooses to be emasculated, the doctor is liable for punishment under this provision and the person undergoing the emasculation could also be punished for 'abetting' this offence. However, under Sec 88 of the IPC an exception is made in case an action is undertaken in good faith and the person gives consent to suffer that harm. The section reads

Nothing which is not intended to cause death is an offence by reason

of any harm which it may cause or be intended by the doer to cause
to any person for whose benefit it is done in good faith, and who has
given a consent...to suffer that harm, or to take the risk of that harm.

In actuality, however, the legal process is set in motion by
someone filing either an FIR in the concerned police station or by
filing a private complaint. This does not happen in the case of SRS/
castration as both the doctor and patient are consenting parties to
the transaction, and it is extremely unlikely that they will activate
the criminal law process. Thus there is no documented case in India
of doctors and patients having been prosecuted for causing grievous
hurt or abetting the causing of grievous hurt through SRS. In the
unlikely case that such a process is activated, a qualified doctor who
does the SRS would be protected by the general exception under
Section 88 of the IPC.

However the lack of clarity about the law has had its impact
on the medical establishment. Hijras are unable to legally access
safe and sanitised medical facilities for castration. The few hijras
who can find the resources and a willing doctor manage to obtain
a surgery-like castration which however is performed in highly
surreptitious circumstances, leaving little space for quality, efficiency
and accountability.

SRS is available in India but very surreptiously. Doctors in India
get transsexuals and hijras to sign consent forms stating that they have
cancer-related complications and thus need the required surgery.
Dr. C. Venkatesan observes, 'previously "neovagina" creation
[creating a vagina-like path in an emasculated person] was being done
in the Government General Hospital in Chennai. But nowadays, it is
not being done because of lack of interest and expertise in Urology/
Plastic surgery department of the hospital and also because of the
ambiguous legal status of SRS.'

Apart from the 'grievous hurt' provisions in IPC, doctors are
also worried about the validity of the consent which the patient
gives to the SRS process. In the unlikely eventuality of a case being
filed against a doctor the general exception under Sec 88 only comes
into play if there is valid consent. In the case of a transsexual, this
consent clause could be challenged since the transsexual is diagnosed

as suffering from GID which is classified as a psychiatric disorder. Further if the person is a child, the absence of support from parents or legal guardians can mean that treatment itself becomes an unviable option.

Even the Indian Medical Council (IMC) and Indian Council for Medical Research (ICMR) have not really responded to the issue of transexualism. SRS is a highly complex surgery that requires strict protocols and guidelines to be followed. However, neither the ICMR nor the IMC have formulated any codes or guidelines and this lack in India is producing various ad hoc and incomplete responses. For example, counselling constitutes an important component of the whole surgery, which is often never made available to transgender people.

Thus if one were to summarise the interface of the medical establishment with hijras, it's clear that SRS is very expensive and therefore very difficult to access, making it almost a luxury and beyond the reach of a common person. Hence hijras fall back on those who are willling to operate under conditions which endanger their health and even their lives.

In this context the first responsibility of both the state and the judiciary is to decriminalise 'voluntary emasculation' and set legal and ethical protocols for performance of SRS and castration facilities in order to avoid any incomplete and ad hoc responses. A clear strategy that seeks de-criminalisation and legalisation needs to be evolved to make these surgeries comprehensive, efficient, accessible and affordable.

Dr. C. Venkatesan observes,

> Many hijras want SRS to be done freely in government hospitals. Also, many want mammoplasty, vaginoplasty as well as procedures for facial hair removal, scalp hair growth and changing their voice. Many hijras take hormonal tablets/injections since hormonal therapy is not offered by government or private doctors.

The non-availability of these facilities combined with the hazards and risks listed above mean that the medical establishment produces the effect of reinforcing the low sense of self-worth that hijras in general feel. In fact due to this low sense of self-worth and due to non-acceptance by their families, many hijras we met had thought about or attempted suicide and many were consuming alcohol. The shabby treatment that the hijra receives at the hands of the medical establishment ends up eroding the hijra's sense of self instead of nourishing it.

Recommendations

What became apparent in the course of our study is that discrimination against hijras and kothis is embedded in both state and civil society. The violence that this community faces is not only due to the state but also has deep societal roots. As has been argued in the course of the Report, wider change is premised on changing existing social relations. Any proposal which tries to ensure that the dignity and selfhood of kothis and hijras is respected, has to deal with a complex reality in which class, gender and sexuality play a crucial role. Apart from shifts in class relations, change would also crucially hinge upon overturning the existing regime of both gender and sexuality that enforces its own hierarchies, (e.g., heterosexuality over homosexuality), exclusions (e.g., hijras as the excluded category) and oppressions. While keeping in mind this wider context, a human rights approach has to deal with the various institutional contexts and think through ways in which change can be brought about. In this context the following proposals are made. These recommendations are also based on the demands made by the hijra kothi community in meetings held with them. Some of the demands made by them require us to reorient our very imagination to conceptualise the nature of violation suffered by them. In this context the demand for recognition of the discrimination suffered by them as a form of untouchability (in terms of access to public spaces, employment, as well as the forms of violence they suffer) needs to be taken seriously.

Legal measures

1. Every person must have the right to decide their gender expression and identity, including transsexuals, transgenders,

transvestites and hijras. They should also have the right to freely express their gender identity. This includes the demand for hijras to be considered female as well as a third sex.

2. Comprehensive civil rights legislation should be enacted to offer hijras and kothis the same protection and rights now guaranteed to others on the basis of sex, caste, creed and colour. The Constitution should be amended to include sexual orientation/ gender identity as a ground of non-discrimination

3. There should be a special legal protection against this form of discrimination inflicted by both state and civil society which is very akin to the offence of practising untouchability.

4. Same-sex marriages should be recognised as legal and valid; all legal benefits, including property rights that accrue to heterosexual married people should be made available to same-sex unions.

5. The Immoral Trafficking in Persons Act, 1956 should be repealed. Sex work should be decriminalised, and legal and other kinds of discrimination against kothis and hijras should stop.

6. Section 377 of the IPC and other discriminatory legislations that single out same-sexual acts between consenting adults should be repealed.

7. Section 375 of the IPC should be amended to punish all kinds of sexual violence, including sexual abuse of children. A comprehensive sexual assault law should be enacted applying to all persons irrespective of their sexual orientation and marital status.

8. Civil rights under law such as the right to get a passport, ration card, make a will, inherit property and adopt children must be available to all regardless of change in gender/sex identities.

9. Reservation in educational institutions such as schools and colleges as well as in government employment.

Police reforms

1. The police administration should appoint a standing committee comprising Station House Officers and human rights and social

activists to promptly investigate reports of gross abuses by the police against kothis and hijras in public areas and police stations, and the guilty policeman immediately punished.

2. The police administration should adopt transparency in their dealings with hijras and kothis ; make available all information relating to procedures and penalties used in detaining kothis and hijras in public places.

3. Protection and safety should be ensured for hijras and kothis to prevent rape in police custody and in jail. Hijras should not be sent into male cells with other men in order to prevent harassment, abuse and rape.

4. The police at all levels should undergo sensitisation workshops by human rights groups/queer groups in order to break down their social prejudices and to train them to treat hijras and kothis in the same courteous and humane manner in which they would treat the general public.

Reforming the medical establishment

1. Initiate a debate on whether being transgender should be classified as a gender identity disorder or whether it should be seen as a choice.

2. The Medical Council of India should issue guidelines to ensure that discrimination in medical treatment of hijras and kothis, which would include refusal to treat a person on the basis of their gender identity, is handled as professional misconduct.

3. Reform medical curriculum in medical colleges so that it moves beyond seeing transgenderism as a disease and a deviance.

4. Free SRS services for hijras should be provided in government hospitals.

Interventions by civil society

1. Human rights and social action organisations should take up the issues of hijras and kothis as a part of their mandate for social change. Socialist and Marxist organisations, Gandhian organisations, environmental organisations, dalit organisations and women's organisations, among others, which have played

a key role in initiating social change, should integrate the concerns of hijras and kothis as part of their mandate in sites such as the family, religion and the media which foster extreme forms of intolerance to gender non-conformity.

2. A comprehensive sex-education programme should be included as part of the school curricula that alters the heterosexist bias in education and provides judgement-free information and fosters a liberal outlook with regard to matters of sexuality, including orientation, identity and behaviour of all sexualities.

3. The Press Council of India and other watchdog institutions of various popular media (including film, video and TV) should issue guidelines to ensure sensitive and respectful treatment of these issues.

4. Setting up of counselling centres to enable families to understand issues of gender non-conformity in their children.

5. Setting up of short-stay homes for hijras and kothis in crises.

Pushing the Boundaries of Transgender and Intersex Persons Rights
Further resources

It is clear that there have been enormous positive developments in the field of human rights relating to sexual orientation and gender identity. The Naz judgement decriminalising homosexuality has its counterpart in numerous developments with respect to transgender persons.

There have been substantial efforts made to address the state's policy of recognising only two sexes and refusing to recognise hijras as women, or as a third sex. The passport form recognises that transgender persons can apply for a passport in a sex/gender category referred to as 'Other'.[1] Similarly, for the purposes of securing an Election ID card, persons can use the category called 'Other'.[2] The recognition of transgenders as 'Other' is also being contemplated in new identity documents such as the Unique Identification Number with the gender category including male, female and transgender.[3] In the southern state of Tamil Nadu, the Government has set up a Transgender Welfare Board which looks into issues pertaining to the transgender community.[4]

However, much still remains to be done. Transgender persons are not protected by the provisions that deal with rape in the Indian Penal Code. The current government proposals related to sexual assault[5] do not aim to protect transgender victims despite documented evidence of horrific cases of violence and sexual assault against transgender persons in police stations and by private gangs.[6] Further, there is no provision which deals with the particular situation of intersex persons and the forcible imposition of gender identity at birth.

As a way of thinking about some of these complex issues as well as to enable a broadening of what might be possible in terms of rights for transgender and intersex persons, below are extracted two documents which try to push the boundaries of transgender rights as it comes in conflict with medical science.

In the first, the Yogyakarta Principles articulate the existing recognition of rights in international law with respect to sexual orientation and gender identity. The purpose of the Yogyakarta Principles would be to serve as a road map to nation states to enact laws and implement policies, which protect rights of those who are discriminated against on the basis of their sexual orientation and gender identity. In particular, Principles 17 and 18 articulate the position in international law when it comes to the rights of transgender and intersex persons particularly as they interface with the medical system. Needless to say, Principles 17 and 18 remain an unfulfilled aspiration in many regions around the world.

The second, the International Bill on Gender Rights, 1995 is a very powerful aspirational document which enlarges the horizon within which one conceptualises the rights of transgender and intersex persons. Its value lies in being able to articulate demands which have not yet found a legal form such as the right to control and change one's body and the right to freely express one's gender. One hopes that a document such as this can play a role in widening our own conceptions of rights itself.

The Yogyakarta principles on the application of international human rights law in relation to sexual orientation and gender identity[7]

Principle 17. The Right to the Highest Attainable Standard of Health
Everyone has the right to the highest attainable standard of physical and mental health, without discrimination on the basis of sexual orientation or gender identity. Sexual and reproductive health is a fundamental aspect of this right.

States shall:

a) Take all necessary legislative, administrative and other measures to ensure enjoyment of the right to the highest attainable standard of health, without discrimination on the basis of sexual orientation or gender identity;

b) Take all necessary legislative, administrative and other measures to ensure that all persons have access to healthcare facilities, goods and services, including in relation to sexual and reproductive health, and to their own medical records, without discrimination on the basis of sexual orientation or gender identity;

c) Ensure that healthcare facilities, goods and services are designed to improve the health status of, and respond to the needs of, all persons without discrimination on the basis of, and taking into account, sexual orientation and gender identity, and that medical records in this respect are treated with confidentiality;

d) Develop and implement programmes to address discrimination, prejudice and other social factors which undermine the health of persons because of their sexual orientation or gender identity;

e) Ensure that all persons are informed and empowered to make their own decisions regarding medical treatment and care, on the basis of genuinely informed consent, without discrimination on the basis of sexual orientation or gender identity;

f) Ensure that all sexual and reproductive health, education, prevention, care and treatment programmes and services respect the diversity of sexual orientations and gender identities, and are equally available to all without discrimination;

g) Facilitate access by those seeking body modifications related to gender reassignment to competent, non-discriminatory treatment, care and support;

h) Ensure that all health service providers treat clients and their partners without discrimination on the basis of sexual orientation or gender identity, including with regard to recognition as next of kin;

i) Adopt the policies, and programmes of education and training, necessary to enable persons working in the healthcare sector to deliver the highest attainable standard of healthcare to all persons, with full respect for each person's sexual orientation and gender identity.

PRINCIPLE 18. *Protection from medical abuses*

No person may be forced to undergo any form of medical or psychological treatment, procedure, testing, or be confined to a medical facility, based on sexual orientation or gender identity. Notwithstanding any classifications to the contrary, a person's sexual orientation and gender identity are not, in and of themselves, medical conditions and are not to be treated, cured or suppressed.

States shall:

a) Take all necessary legislative, administrative and other measures to ensure full protection against harmful medical practices based on sexual orientation or gender identity, including on the basis of stereotypes, whether derived from culture or otherwise, regarding conduct, physical appearance or perceived gender norms;

b) Take all necessary legislative, administrative and other measures to ensure that no child's body is irreversibly altered by medical procedures in an attempt to impose a gender identity without the full, free and informed consent of the child in accordance with the age and maturity of the child and guided by the principle that in all actions concerning children, the best interests of the child shall be a primary consideration;

c) Establish child protection mechanisms whereby no child is at risk of, or subjected to, medical abuse;

d) Ensure protection of persons of diverse sexual orientations and gender identities against unethical or involuntary medical procedures or research, including in relation to vaccines, treatments or microbicides for HIV / AIDS or other diseases;

e) Review and amend any health funding provisions or programmes, including those of a development-assistance nature, which may promote, facilitate or in any other way render possible such abuses;

f) Ensure that any medical or psychological treatment or

counselling does not, explicitly or implicitly, treat sexual orientation and gender identity as medical conditions to be treated, cured or suppressed.

The International Bill of Gender Rights[8] (As adopted 17 June 1995 Houston, Texas, USA)

'The International Bill of Gender Rights (IBGR) strives to express human and civil rights from a gender perspective. However, the ten rights enunciated below are not to be viewed as special rights applicable to a particular interest group. Nor are these rights limited in application to persons for whom gender identity and gender role issues are of paramount concern. All ten sections of the IBGR are universal rights which can be claimed and exercised by every human being.'

The International Bill of Gender Rights (IBGR) was first drafted in committee and adopted by the International Conference on Transgender Law and Employment Policy (ICTLEP) at that organisation's second annual meeting, held in Houston, Texas, 26–29 August 1993.

The IBGR has been reviewed and amended in committee and adopted with revisions at subsequent annual meetings of ICTLEP in 1994 and 1995.

The IBGR is a theoretical construction which has no force of law absent its adoption by legislative bodies and recognition of its principles by courts of law, administrative agencies and international bodies such as the United Nations.

However, individuals are free to adopt the truths and principles expressed in the IBGR, and to lead their lives accordingly. In this fashion, the truths expressed in the IBGR will liberate and empower humankind in ways and to an extent beyond the reach of legislators, judges, officials and diplomats.

When the truths expressed in the IBGR are embraced and given expression by humankind, the acts of legislatures and pronouncements of courts and other governing structures will necessarily follow. Thus, the paths of free expression trodden by millions of human beings, all seeking to define themselves and give meaning to their lives, will ultimately determine the course of governing bodies.

The IBGR is a transformative and revolutionary document but it is grounded in the bedrock of individual liberty and free expression. As our lives unfold these kernels of truth are here for all who would claim and exercise them.

This document, though copyrighted, may be reproduced by any means and freely distributed by anyone supporting the principles and statements contained in the International Bill of Gender Rights.

The right to define gender identity

All human beings carry within themselves an ever-unfolding idea of who they are and what they are capable of achieving. The individual's sense of self is not determined by chromosomal sex, genitalia, assigned birth sex, or initial gender role. Thus, the individual's identity and capabilities cannot be circumscribed by what society deems to be masculine or feminine behaviour. It is fundamental that individuals have the right to define, and to redefine as their lives unfold, their own gender identities, without regard to chromosomal sex, genitalia, assigned birth sex, or initial gender role.

Therefore, all human beings have the right to define their own gender identity regardless of chromosomal sex, genitalia, assigned birth sex, or initial gender role; and further, no individual shall be denied Human or Civil Rights by virtue of a self-defined gender identity which is not in accord with chromosomal sex, genitalia, assigned birth sex, or initial gender role.

The right to free expression of gender identity

Given the right to define one's own gender identity, all human beings have the corresponding right to free expression of their self-defined gender identity.

Therefore, all human beings have the right to free expression of their self-defined gender identity; and further, no individual shall be denied Human or Civil Rights by virtue of the expression of a self-defined gender identity.

The right to secure and retain employment and to receive just compensation

Given the economic structure of modern society, all human beings have a right to train for and to pursue an occupation or profession as a means of providing shelter, sustenance, and the necessities and bounty of life, for themselves and for those dependent upon them, to secure and retain employment, and to receive just compensation for their labour regardless of gender identity, chromosomal sex, genitalia, assigned birth sex, or initial gender role.

Therefore, individuals shall not be denied the right to train for and to pursue an occupation or profession, nor be denied the right to secure and retain employment, nor be denied just compensation for their labour, by virtue of their chromosomal sex, genitalia, assigned birth sex, or initial gender role, or on the basis of a self-defined gender identity or the expression thereof.

The right of access to gendered space and participation in gendered activity

Given the right to define one's own gender identity and the corresponding right to free expression of a self-defined gender identity, no individual should be denied access to a space or denied participation in an activity by virtue of a self-defined gender identity which is not in accord with chromosomal sex, genitalia, assigned birth sex, or initial gender role.

Therefore, no individual shall be denied access to a space or denied participation in an activity by virtue of a self-defined gender identity which is not in accord with chromosomal sex, genitalia, assigned birth sex, or initial gender role.

The right to control and change one's uwn body

All human beings have the right to control their bodies, which includes the right to change their bodies cosmetically, chemically, or surgically, so as to express a self-defined gender identity.

Therefore, individuals shall not be denied the right to change their bodies as a means of expressing a self-defined gender identity; and further, individuals shall not be denied Human or Civil Rights on the basis that they have changed their bodies cosmetically, chemically, or surgically, or desire to do so as a means of expressing a self-defined gender identity.

The right to competent medical and professional care

Given the individual's right to define one's own gender identity, and the right to change one's own body as a means of expressing a self-defined gender identity, no individual should be denied access to competent medical or other professional care on the basis of the individual's chromosomal sex, genitalia, assigned birth sex, or initial gender role.

Therefore, individuals shall not be denied the right to competent medical or other professional care when changing their bodies cosmetically, chemically, or surgically, on the basis of chromosomal sex, genitalia, assigned birth sex, or initial gender role.

The right to freedom from psychiatric diagnosis or treatment

Given the right to define one's own gender identity, individuals should not be subject to psychiatric diagnosis or treatment solely on the basis of their gender identity or role.

Therefore, individuals shall not be subject to psychiatric diagnosis or treatment as mentally disordered or diseased solely on the basis of a self-defined gender identity or the expression thereof.

The right to sexual expression

Given the right to a self-defined gender identity, every consenting adult has a corresponding right to free sexual expression.

Therefore, no individual's Human or Civil Rights shall be denied on the basis of sexual orientation; and further, no individual shall be denied Human or Civil Rights for expression of a self-defined gender identity through sexual acts between consenting adults.

The right to form committed, loving relationships and enter into marital contracts

Given that all human beings have the right to free expression of self-defined gender identities, and the right to sexual expression as a form of gender expression, all human beings have a corresponding right to form committed, loving relationships with one another, and to enter into marital contracts, regardless of their own or their partner's chromosomal sex, genitalia, assigned birth sex, or initial gender role.

Therefore, individuals shall not be denied the right to form committed, loving relationships with one another or to enter into marital contracts by virtue of their own or their partner's chromosomal sex, genitalia, assigned birth sex, or initial gender role, or on the basis of their expression of a self-defined gender identity.

The right to conceive, bear, or adopt children; the right to nurture and have custody of children and to exercise parental capacity

Given the right to form a committed, loving relationship with another, and to enter into marital contracts, together with the right to express a self-defined gender identity and the right to sexual expression, individuals have a corresponding right to conceive and bear children, to adopt children, to nurture children, to have custody of children, and to exercise parental capacity with respect to children, natural or adopted, without regard to chromosomal sex, genitalia, assigned birth sex, or initial gender role, or by virtue of a self-defined gender identity or the expression thereof.

Therefore, individuals shall not be denied the right to conceive, bear, or adopt children, nor to nurture and have custody of children, nor to exercise parental capacity with respect to children, natural or adopted, on the basis of their own, their partner's, or their children's chromosomal sex, genitalia, assigned birth sex, initial gender role, or by virtue of a self-defined gender identity or the expression thereof.

Notes

[1] See http://passport.gov.in/cpv/ppapp1.pdf (accessed on 29 April 2010).
[2] During months of hearings, the election commission heard written and oral testimony (or 'representations') from 'various individuals and interest groups', according to *TOI*. Election commissioner S.Y. Qureishi explained, 'When the representation came, we readily agreed. Why should a section of the population be left out? The decision will help in mainstreaming a section of the population. I am sure even government would like to do the same.' See http://lgbtqnews.com/gaynews/eunuchs-transsexuals-given-third-gender-

option-india-election-forms_BYN.aspx (accessed on 28 April 2010).

[3] See Demographic Data Standards and Verification procedure (DDSVP) Committee Report, Unique Identification Authority of India, Dec. 2009.

[4] See http://www.tn.gov.in/pressrelease/archives/pr2008/pr260508/pr260508c. htm (accessed on 28 April 2010).

[5] Draft Criminal Law Amendment Bill (2010). See http://www.prsindia.org/ uploads/media/draft/Draft%20Criminal%20Law%20(Amendment)%20 Bill%202010.pdf (accessed on 19 April 2010).

[6] See People's Union for Civil Liberties (Karnataka) Report, Human Rights Violation Against the Transgender Community, 2nd Ed., 2005, http://ai.eecs. umich.edu/people/conway/TS/PUCL/PUCL%20Report.html (accessed on 21 May 2010).

[7] www.yogyakartaprinciples.org

[8] Accessed at http://my.execpc.com/~dmmunson/billrights.htm. April 2013.

About the Editors and Contributors

About the Editors

VINAY CHANDRAN is a counsellor and Executive Director of Swabhava Trust, Bangalore, a non-governmental organisation working with issues related to gay, lesbian, bisexual, transgender and similar (LGBT) populations. He set up the Bangalore-based telephone helpline called Sahaya in 2000, and has worked on linking support services with LGBT communities. His areas of research and interest include sexuality, sexual health, counselling, gender, masculinities and ethics. He is also a trainer on all these issues and has worked with various state AIDS prevention organisations to train diverse groups on working with sexuality, sexual health, counselling and HIV.

ARVIND NARRAIN is an advocate and founder member of the Alternative Law Forum, Bangalore. He is the author of *Queer: Despised Sexuality, Law and Social Change* and co-editor of *Because I Have a Voice: Queer Politics in India*, along with Gautam Bhan. He has also co-edited *Law Like Love* with Alok Gupta. Arvind was one of the team of lawyers representing those who challenged Section 377 both in the High Court of Delhi and the Supreme Court of India.

334 Nothing to Fix

About the Contributors

DR. POORNIMA BHOLA works as Associate Professor, Department of Clinical Psychology at the National Institute of Mental Health and Neuro Sciences, Bangalore. She is currently engaged in developing a transgender care protocol for use in mental health settings. Her interests include the provision of inclusive and informed psychotherapy training and practice for individuals considering sex-reassignment surgery. Some additional research areas are focused on psychotherapy processes, training and psychotherapist development and on youth mental health and suicidality.

DR. VENKATESAN CHAKRAPANI, M.D., is a medical doctor with a specialisation in sexually transmitted infections and HIV. He is the director of Centre for Sexuality and Health Research and Policy (C-SHaRP), Chennai. For the past 10 years, Dr. Chakrapani's research studies among men who have sex with men (MSM) and transgender people in India have focused on barriers to access and use of health services, HIV-related risk behaviours, social and sexual networks, stigma/discrimination and structural violence, and influence of stigma on mental health and sexual risk. He has authored and co-authored 23 peer-reviewed academic articles, 35 research/policy reports, and four book chapters. He has trained several government and non-governmental healthcare providers on the sexual health issues of MSM and transgender people and has prepared training materials on the same. He has served as consultant to India's National AIDS Control Organization and United Nations agencies in India (UNDP-India, UNODC-India, and UNAIDS-India). He is the recipient of several fellowships and awards including the National Institute of Health's Fogarty fellowship from Yale University (2003), and the Fund for Leadership Development (FLD) fellowship of the John D. and Catherine T. MacArthur Foundation (2003/05).

RADHIKA CHANDIRAMANI trained as a clinical psychologist at the National Institute of Mental Health and Neurosciences (NIMHANS). She founded Talking About Reproductive and Sexual Health Issues (TARSHI) in 1996. Her main areas of interest are sexuality and rights. She is a recipient of the MacArthur Fellowship for Leadership Development and the Soros Reproductive Health and Rights Fellowship. Radhika is Executive Director of TARSHI, the South and Southeast Asia Resource Centre on Sexuality, and co-Director of The Sexuality and Rights Institute in India.

DR. C. R. CHANDRASHEKAR is Senior Professor in the Department of Psychiatry at the National Institute of Mental Health and Neuro Sciences (NIMHANS). His areas of interest include cultural issues, somatisation, legal and community psychiatry and mental health education.

BINA FERNANDEZ is a lecturer in Development Studies at the University of Melbourne. Prior to this, she taught development studies for three years at the University of Leeds, UK. She has also taught at the Institute of Development Studies, Sussex, and the Universities of Oxford and Oxford-Brookes. Bina has considerable professional experience as a development practitioner, obtained through eight years of working with rural development and human rights NGOs in India, in addition to research and evaluation consultancies with international NGOs. Bina is also interested in research on social movements, human rights and identity politics as they pertain to communities marginalised by ethnic, caste and sexual identities. Her research in this area has focussed on lesbian and gay rights, and violence against lesbians in India.

DR. LATA HEMCHAND is a consultant clinical psychologist with over 30 years of experience. She is also Professor at the Richmond Fellowship Post Graduate College and a consultant trainer on counselling, particularly for HIV/AIDS. She is a fellow at the Indian Association of Clinical Psychologists (IACP) and also the former President and office bearer of the Karnataka Association of Clinical Psychologists (KACP).

DR. AMI SEBASTIAN MAROKY is a psychiatrist who completed her training from the National Institute of Mental Health and Neurosciences, Bangalore, and her research interests include alternate sexuality and mental health aspects. Her thesis, 'The Validity of Ego

Dystonicity in Homosexuality: An Indian perspective', explores the causes implicated in discomfort associated with one's gay identity. She is currently a full-time mother and homemaker.

DR. SURESH BADA MATH works as Additional Professor, Department of Psychiatry, National Institute of Mental Health and Neuro Sciences (NIMHANS), Bangalore. After completing his master's degree in psychiatry from NIMHANS and Diplomat of National Board in Psychiatry, he got post-graduate diplomas in Medical Law and Ethics and in Human Rights and Law, from National Law School of India University (NLSIU), Bangalore. Currently, he is pursuing his PhD thesis, titled 'Mental Health and Law' from NLSIU, Bangalore. His areas of research are obsessive compulsive disorder, disaster management, human rights and forensic psychiatry. He has written two books on prison and mental health.

KETKI RANADE works as Assistant Professor at the Center for Health and Mental Health, School of Social Work, Tata Institute of Social Sciences, Mumbai. She is currently working on her PhD thesis, titled '"Growing Up Gay" in a Heterosexually Constructed World: Developmental life histories of young lesbian and gay persons in urban India'. Some of the other research studies that she is engaged in are focused on gay affirmative counselling practice, understanding familial responses to same-sex sexuality.

DR. ASWIN RATHEESH is a consultant psychiatrist and a gay man. He has trained in psychiatry at the National Institute of Mental Health and Neurosciences, Bangalore, and is currently working in Melbourne, Australia. He has been involved in research and discourse in the area of sexuality and its relationship with mental health. He is also interested in research in mood disorders and early intervention for young people with mental illnesses.

DR. K. R. BHARATH KUMAR REDDY is a medical consultant with a specialisation in paediatrics. He currently works as a clinical fellow at the National University Hospital, Singapore. He holds a Diploma in Medical Law and Ethics from the National Law School of India

University (NLSIU), Bangalore. His areas of interest include child advocacy, child rights law and others.

DR. VIDYA SATHYANARAYANAN is Associate Professor of Clinical Psychology and Consultant Clinical Psychologist in the Department of Psychiatry, St. John's Medical College Hospital, Bangalore. Her work in this consultation-liaison setting incorporates evaluation, assessment and psychotherapeutic management for individuals with gender dysphoria, transgender issues and those considering sex-reassignment surgery. In addition, her clinical interests include mental health issues and concerns in medical/surgical disorders.

DR. SHEKHAR P. SESHADRI is Professor in the Department of Child and Adolescent Psychiatry at the National Institute of Mental Health and Neuro Sciences (NIMHANS), Bangalore. He has co-authored *Parenting: The Art and Science of Nurturing* with Nirupama Rao and co-edited *Play: Experiential Methodologies in Developmental and Therapeutic Settings* with Shubhada Maitra. He has a wide array of research interests which include child and adolescent psychiatry (adolescent mental health), therapy and therapy training, gender, sexuality, sexual abuse, difficult populations like street children, qualitative research and experiential methodology, life skills education, school programmes and others.

MAYUR SURESH is currently a doctoral candidate at Birkbeck, School of Law, University of London. Previously, he practiced law before courts in Delhi and was involved in the Section 377 related litigation before the Delhi High Court and the Supreme Court of India. His current research involves looking at the ideas of hope and fear in relation to sovereignty through an ethnography of terrorism trials in Delhi.

DR. BIJU VISWANATH is currently a Post-Doctoral Fellow and Senior Resident in the Department of Psychiatry at the National Institute of Mental Health and Neurosciences, Bangalore, where he has trained in psychiatry. His research areas include mental health disorders and social psychiatry.